Beyond the Impasse

Beyond the Impasse

Toward a Pneumatological Theology of Religions

Amos Yong

Published by Baker Academic
a division of Baker Book House Company
P.O. Box 6287, Grand Rapids, MI 49516-6287
www.bakeracademic.com

and

Paternoster Press
an imprint of Authentic Media
P.O. Box 300, Carlisle, Cumbria CA3 0QS, UK
www.paternoster-publishing.com

Printed in the United States of America

Library of Congress Cataloging-in-Publication Data
Yong, Amos.
Beyond the impasse : toward a pneumatological theology of religions / Amos Yong.
p. cm.
Includes bibliographical references and indexes.
ISBN 0-8010-2612-1 (pbk.)
1. Theology of religions (Christian theology) 2. Holy Spirit. I. Title.
BT83.85 .Y66 2003
261.2—dc21 2002038608

British Library Cataloguing in Publication Data
A catalogue record for this book is available from the British Library
ISBN 1-84227-208-4

For
Rev. Joseph and Irene Yong

Contents

Preface

I vaguely recall a conversation I had one day in grade school with my parents, the Reverend and Mrs. Joseph Yong, about what culture I belonged to. This was, as I recall, shortly after our family had emigrated to the United States from Malaysia, where I was born. It went, generally, something like this:

Me:	So, what is our culture? Chinese? Malaysian? American?
Them:	None of the above; we're Christians.
Me:	Christians? But we're also Chinese, right? And I'm a Malaysian citizen, right?
Them:	Well, yes. But since we're Christians, we pay supreme allegiance to Jesus, not to the norms or conventions of any particular culture.
Me:	So, we're just Christians? We don't belong to any culture?
Them:	Well, we're Christians, and we belong to the Christian culture.

When I learned about the Chinese religions in graduate school, however, I saw that my parents had, intentionally or not, passed on to me the familial piety, respect for elders, and wholesome and balanced life characteristic of the Taoist-Confucian-Buddhist synthesis that emerged out of the meeting of these three traditions during and after the Later Han dynasty in China (23–220 C.E.). Yet my parents were also right, for they understood clearly as first-generation converts from South Asian (Theravadan) Buddhism to Christianity that while they were in the world, they did not belong to the world (cf. John 17:6–19). As such, my parents had handed down to me both Confucian values and Christian faith. This book reflects part of my own quest to learn about the Christian culture they handed down to me, even as I have come to appreciate the truths, beauty, goodness, and values of other cultural-religious traditions, some of which I also received from them. As such, I dedicate this volume to my mom and dad with affection and gratitude.

At the same time, it is quite safe to say that this book would not have come together as it has without the persistence of Bob Hosack, senior acquisitions editor at Baker Academic, who was relentless (in his own low-key way) in pursuing me for a book. Bob, the vision you have for Baker specifically and for evangelical theology in general is to be commended.

Many others have contributed to this volume. Chapter 2 was written during the summer before the Regent College Fall Theology Conference on "Evangelicalism and the World Religions" held in October 2001 and later published as "Discerning the Spirit(s) in the World of Religions: Toward a Pneumatological Theology of Religions," in John G. Stackhouse Jr., ed., *No Other Gods before Me? Evangelicals and the Challenge of World Religions* (Grand Rapids: Baker, 2001). My thanks to Mark Reasoner, my colleague and conversation partner in the department of biblical and theological studies at Bethel College, for reading and commenting on one of the original drafts for this chapter.

The earliest version of chapter 3 was presented at the twenty-eighth annual meeting of the Society for Pentecostal Studies held at Evangel University, Springfield, Missouri, 13–15 March 1999 and published later as "On Divine Presence and Divine Agency: Toward a Foundational Pneumatology" in *Asian Journal of Pentecostal Studies* 3.2 (July 2000). My thanks to Koo Dung Yun (Bethany College, Santa Cruz, California) for his remarks and comments at the conference.

Chapter 4 was originally written for a graduate seminar at Boston University during the spring of 1997 and published as "The Turn to Pneumatology in Christian Theology of Religions: Conduit or Detour?" in *Journal of Ecumenical Studies* 35.3–4 (1998). My thanks to Professor Lucien Richard, who guided me in this critical early stage of my research with ecumenical awareness, Catholic depth, and theological sophistication. The nomenclature of "pneumatological imagination" I have developed in this study and elsewhere has its origins in Professor Richard's observation that what

I was up to as a Pentecostal theologian was parallel to the "analogical imagination" developed by David Tracy in order to identify the substance of Catholic theological method. Thanks also to my brother, Eben Yong, for helping me with the "academese" of the original paper.

I. Howard Marshall saw the potential of a much longer version of chapter 5, originally written during the summer of 1997. The shorter version appeared as "Whither Theological Inclusivism? The Development and Critique of an Evangelical Theology of Religions" in *Evangelical Quarterly* 71.4 (October 1999). Dennis Cheek (formerly of the University of Rhode Island, now at the John Templeton Foundation) and R. Douglas Geivett (Biola University) commented on earlier drafts of the *EQ* essay. Thanks also to Clark Pinnock for his response in the same issue of *EQ*. I have incorporated some of his ideas at the appropriate place in chapter 5 of this volume.

This book may appear with chapter 6 before another version of that chapter appears in a Festschrift for Russell Spittler of Fuller Theological Seminary, for whom it was originally written during the summer of 1999. At present, it is scheduled to appear under the title *The Spirit and Spirituality: Essays in Honor of Russell P. Spittler*, edited by Wonsuk Ma and Robert P. Menzies for the Journal of Pentecostal Theology Supplement Series (Sheffield: Sheffield Academic Press). I am grateful to Ettien Kofi (formerly of Houghton College, now at St. Cloud State University) and Mark Reasoner (again) for their critical comments on the Festschrift version of this essay.

I was also counseled and encouraged in various ways in collecting these essays for Baker Academic by Jim Beilby (Bethel College), John Sanders (Huntington College), and John G. Stackhouse Jr. (Regent College). Mike Holmes, chair of the biblical and theological studies department at Bethel, has also been supportive of this project. Recent discussions with Dale Irvin (New York Theological Seminary), Ralph Del Colle (Marquette University), and Frank Macchia (Vanguard University) have helped nuance my discussion of the trinitarian missions. Glen Menzies (North Central University) read through and commented on the entire manuscript at a late stage. And, the editorial staff at Baker, especially Brian Bolger, clarified numerous factual and interpretive blunders on my part and prevented at least some of the obscurities in the text.

Of course, none of the aforementioned persons should be held responsible for the content of this book. I am grateful to the publishers and editors for permission to bring these previous publications together for this volume. In some cases, the material has been thoroughly reworked. The introductory chapter and part of the concluding chapter are newly written (the other part of the last chapter being a reworking of sections of the *JES* and *EQ* articles mentioned above).

Annalisa, Alyssa, and Aizaiah have been patient with daddy working on yet another book this last month or so, including over Christmas break this time! May the Spirit lead them to both give witness to Jesus and learn from their non-Christian friends as they negotiate life in this religiously plural world. My wife, Alma, has shared the home computer with me as she's worked her way through her master's degree at Bethel. From the day she said "I do!" over fourteen years ago, she has been a source of inspiration, support, and encouragement and has been patient far beyond the call of duty in sharing her husband with books and ideas. I could not do what I do without her. Once again, Alma, thank you for your love.

Crystal, Minnesota
Epiphany 2002

1

Introduction

Toward a Pneumatological Paradigm in Christian Theology of Religions

Historians of religion have debated over the last few generations whether *homo religiosus* was originally monotheistic, henotheistic, polytheistic, or even theistic at all.[1] However this question may be finally decided, it is certainly the case that there has been a diversity of religions at least since the time of the biblical patriarchs. It is also fair to say that the concept of "world religion" is a more recent attempt to draw attention to those religious phenomena that are not simply local expressions of faith but have expanded beyond their locations of origin across the globe. This expansion, of course, could not have occurred before the time of Columbus, and in that sense, the emergence of world religions is a relatively recent one in the history of humankind. In the West, perhaps no event has been as instrumental in raising awareness of the plurality and explanatory power of world faiths as the Parliament of Religions, which convened at the Chicago World's Fair in 1893.[2]

1. Most histories of religion written during the past generation include chapters on primeval or pre-historic religiousness; see, e.g., John D. Loftin, *The Big Picture: A Short World History of Religions* (Jefferson, N.C., and London: McFarland, 2000), chaps. 1 and 2.

2. Eric J. Ziolkowski, ed., *A Museum of Faiths: Histories and Legacies of the 1893 World's Parliament of Religions* (Atlanta: Scholars Press, 1993); Richard Hughes Seager, *The Dawn of Religious Pluralism: Voices from the World's Parliament of Religions, 1893* (La

Not surprisingly, there has certainly been a plurality of Christian responses to religious diversity since the time of the apostles.[3] In one sense, these responses have all presumed, if not explicitly derived from, a consciously developed theological perspective. Insofar as theology is itself the intellectual pursuit of understanding God and the relationship between God and the world, and insofar as the phenomenon of religion is one dimension of the human experience, Christian theology of religions is the attempt to reflect on the relationship between God and the phenomenon of the religions from the standpoint of Christian faith.

The purpose of this book is to propose and begin to explore the possibility of a pneumatological approach to Christian theology of religions. While having been previously suggested by a number of theologians, such a proposal remains to be explored at length.[4] In this introductory chapter, I lay out the fundamental objective for this project (the what), its primary rationale (the why), and its anticipated audiences (the who).

Toward a Pneumatological Theology of Religions (The What)

There are actually three questions here. What is religion? What is a theology of religions? And, what is a pneumatological theology of religions? I will deal briefly with each question in order.

Salle, Ill.: Open Court, 1993); idem, *The World's Parliament of Religions: The East/West Encounter, Chicago, 1893* (Bloomington: Indiana University Press, 1995); and James A. Kirk, "The World's Parliament of Religions Revisited," in *New Essays in Religious Naturalism*, ed. W. Creighton Peden and Larry E. Axel, Highlands Institute Series 2 (Macon, Ga.: Mercer University Press, 1993), 161–72.

3. See Richard J. Plantinga, ed., *Christianity and Plurality: Classic and Contemporary Readings* (Oxford: Blackwell, 1999), and the literature cited there.

4. To my knowledge, there is no booklength discussion to date except for my *Discerning the Spirit(s): A Pentecostal-Charismatic Contribution to Christian Theology of Religions*, Journal of Pentecostal Theology Supplement Series 20 (Sheffield: Sheffield Academic Press, 2000). Clark Pinnock's *Flame of Love: A Theology of the Holy Spirit* (Downers Grove, Ill.: InterVarsity, 1996) comes closest, even if Pinnock himself considers this more of a systematic pneumatological theology than of the *theologia religionum* genre (see chapter 5). Michael E. Lodahl, *Shekhinah Spirit/Spirit: Divine Presence in Jewish and Christian Religion* (New York: Paulist Press, 1992), has a restricted focus on one pneumatological theme in two religious traditions. Deserving of mention is Horst Georg Pöhlmann, *Heiliger Geist: Gottesgeist, Zeitgeist oder Weltgeist*, Reihe Apologetische Themen 10 (Neukirchen-Vluyn: Friedrich Bahn, 1998), who devotes one chapter (4) explicitly to this question of a pneumatological theology of religions. Others who have suggested but not carried out pneumatological approaches to theology of religions will be discussed in chapter 4.

What Is Religion?

One of the most complex questions in the academic study of religion today is itself the question, What is religion? The positivistic answer to this question is, "superstition." The answer provided within Christian pietistic circles is something to the effect that "religion is the human effort to reach God; Christianity, on the other hand, is not a 'religion,' but rather a relationship with the God-man, Jesus Christ" (thus representing divinity reaching down to human beings instead). I certainly do not intend to discuss this question exhaustively here. Let me, however, say three things about the question, What is religion?

First, religion is a complex aspect of human experience that is manifested through and inseparable from other dimensions of human life. The Western preoccupation with definition, expressed most clearly in its atomistic division of research and intellectual labor in the departments of universities and other institutions of higher learning, simply has not been able to do justice to the phenomenon of religion through this approach since human religious activity can be isolated only in abstraction. Even the biblical description of pure religion—as caring for orphans and widows, and keeping oneself "unstained by the world" (James 1:27)—points to another dimension, its sociality. Minimally, is not the religious dimension of human experience always embedded in or intertwined with the cultural, social, political, and economic dimensions of life? Put another way, can we understand human religious experience apart from understanding the cultural, social, political, and economic elements with which it is associated? If this is the case, then whatever religion is, the study of religion is, effectively, the study of what it means to be human. This would include, of course, the study of human history, society, and culture. Historical approaches to religion, for example, would focus on the development of religious practices and beliefs and on the influences that various religious traditions have had on each other. Sociological analyses would highlight the interrelationship between religion and society, politics and economics, and the interconnectedness between them. Cultural studies would explore the texts, works of art, rituals, and other behavioral expressions of the human religious impulse.

The second point naturally follows, namely that religion is

irreducible to any one dimension of human experience and the study of religion to any one method or approach. Here I am resisting the attempts that have been made over the last century to reduce religion to an opiate for the weak (Marx and Nietzsche), that which is representative of the mind of society (Durkheim), a projection of the subconscious (Freud), or any other one explanation.[5] I agree that there is an important place for the hermeneutics of suspicion with regard to defining religion, even as I agree that in some specific cases the masters of suspicion have diagnosed the religious phenomenon accurately. That said, there is no neutral place from which one can pontificate about the religions precisely because the student of religion cannot disentangle completely either himself or herself or the phenomenon of religion from the complex web of human life. Insofar as this is the case, the definition of religion is always informed by the values resident in the various dimensions of human life through which religious experience is mediated, by the values implicit in the tools of analysis that are employed, and by the perspectives, biases, and historical situatedness of the investigator. This alerts us to two facts: that there is no such thing as religion in its purity that can be isolated for discussion or investigation and that no inquiry into religious experience is value-free.

But if that is all that can be said, can we ever get objectively at what we might conceive of as the "core" of religion? This leads to a third point, my adoption of Paul Tillich's definition of religion as ultimate concern. In his words, religion is "the state of being grasped by an ultimate concern which qualifies all other concerns as preliminary and which itself contains the answer to the question of the meaning of our life."[6] I use Tillich's definition fully aware of the existentialist framework in which it was formulated. At the same time, I believe it is useful for at least two reasons. First, there is room in Tillich's definition for all of the other

5. On religion and these masters of suspicion, see the overview provided in Daniel Pals, *Seven Theories of Religion* (New York and Oxford: Oxford University Press, 1996), esp. chaps. 2–4.

6. Paul Tillich, *Christianity and the Encounter of World Religions* (1963; reprint, Minneapolis: Fortress, 1994), 3. This definition of Tillich's goes back to his *Systematic Theology*, vol. 1 (Chicago: University of Chicago Press, 1951), passim, esp. 11–14. Cf. also his definition of religion as the substantive depth of culture and culture as the expression or form of religion; idem, "Aspects of a Religious Analysis of Culture," in *Theology of Culture*, ed. Robert C. Kimball (London: Oxford University Press, 1959), 40–51.

(penultimate) concerns with which religion, as the ultimate concern, engages. One could, after all, define religion in a variety of other ways—for example, according to its origins, whether it be from demonic influence or from primordial UFOs. In these cases, then, the discussion of religion would be, de facto, the discussion of demonology or space travelers. My point is that a definition of religion that is not sufficiently flexible to account for its complexity will ultimately be reductive and thus useless. I prefer a definition that allows discussion of its relationship to demonic activity or, for that matter, to alien beings rather than one that decides in an a priori sense either to include or exclude these elements.

The second reason for the appeal of Tillich's definition is its amenability to theological analysis. Tillich was, after all, a theologian who reflected at great length, and often great depth, on the human religious experience. My interests are predominantly theological, even if I approach the subject fully aware that no discussion of religious experience can be *only* theological but must also be anthropological, historical, social, and cultural.

What Is a Theology of Religions?

Building on Tillich's definition, I suggest that in generalist terms a theology of religions is the attempt to understand the human ultimate concern within a theistic framework. Would Buddhists be able to develop a theology of religions? This depends in part on what Buddhists understand by the theistic reference. My point here is simply that a theology of religions attempts to understand how the phenomenon of human religiousness in all its complexity relates to God.

Christian theology of religions is informed specifically by faith commitments arising out of the Christian experience of Jesus Christ and his Spirit. Given the Christian conviction that such experience is definitively set forth in the Hebrew Bible and the Christian Scriptures, Christian theology of religions inevitably includes an investigation of "what the Bible says" about the phenomenon of religion. Yet here again, the study of "what the Bible says" is both hermeneutical and axiological. According to the brief analysis above, as a religious document, the Bible itself is (at least) historically, culturally, and socially mediated. For this reason, contemporary biblical studies includes a variety of tools drawn from the social and humanistic sciences designed to uncover the context of the world of the Bible.

A biblical theology of religions then also includes a biblical theology of history, a biblical theology of society, a biblical theology of culture, and so on. Even with its source document as a starting point, a Christian theology of religions nevertheless remains a complex endeavor. And why should this not be the case? Because Christians believe that God is revealed not a-historically, a-socially, or a-culturally, but in the Word made "flesh" (John 1:14) and in the Spirit poured out on "all flesh" (Acts 2:17), a Christian theology of religions is alert to the multidimensionality of human experience and religiosity.

This has certainly been the case historically. I would suggest, for example, that Clement of Alexandria's reference to the Buddha (*Stromata* 1.15) cannot be understood apart from Justin Martyr's discussion of the activity of the *Logos spermatikos* in all persons, including the Greek philosophers (*1 Apology* 20; *2 Apology* 13). Further, can Augustine's discussion of the Manicheans be completely divorced from his reflections on the two cities and from his dependence on Neoplatonism? Is the theology of the medieval Scholastics qualitatively different from that of the theological reflections of Al-Ghazali or Maimonides, or did these systems not mutually interact and perhaps influence each other? These are horrible generalizations. My point, however, is that there can never be a "pure" theology of religions completely separated from a theology of culture, or a philosophical theology, or a theology of history, and so on.

Of course, this also means that there is never a "pure" Christianity in the sense of an unacculturated Christianity. It is not even a matter of missionaries taking the pure gospel to the two-thirds world. In point of fact, we now realize that to search for such a pure "essence of Christianity" as did Harnack and other modernist liberals was a mistake, precisely because to think in these terms is to misconceive how our cognitive categories transfer neatly into reality.[7] Rather, the gospel has always already been translated into the categories of first-century Palestine, then later into those of Samaria, Rome, and even into those of the ends of the earth.

7. Cf. Stephen Sykes, *The Identity of Christianity: Theologians and the Essence of Christianity from Schleiermacher to Barth* (Philadelphia: Fortress, 1984).

In another sense, then, a Christian theology of religions is also a Christian theology of mission.[8] The goal here is the translation or contextualization of the gospel in the cultural-linguistic idiom of the religious other, be it Buddhist, Hindu, or Muslim. Of course, there is always a fine line between contextualization and syncretism. Yet this line needs to be recognized as a dynamic one, to be renegotiated at every turn as Christians encounter religious others afresh. A robust Christian theology of religions is required precisely because the Christian mission in a postcolonial, postfoundationalist, and postmodern world needs to be rethought, perhaps from the ground up.[9] There is no longer a centrally authoritative epistemic structure to adjudicate religious disputes (even the Pope cannot resolve interreligious disputes on his own). Rather, our situation may well be characterized as one in which epistemological and hermeneutical power emerges instead from the margins. Local voices, readings, and interpretations are vying for the right to redefine the "great traditions"—whether Christian, Buddhist, Islamic, etc.—as they have been handed down.[10]

What does this mean for a Christian theology of religions? For one thing, it means that Christian thinking about the religions can no longer be done in an a priori manner, from the theological armchair, as it were. Rather, theologizing about the religions requires engaging them. The days when one could pontificate about the religious others without knowing anything about them or without having interacted with them at all are over. In short, a Christian theology of religions needs to emerge out of a genuine dialogue with the religions. Such a dialogue, of course, needs to steer

8. On this point, see also Gerald H. Anderson, "Theology of Religions: The Epitome of Mission Theology," in *Mission in Bold Humility: David Bosch's Work Considered*, ed. Willem Saayman and Klippies Kritzinger (Maryknoll: Orbis, 1996), 113–20.

9. These issues are laid out nicely in Harold Netland, *Encountering Religious Pluralism: The Challenge to Christian Faith and Mission* (Downers Grove, Ill.: InterVarsity, 2001), esp. part 1; cf. also Kenneth Cracknell, *Toward a New Relationship: Christians and People of Other Faith* (London: Epworth, 1986).

10. With regard to Christianity, one needs only to think about the emergence of Asian, African, and Latin American theologies that have countered Western definitions of the gospel in Eurocentric terms. The result is that there is no longer a "Christianity," but rather many different "christianities." Of course, what has been happening with regard to Christian awareness of the diversity within its own house is also happening in other world religious traditions. See, e.g., Hans Küng, *Christianity: Essence, History and Future* (New York: Continuum, 1995); and idem, *Judaism: Between Yesterday and Tomorrow* (New York: Crossroad, 1992), along with any textbook on the world religions carried by a reputable university publisher that has appeared during the past two decades.

between the Scylla of a monologistic, a prioristic, and colonialistic/imperialistic defining of religious others on the one hand, and the Charybdis of a syncretistic, (simply) empiricistic, and relativistic attitude on the other. Is Christian theology today equipped for such a project?

What Is a Pneumatological Theology of Religions?

It is precisely at this point that I believe a pneumatological approach to Christian theology of religions can make a contribution. While I will later return to a more thorough engagement with the question, What is a pneumatological theology of religions? for now, let me briefly indicate its promise by providing a preliminary response along three lines.

First, a pneumatological theology is a robustly trinitarian theology. I argue elsewhere that pneumatology completes and fills out the Christian doctrine of the Trinity.[11] As such, not only does a pneumatological theology of religions contribute to the recent renaissance of pneumatology in Christian theological reflection,[12] but it also engages the current attempts to develop trinitarian approaches to understanding the religions.[13]

Second, given the contemporary situation in theological method in which emphasis is placed on local or marginal epistemologies and hermeneutics, and given the requirement that *theologia*

11. See Yong, *Spirit-Word-Community: Theological Hermeneutics in Trinitarian Perspective*, New Critical Thinking in Theology and Biblical Studies (Aldershot, Hampshire, UK, and Burlington, Vt.: Ashgate, 2002), chap. 2.

12. The literature on pneumatology that has emerged during the last generation is immense. For introductions to the current discussion, see John McIntyre, *The Shape of Pneumatology: Studies in the Doctrine of the Holy Spirit* (Edinburgh: Clark, 1997); Gary D. Badcock, *Light of Truth and Fire of Love: A Theology of the Holy Spirit* (Grand Rapids: Eerdmans, 1997); Nancy Victorin-Vangerud, *The Raging Hearth: Spirit in the Household of God* (St. Louis: Chalice, 2000); Donald G. Bloesch, *The Holy Spirit: Works and Gifts* (Downers Grove, Ill.: InterVarsity, 2000); and Veli-Matti Kärkkäinen, *Pneumatology: The Holy Spirit in Ecumenical, International, and Contextual Perspective* (Grand Rapids: Baker, 2002).

13. For suggestions toward a trinitarian theology of religions, see, e.g., Kevin Vanhoozer, "Does the Trinity Belong in a Theology of Religions? On Angling the Rubicon in the 'Identity' of God," in *The Trinity in a Pluralistic Age*, ed. Kevin Vanhoozer (Grand Rapids: Eerdmans, 1997), 41–71; and the three essays by Rowan Williams, Gavin D'Costa, and Christoph Schwöbel on the promise of trinitarian theology for theology of religions in part 1 of *Christian Uniqueness Reconsidered: The Myth of a Pluralistic Theology of Religions*, ed. Gavin D'Costa (Maryknoll, N.Y.: Orbis, 1990). D'Costa advances the discussion substantively in his recent book, *The Meeting of Religions and the Trinity* (Maryknoll, N.Y.: Orbis, 2000), as does S. Mark Heim, *The Depths of the Riches: A Trinitarian Theology of Religious Ends* (Grand Rapids: Eerdmans, 2001). An older, much smaller, but still suggestive work is Raimundo Panikkar, *The Trinity and the Religious Experience of Man* (Maryknoll, N.Y.: Orbis, 1973).

religionum today needs to genuinely engage the world of the religions, perhaps pneumatology can contribute to this task where previous approaches have fallen short. Might it be that a theology of the first article with the emphasis on God the Creator has led to an undue optimism with regard to common grace and that a theology of the second article with an emphasis on Christ the Redeemer has led to an undue pessimism with regard to theological anthropology (and, perhaps, an ecclesiocentrism with regard to the soteriological question)? If there is any truth at all to these generalizations, what might a theology of the third article focused on the Spirit as the eschatological arrival of God and the divine kingdom contribute to the question of theology of religions?[14] I will argue that it is precisely because the Spirit is both universal and particular, both the Spirit of God and the Spirit of Jesus the Christ, that pneumatology provides the kind of relational framework wherein the radical alterity—otherness—of the religions can be taken seriously even within the task of Christian theology. The result, perhaps, is the emergence of a new set of categories that may chart the way forward.

This leads to a third point, that a pneumatological theology of religions allows us to ask the soteriological question within a different, and perhaps broader, framework. Certainly, since the Spirit is the Spirit of Jesus, a pneumatological *theologia religionum* takes the soteriological question seriously with regard to the person and name of Jesus. But does the soteriological question therefore become subordinated to the ecclesiological question? In other words, is the Spirit at work only in and through the church, and is salvation therefore available only ecclesiocentrically (*extra ecclesia nulla salus*, or "no salvation outside the church")? This, of course, raises the question of what it means to talk about the church as well as the question of how, if at all, the church mediates Christian salvation. But of course, the Spirit cannot be limited to

14. The distinctions between theologies of the first, second, and third articles are derived from the work of D. Lyle Dabney, "Otherwise Engaged in the Spirit: A First Theology for the Twenty-First Century," in *The Future of Theology: Essays in Honor of Jürgen Moltmann*, ed. Miroslav Volf, Carmen Krieg, and Thomas Kucharz (Grand Rapids: Eerdmans, 1996), 154–63; and idem, "Starting with the Spirit: Why the Last Should Now Be First," in *Starting with the Spirit*, ed. Stephen Pickard and Gordon Preece, Task of Theology Today 2 (Hindmarsh, Australia: Australian Theological Forum; Adelaide, Australia: Openbook, 2001), 3–27. On the Spirit as the possibility of God, see Dabney, "The Nature of the Spirit: Creation as a Premonition of God," in *Starting with the Spirit*, ed. Pickard and Preece, 83–110, esp. 101–9.

the institutional forms of the church, and in that sense the Spirit "blows where it chooses" (John 3:8).[15] If that is the case, why would the Spirit blow "outside" the church but not at all in the religions, especially if the religions themselves are never only (or purely) the religions but are already culturally, socially, and politically informed in some way? Yet it is also certainly the case that because the Spirit is the Spirit of Jesus, any desire to bracket the soteriological question can only be momentary. The promise of a pneumatological approach to the religions, however, is that even a temporary bracketing of the question may open up new lines of dialogue and engagement with the religious other so that returning to the soteriological question later may mean returning to a different set of questions within a different framework. In this case, of course, a pneumatological *theologia religionum* would have succeeded in its objective: to push the question of Christian theology of religions farther along.

From a "Soteriology of the Unevangelized" to a "Theology of Religions" (The Why)

At this point, however, the question may arise as to why such a development may be considered an advance in the discussion of Christian theology of religions. In order for me to argue this case, let me briefly summarize the dominant categories that have been featured in the theology of religions discussion so far and explain why they may have outworn their usefulness and are no longer viable.

The Categories: Exclusivism, Inclusivism, Pluralism

By the mid-1980s, the discussion of Christian theology of religions was dominated by the categories of exclusivism, inclusivism, and pluralism.[16] Exclusivism was the convenient label given to the traditional Christian position of *extra ecclesia nulla salus.* This explains, of course, the importance of infant baptism from Augustine through to the Reformation. Apart from Christian baptism, the stain of original sin on human lives was sufficient for damnation. During the Reformation, however, this consensus was

15. See Hans Schwarz, "Reflections on the Work of the Spirit outside the Church," in *Credo in Spiritum Sanctum* (Vatican City: Libreria Editrice Vaticana, 1982), 2:1455–72.

16. The landmark historical study here is Alan Race, *Christians and Religious Pluralism: Patterns in the Christian Theology of Religions* (Maryknoll, N.Y.: Orbis, 1983).

broken on two fronts. On the one hand, the doctrine of baptism was itself radically reconceived. On the other hand, the doctrine of the church was itself shaken to its foundations. By the twentieth century, then, the exclusivistic position had been revised in at least two directions. Karl Barth, for example, was certainly an exclusivist, but his christomonistic exclusivism affirmed salvation as revealed in Christ even while denying that salvation is to be found in "Christianity," the latter being, like any other religious tradition, representative of the human attempt to reach God.[17] Alternatively, evangelical exclusivists, of whom I will have more to say later, have focused on the necessity of confession of the name of Jesus as constitutive of salvation (cf. Rom. 10:9–13).

Inclusivism, by contrast, has always affirmed the distinction between salvation as ontologically secured (through the person and work of Christ) and as epistemically accessed (through the preaching of the gospel, among other providential means of God). During the post–Vatican II period, Karl Rahner developed the inclusivistic argument further than it had ever been before.[18] It must be possible for those who have either never heard or never understood the gospel to be saved since God desires that none should perish and has made salvation available to all persons in his own mysterious ways (e.g., 1 Tim. 2:3–4; John 3:16; 1 John 2:2). As such, the Christology of John's Gospel that emphasizes the Logos as the true light "which enlightens everyone" (John 1:9) is central to theological inclusivism. While the religions may or may not be mediators of salvation, the key is not the religious tradition as such but whether or not the individual responds to God (or whatever the person considers to be religiously

17. See Karl Barth, "The Revelation of God as the Abolition of Religion," in *The Doctrine of the Word of God*, vol. 1, pt. 2 of *Church Dogmatics*, trans. G. T. Thomson and Harold Knight (Edinburgh: Clark, 1956), §17. See also Hendrik Kraemer, *The Christian Message in a Non-Christian World* (London: International Missionary Council, 1938).

18. See Karl Rahner, "Anonymous Christians," in *Theological Investigations*, trans. Karl and Boniface Kruger (Baltimore: Helicon; London: Darton, Longman and Todd, 1969), 6:390–98, along with numerous other essays on the "anonymous Christianity" motif scattered throughout his *Theological Investigations*. The literature on Rahner's proposal is voluminous. For starters, see the summary and critique in Gavin D'Costa, *Theology and Religious Pluralism: The Challenge of Other Religions* (Oxford: Blackwell, 1986), chap. 4; cf. also John Peter Kenny, *Roman Catholicism, Christianity and Anonymous Christianity: The Role of the Christian Today*, Theology Today 44 (Hales Corners, Wis.: Clergy, 1973); and Eamonn Conway, *The Anonymous Christian—A Relativized Christianity?* European University Studies, Series 23, Theology 485 (Frankfurt and New York: Lang, 1993).

ultimate) according to the light that the individual has received (cf. Rom. 2:12–16).

From this, the natural progression has been to move toward what has come to be known as the pluralist position. Championed most vigorously by John Hick and Paul F. Knitter, pluralism sought to move beyond Rahner's inclusivistic christocentrism toward what they call a pluralistic theocentrism.[19] Presupposing the notion of epistemic parity—that salvation needs to be universally accessible to all persons regardless of where or when they were born, the cultural-linguistic framework they have been socialized into, or the religious tradition that has nurtured them—pluralists have suggested that salvation should be understood as available through the various religions in the same way as the rays of the sun hit all persons without prejudice. Within this framework, the moral or ethical criterion becomes the most important with regard to discerning the salvific power of any religious tradition.[20]

It is no accident that the popularity of pluralism coincided with the emergence of postmodern relativism. As such, critics of the pluralist position have pointed out that the question of epistemic parity need not be confused with either the soteriological or ontological questions. Further, critics have also suggested that since pluralists have sought to include all persons within the plan of Christian salvation, they have imperialistically imposed a particular soteriological vision on the other faiths. Finally, even the question of epistemic relativism still begs the question of how it is that pluralists know the character of God around which their theocentrism revolves apart from its specifically revealed (for Christians: incarnational and pentecostal) forms.[21] For these and other reasons, the pluralist paradigm is no longer as appealing as it used to be.

19. See John Hick, "Jesus and the World Religions," in *The Myth of God Incarnate*, ed. John Hick (Philadelphia: Westminster, 1977), 167–85. The pluralist paradigm was at its height in the mid-1980s, led by Paul F. Knitter, *No Other Name? A Critical Survey of Christian Attitudes toward the World Religions* (Maryknoll, N.Y.: Orbis, 1985), 171–204, and John Hick, *An Interpretation of Religion: Human Responses to the Transcendent* (New Haven and London: Yale University Press, 1989); cf. also *The Myth of Christian Uniqueness: Toward a Pluralistic Theology of Religions*, ed. John Hick and Paul F. Knitter (Maryknoll, N.Y.: Orbis, 1987).

20. See John Hick, "On Grading Religions," *Religious Studies* 17 (1981): 451–67; and Paul F. Knitter, "Dialogue and Liberation: Foundations for a Pluralist Theology of Religions," *Drew Gateway* 58 (1988): 1–53, and *One Earth, Many Religions: Multifaith Dialogue and Global Responsibility* (Maryknoll, N.Y.: Orbis, 1995).

21. For a sampling of the extensive critique of the relativism and incoherence of the pluralist proposal, see, e.g., the responses in D'Costa, ed., *Christian Uniqueness Reconsidered*;

Questions for Exclusivism

But what about either exclusivism or inclusivism? There are many stripes of inclusivists and exclusivists, as there are pluralists or relativists who generally hold the "all roads lead to Rome" theory of religion. To simplify matters and to be consistent, I will retain the use of *exclusivism, traditionalism, restrictivism, particularism*, and their cognates throughout this book to refer to the more conservative Christians who object to both inclusivism and pluralism by espousing the position that salvation comes only through faith engendered by the hearing of the gospel, even while noting important nuances in these positions at the appropriate places.

While it is certainly true that all religious traditions espouse exclusivism at some level—for example, minimally, to make a truth claim, *A*, is to make an exclusive claim with regard to *not-A*—the claim that Christian salvation is dependent on access to a particular experience or set of beliefs is a central feature of theological exclusivism. The latter position, what I will call epistemological restrictivism, raises the following sets of questions. First, the exegetical: What grounds are there to read Acts 4:12 as ontological rather than epistemological? Why should not Romans 10:10–13 be read in light of Romans 2:12–16? Does John 3:17–18 say anything about the fate of the unevangelized? With regard to the exegesis of Scripture itself, I believe Gordon Smith to be on the right track in saying that "the Bible is not explicit on what happens to one who has never heard or had the opportunity to hear specifically of Jesus."[22] In that case, no amount of biblical prooftexting can

---

S. Mark Heim, *Salvations: Truth and Difference in Religion* (Maryknoll, N.Y.: Orbis, 1995), part 1; D. A. Carson, *The Gagging of God: Christianity Confronts Pluralism* (Grand Rapids: Zondervan, 1996); Vinoth Ramachandra, *The Recovery of Mission: Beyond the Pluralist Paradigm* (Grand Rapids: Eerdmans, 1996); James L. Fredericks, *Faith among Faiths: Christian Theology and Non-Christian Religions* (New York: Paulist Press, 1999); and, at length, Paul R. Eddy, *John Hick's Pluralist Philosophy of World Religions*, New Critical Thinking in Theology and Biblical Studies (Aldershot, Hampshire, UK, and Burlington, Vt.: Ashgate, 2002).

22. Gordon T. Smith, "Religions and the Bible: An Agenda for Evangelicals," in *Christianity and the Religions: A Biblical Theology of World Religions*, ed. Edward Rommen and Harold Netland, Evangelical Missiological Society Series 2 (Pasadena, Calif.: William Carey, 1995), 9–29, quote from p. 25. Cf. also the tentative "agnosticism" of Alister E. McGrath, "A Particularist View: A Post-enlightenment Approach," in *More Than One Way? Four Views on Salvation in a Pluralistic World*, ed. Dennis L. Okholm and Timothy R. Phillips (Grand Rapids: Zondervan, 1995), 149–80, esp. 176–80.

deliver an irrefutable answer to the question about the unevangelized. Epistemological restrictivism will therefore need to be argued on theological rather than exegetical grounds.

Second, the practical: Is not the logic of epistemological restrictivism that of motivating Christian evangelism and missions? In fact, does not evangelical exclusivism turn out to be a species of the traditional *extra ecclesia nulla salus* position since the experience of salvation is ecclesially mediated through Christian proclamation (even if its ecclesiology is reconceived within individualistic rather than communitarian categories)? Now even if the exclusivist or restrictivist position is rejected on this count, it by no means follows that the policy for Christian mission should be "don't tell the non-Christian since what she does not know will not hurt her" since Christian mission should be driven by obedience to the gospel rather than by the fear of hell. (In fact, I do not see any scriptural justification for connecting evangelism and missions with the fear of eternal damnation, although I am open to being shown otherwise.) My point here, however, is to raise the question of whether or not our theology (in this case, theology of religions) should be motivated by solely pragmatic concerns, and I would hope that our answer would be a unanimous no!

Third, and most important regarding my argument, are the categorical questions: Is not the function of "exclusivism" directed inwardly rather than externally? Is not religious exclusivism a claim made on behalf of one's home tradition rather than with regard to other faiths? If so, then at best, exclusivism concerns one religious tradition—one's own—and says nothing about other traditions except that they do not lead to salvation. Here, we come to the core of the issue: that exclusivism is first and foremost a soteriological category. In fact, it is concerned primarily with questions like who can be saved, how salvation occurs, and what is the fate of the unevangelized or the inadequately evangelized. Since it is arguable that the central purpose of religion is the attainment of salvation, it is certainly the case that any broadly construed theology of religions needs to deal with this set of soteriological questions. I would suggest, however, that either to limit theology of religions to the soteriological question, especially that concerning (as exclusivism focuses on) those who have never heard, or even to begin with it, leads to a reductionist view of the phenomenon of the religions. As such, while exclusivism may enable us to deal with the question concerning the unevangelized, it is not well equipped for engaging the task of theology of religions broadly considered.

Beyond Inclusivism toward Theology of Religions

The same goes for inclusivism. As I will make clear later (chap. 5), inclusivism, at least of the evangelical type, labors to demonstrate how those who have not heard may be saved even while they may be adherents of other religious traditions. The focus, however, is not on the non-Christian religious tradition as such but rather on Christian faith and the accessibility of its saving experience to those who have not heard. But again, this question concerns the soteriology of the unevangelized, strictly delimited, rather than the theology of religions. The focus remains on whether or not those in other faiths can experience Christian salvation and if so, how, rather than on understanding religious otherness as such.

I am unsure that the theological position to be developed in this book is best categorized under the label "inclusivism." I certainly am not an exclusivist if one means by this not only that salvation is dependent in an ontological sense on the person and work of Christ but also that one has to cognitively recognize that dependence. I am also not a pluralist who would deny both the latter epistemic condition as well as the former ontological premise. Perhaps I am close to the inclusivist position that affirms the ontological normativity of Christ for salvation without insisting that persons who have never heard the gospel or verbally confess Christ have absolutely no hope of this great salvation. Yet since the inclusivist category is more concerned with the question of salvation with regard to those who have not heard the gospel than with the question of religious others and the world's religions, it also proceeds from a christological starting point and is therefore closely intertwined with christological assumptions. But what if one begins with pneumatology rather than christology? I will argue in this book that a pneumatological paradigm transcends these categories.

That is exactly the promise, and the potential problem, of a pneumatological approach to theology of religions. In one sense, a pneumatological *theologia religionum* attempts to mediate between a narrow focus on what may be called the soteriology of religions on the one side and a purely descriptive account of either a phenomenology or a history of religions on the other. It is thereby motivated by the conviction that a richer theological account of the religions is called for than can be provided within a purely soteriological framework. Granted that soteriological concerns cannot be entirely disengaged from the theological task, yet is it fair to the explication of theology of religions that the soteriological issue has dominated the field of inquiry to date?[23]

In sum, then, the exclusivist-inclusivist-pluralist categories may have outlived their usefulness. They represent one approach to the theology of religions but not self-evidently the least problematic or most productive one. Is it not true, for example, that many of us are exclusivist, inclusivist, and pluralist in different respects? One could be an exclusivist regarding the foundations of salvation, an inclusivist regarding the question of the unevangelized, and a pluralist regarding the fact of religious diversity.[24] Further, the categories themselves are becoming murky through a variety of qualifications. Epistemological restrictivism and cautious agnosticism are now two forms of exclusivism.[25] Inclusivism itself also now features closed and open types, directed at not only the question of salvation but also the question of truth. And the question arises about just how helpful the categories are at this state of the discussion when versions of exclusivism such as epistemological restrictivism are said to be structurally equivalent to versions of pluralism such as universalism.[26] Given this state of affairs—that

23. The titles of the landmark publications in this area over the last generation are indicative of the motivating importance of the soteriological question: e.g., W. A. Visser't Hooft, *No Other Name: The Choice between Syncretism and Christian Universalism* (Philadelphia: Westminster, 1963); Russell F. Aldwinckle, *Jesus—A Savior or The Savior? Religious Pluralism in Christian Perspective* (Macon, Ga.: Mercer University Press, 1982); S. Mark Heim, *Is Christ the Only Way? Christian Faith in a Pluralistic World* (Valley Forge, Pa.: Judson, 1985); Carl E. Braaten, *No Other Gospel! Christianity among the Religions of the World* (Minneapolis: Fortress, 1992); and Schubert M. Ogden, *Is There Only One True Religion or Are There Many?* (Dallas: Southern Methodist University Press, 1992).

24. Clark H. Pinnock makes a similar claim in his *A Wideness in God's Mercy: The Finality of Jesus Christ in a World of Religions* (Grand Rapids: Zondervan, 1992), 15.

25. Alister McGrath defends a tentatively agnostic version of exclusivism while R. Douglas Geivett and Gary H. Phillips defend a more restrictivist view, both in *More Than One Way?* ed. Okholm and Phillips.

26. On open and closed inclusivism, and the discussion of restrictivism alongside universalism, see Paul J. Griffiths, *Problems of Religious Diversity* (Oxford: Blackwell, 2001), 56–65, 161–69. I am here not denigrating the extremely valuable work of Griffiths but rather suggesting that revisioning of these categories in a variety of directions lends credence to my call to bracket them long enough for us to address other theological questions before returning to the soteriological issue.

these exclusivist-inclusivist-pluralist categories are too narrowly focused on the soteriological question; that they are no longer seen to be adequate without serious qualification even with regard to the soteriological question they were originally designed to respond to; that they are being stretched beyond their originally proposed usage—is it not the case that this approach to Christian theology of religions has been found wanting and that another way needs to be explored in order to push the conversation forward?

The goal of this project is to find a valid theological method and rationale to bracket, at least temporarily, the soteriological question so that other questions can be pursued. However, in that case, the framework of inquiry needs to allow just such a research program to proceed. For this to occur, legitimately theological categories should be employed that foster rather than inhibit such inquiry. I submit that a pneumatological starting point for Christian theology of religions provides this kind of alternative categorical framework that remains resolutely Christian and still theological on the one hand, even while allowing for the religions to be heard on their own terms on the other.

The Guiding Questions (The Who)

The preceding established the framework of inquiry that is charted in this volume. To lay out the guiding questions, as I have done, is to identify one's dialogue partners, at least implicitly. In this section, I want to come clean with the latter, and I do so biographically. Along the way, an outline of the book's contents will be provided.

The Ecumenical Audience

I grew up in a Pentecostal denomination, the Assemblies of God, in both Malaysia and Northern California. I was led to believe early on that Pentecostalism in general and the Assemblies of God variety in particular was not only the supreme expression of Christian faith (if indeed other forms of the faith were even Christian at all) but also, of course, most conducive to Christian salvation. My undergraduate training at a Pentecostal Bible college did not do much to unsettle my Pentecostal confidence.

This confidence was radically shaken, however, during graduate studies at a conservative Wesleyan-Holiness seminary, and that along two fronts. First, awakening to historical awareness raised questions about the Pentecostalism that I had previously thought "fell directly from heaven."[27] Second, exposure to non-Pentecostal forms of Christian faith challenged my smugly elitist attitude. Together, these experiences combined to raise the ecumenical question in full force: How can I be so sure that my Pentecostal beliefs are reliable when they have emerged through historically contingent routes, and when central Pentecostal doctrines, even soteriologically connected ones, are not accepted by others whose Christian identity I could not easily deny? Of course, these are predominantly soteriological questions. But the trajectory of inquiry was already established.

I went on to pursue a second master's degree, this time at a secular university in the field of history, in order to fortify my background for doctoral work. The ecumenical question opened up to the interreligious question explicitly when I encountered, through the study of process philosophy, the Eastern religious traditions. My thesis this time explored one facet of the emergence of a religiously plural Christian consciousness during the late nineteenth and early twentieth centuries.[28]

Doctoral studies at Boston University gave me the opportunity to inquire further into these issues within an ecumenical context. I had both Protestant and Catholic theologians as teachers. Chapters 3 and 4 of this volume directly reflect my negotiating the issues at the intersection of Christian ecumenism and the interreligious dialogue.

The Pentecostal Audience

I was also providentially blessed at Boston University with mentors who gave me the space to research and explore the question of religious pluralism on my own terms rather than according to their agendas. Along the way, of course, the question of theological method was raised. I was able to return to the wellsprings of my own Pentecostal experience and tradition and ask the question: What can a Pentecostal perspective contribute to the discussion of Christian theology of religions? The result was my doctoral

27. My master's thesis originally focused on the question of the Christology of Oneness Pentecostalism but developed into a history of Christology centered on the Chalcedonian doctrine of the two natures of Christ: "The Doctrine of the Two Natures of Christ: A Historical and Critical Analysis" (master's thesis, Western Evangelical Seminary, 1993).

28. Yong, "From Pietism to Pluralism: Boston Personalism and the Liberal Era in American Methodist Theology, 1872–1952" (master's thesis, Portland State University, 1995).

thesis, now published in book form as *Discerning the Spirit(s): A Pentecostal-Charismatic Contribution to Christian Theology of Religions*. While the audience for this volume included my Pentecostal friends and colleagues, I was also interested in the broader ecumenical and interreligious discussions for their own sake. These latter groups remain important dialogue partners for me.

The methodological question, however, begged for more in-depth analysis. It is treated throughout this volume at least indirectly, albeit most intentionally in chapter 3. What is found in rudimentary form here is explicated at length in *Spirit-Word-Community: Theological Hermeneutics in Trinitarian Perspective*. There, the concepts of foundational pneumatology and the pneumatological imagination are central to the question of Christian hermeneutics and theological method. My Pentecostal experience and background are implicitly operative in that volume, even if not specifically spelled out. What is argued, however, is that pneumatological insights into hermeneutical and methodological issues in Christian theology open up the discussion in robustly ecumenical directions. In that sense, my reflections there are both implicitly Pentecostal on the one hand yet broadly ecumenical on the other.

Such remains the case for this book. Chapter 6, for example, emerges explicitly from my own experience as a Pentecostal. Within Pentecostal circles, the question of discernment is acute, both with regard to what might loosely be called charismatic manifestations or phenomena and with regard to the charismatic gift of the discernment of spirits (1 Cor. 12:10). Yet my own ecumenical horizons have challenged me to reconceptualize discernment within the broader framework of what St. Paul calls "life in the Spirit." As such, I see the following discussion as both implicitly Pentecostal and yet broadly ecumenical.

The Evangelical Audience

Growing up Pentecostal in the Assemblies of God during the '60s and '70s in Malaysia and (especially) during the '80s in California meant growing up fundamentalist in part and evangelical in part. The creation narratives, the experience of Jonah, the falling of Satan from heaven—these and other biblical accounts were certainly understood to be historically factual reports. The fundamentalist mentality, however, nurtured in me a love for the Bible. At the Pentecostal Bible college I attended, we read predominantly evangelical authors since as an oral culture, Pentecostals had for the most part neglected to produce intellectually sophisticated theological texts replete with academic apparatus.[29] And, of course, since Pentecostalism and evangelicalism had, since the 1940s and especially through the charismatic renewal movement of the '60s and '70s, been on continuously converging trajectories, my own socialization into the North American version of evangelicalism was subtly yet thoroughly accomplished.[30]

As such, I consider my own evangelical allegiances to be substantive. I am committed to the authority of Scripture, to the importance of a personal relationship with Jesus (as mediated by the Spirit, of course), and to the task of Christian mission and evangelism. If these are, minimally, nonnegotiable aspects of what it means to be evangelical, then I presume I count. Institutionally, I teach in an evangelical context. Chapter 2 of this book was originally written in response to my being invited—undoubtedly in part because of my institutional location—to participate in a conference devoted to discussing a specifically evangelical theology of religions. I believe that in itself is significant regarding my representing an evangelical voice in the *theologia religionum* conversation, at least to some degree. This is important because while evangelicals have been diligent to engage non-evangelical Christian voices, the reverse has not been as evident. I believe this situation is changing, and my hope is that this book will contribute to motivating non-evangelicals to engage at greater length with evangelical thinkers and arguments.

Initially, however, my journey within evangelicalism left me without any significant resources to develop the kind of broad theology of religions I believed to be important for contemporary Christian theology. Until, that is, I encountered the work of Clark Pinnock (and other evangelical theologians) in 1994. Pinnock's

29. Our theological diet consisted of all three volumes of Millard Erickson's *Christian Theology* (Grand Rapids: Baker, 1985), Bernard Ramm's *Protestant Biblical Interpretation*, 3d ed. (Grand Rapids: Baker, 1970), and an assortment of other evangelical authors published predominantly by Baker and Zondervan.

30. Most representative of this "merger" are the many charismatic forms of evangelicalism and the many evangelical expressions of Pentecostalism. Theologically, see Robert P. Menzies and William W. Menzies, *Spirit and Power: Foundations of Pentecostal Experience—A Call to Evangelical Dialogue* (Grand Rapids: Zondervan, 2000). I leave to one side the differences, radical in some places, between the two movements; on this, see my "The Word and the Spirit, or the Spirit and the Word: Exploring the Boundaries of Evangelicalism in Relationship to Modern Pentecostalism," *Trinity Journal* (forthcoming).

evangelical inclusivism inspired me because it seemed to suggest that I did not need to "leave" evangelicalism in order to continue to engage the question of the non-Christian faiths theologically. Further, by 1996, his *Flame of Love: A Theology of the Holy Spirit* revealed more explicitly his own charismatic identity. I devoted the summer of 1997 to an intensive engagement with Pinnock's project, the result of which was a paper published later in *The Evangelical Quarterly* and now revised as chapter 5 of this book. In these pages, then, I wish also to engage evangelical thinkers, not only to spur them on in the task of theology of religions (rather than the soteriology of the unevangelized), but also to enlist their critical and biblical perspectives in the project envisioned here.[31]

Given that the main chapters of this book consist of previously published essays, some repetition of the argument will be found. However, each chapter has been thoroughly reconsidered, if not extensively revised, for this volume. Simply put, my argument for a pneumatological approach to Christian theology of religions spirals toward its goal from biblical and missiological (chapter 2), philosophical (chapter 3), theological (chapters 4 and 5), and practical (chapter 6) perspectives. I prefer to see chapter 7 as transitional rather than concluding since it charts out the kind of research program that needs to be thoroughly engaged if a pneumatological *theologia religionum* is to be fully developed, adequately assessed, and, perhaps, have its promise fulfilled. Now, may the Spirit guide us as we proceed with the argument.

31. Certainly, Pinnock's inclusivism is intricately connected to his relational or open theism. While I am in broad sympathy with Pinnock's theological program, there are substantive differences between us in the details, where things may count the most. I have commented elsewhere on the evangelical debate between open and classical theists—"Possibility and Actuality: The Doctrine of Creation and Its Implications for Divine Omniscience," *Wesleyan Philosophical Society Online Journal* [http://david.snu.edu/~brint.fs/wpsjnl/v1n1.htm] 1.1 (2001), and especially, "Divine Knowledge and Future Contingents: Weighing the Presuppositional Issues in the Contemporary Debate," *Evangelical Review of Theology* 26.2 (2002): 240–64—and refer the interested reader there. That said, I would be remiss not to acknowledge the personal encouragement I have received from Pinnock over the years.

2

A Pneumatological Theology of Religions

Thesis and Overview

In this chapter, I sketch the basic biblical and theological framework of a pneumatological theology of religions as well as deal with a few potential objections to such a project. In the process of defining a pneumatological approach to theology of religions, I suggest that this proposal will play an important part in the further renaissance of contemporary trinitarian theology; that it also has the practical benefit of contributing to the formation of a more dynamic missiology; and that it will enable a more genuine and effective engagement with the post-Christian and postmodern cultures of the twenty-first century. My central claim, however, is a methodological one: that a pneumatological theology of religions not only commits but also enables us to empirically engage the world's religions in a truly substantive manner with theological questions and concerns.

A Biblical Overview

Christian theology begins with Scripture, even if there is a dynamic, dialectical, and dialogical interplay between Scripture and tradition as well as between the canon itself and the horizons of the interpreter and reader of Scripture. In developing a theology of religions, then, one should look to see what the Bible says about religion in general and religions more specifically. While there are not an overwhelming number of references to these topics in the biblical canon, it is fair to conclude that religion and the religions are presented as being divinely providential on the one hand and yet demonically inspired to deceive and turn human beings away from the truth on the other.[1] My goal, however, is to develop a theology of religions that proceeds from a pneumatological starting point. The primary question that emerges, then, is who is the Holy Spirit and what is his function—that is, what has he done, what is he doing, and what will he do?[2] I propose to explore the notion that the Holy Spirit is God present and active, the power of God in creation, re-creation, and final creation. Let us look at each of these categories briefly.[3]

The Spirit of God in Creation

God's presence and activity in creation speaks to the universality of the Holy Spirit. In fact, it is important to emphasize that all things are created by God's Word *and* God's Spirit. The creation narrative clearly portrays God as speaking the world into existence (Gen. 1). Yet sometimes overlooked is the fact that speech requires breath, and it is the breath of God that is first said to have "swept over the face of the waters" (Gen. 1:2). Elsewhere, the psalmist extols the creative and sustaining power of God through

1. For biblical surveys that support this conclusion, see Daniel B. Clendenin, *Many Gods, Many Lords: Christianity Encounters World Religions* (Grand Rapids: Baker, 1995), 117–40, and Clark Pinnock, *A Wideness in God's Mercy: The Finality of Jesus Christ in a World of Religions* (Grand Rapids: Zondervan, 1992), 85–110.

2. Donald L. Gelpi, S.J., *The Divine Mother: A Trinitarian Theology of the Holy Spirit* (Lanham, Md.: University Press of America, 1984), presents many valid reasons why theologians should use the feminine pronoun with regard to the Holy Spirit, the *ruach* of God, with the recognition that the Spirit is not female—or male, for that matter. However, I will use the conventional masculine pronoun since I am addressing a controversial topic—the religions—and there is no need to further complicate an already difficult task.

3. The Spirit as God present and active comes from the biblical scholar, Gordon Fee, *God's Empowering Presence: The Holy Spirit in the Letters of Paul* (Peabody, Mass.: Hendrickson, 1994), xxi and passim. What follows is also indebted in various ways to Jürgen Moltmann, *The Spirit of Life: A Universal Affirmation*, trans. Margaret Kohl (London: SCM, 1992); Michael Welker, *God the Spirit*, trans. John F. Hoffmeyer (Minneapolis: Fortress, 1994); and Lee Snook, *What in the World is God Doing? Re-imagining Spirit and Power* (Minneapolis: Fortress, 1999). The categories of creation, re-creation, and final creation, however, are mine.

the Spirit for both the heavens—"By the word of the Lord the heavens were made, and all their host by the breath [*ruach*] of his mouth" (Ps. 33:6)—and the earth—"When you hide your face, they [the creatures of the world] are dismayed; when you take away their breath, they die and return to their dust. When you send forth your spirit, they are created; and you renew the face of the ground" (Ps. 104:29–30). It is this same breath of God that also bestows *life* to certain creatures formed of clay, thus enabling *ha adam* to become "a living being" (Gen. 2:7; cf. Job 33:4).

Recognition of the Spirit's omnipresence follows from this pneumatological vision of creation and providence. Certainly, there is no place one can go to escape the Spirit of God:

> Where can I go from your spirit?
> Or where can I flee from your presence?
> If I ascend to heaven, you are there;
> if I make my bed in Sheol, you are there.
> If I take the wings of the morning
> and settle at the farthest limits of the sea,
> even there your hand shall lead me,
> and your right hand shall hold me fast. (Ps. 139:7–10)

This is a remarkable portrait of the ubiquitous presence of the divine Spirit. Even more striking is that in the context of this psalm, the Spirit's universal presence is declared by the psalmist's affirming God's exhaustive knowledge of the psalmist himself—both in the depth of his personal subjectivity (vv. 1–6) and across the breadth of his life from conception to last days (vv. 13–16). In other words, the Spirit's universality is intimately connected with God's knowledge of and activity in the world of human beings. This receives confirmation by St. Paul in his sermon at the Areopagus:

> The God who made the world and everything in it, he who is Lord of heaven and earth . . . he himself gives to *all* mortals *life and breath* and all things. From one ancestor he made all nations to inhabit the whole earth, and he allotted the times of their existence and the boundaries of the places where they would live, so that they would search for God and perhaps grope for him and find him—though indeed he is not far from each one of us. For "*in him we live and move and have our being*"; as even some of your own

poets have said, "For we too are his offspring" (Acts 17:24a, 25b–28 [my emphasis]).

From this, it is clear that human life—even that of the pagan poets (or philosophers) quoted here by Paul—is animated by the presence and activity of God by and through the divine Spirit.

The Spirit of God in Re-creation

It is precisely because the divine Spirit is universally present and active that God is not only Creator but also Re-creator, or Redeemer and Savior.[4] This is evident most concretely in the life, work, death, and resurrection of Jesus Christ—the ultimate sequence of pneumatological events in history. Notice the prevalence of the Spirit at key events in the Lukan version of the life of Jesus: conception (1:35), fetal development (1:39–44), dedication (2:25–35), baptism (3:21–22), temptation (4:1–14), ministry (4:18–19; cf. Acts 10:38), death (cf. Heb. 9:14), and resurrection (cf. Rom. 1:2–4). While I believe in the importance of Spirit-christology to the task at hand, space constraints prohibit any further development of this theme.[5] Yet the events of Jesus' life are paradigmatic for the ways in which God redeems and saves humankind individually and as a whole. It is pneumatology that provides for Luke the thread of continuity between his two books—volume one on the life of Jesus and volume two (Acts) on the life of the church, those who are being saved.

The centrality of the Day of Pentecost to Luke's story of the early church therefore should not be overlooked. At Pentecost, God enacted the first step of the divine plan to extend the boundaries of those who could be the people of God. The presence in Jerusalem of "devout Jews from every nation under heaven" (Acts 2:5, 8–11) provided the occasion for the outpouring of the Holy Spirit and the reconstituting of the "new" people of God. Recognizing this

4. It could also be argued that re-creation as a pneumatological motif is typologically prefigured in the Hebrew Bible in the sending of the wind (*ruach*) that causes the receding of the flood waters from the earth (Gen. 8:1).

5. For recent articulations of Spirit-Christology, see, e.g., Paul W. Newman, *A Spirit Christology: Recovering the Biblical Paradigm of Christian Faith* (Lanham, Md.: University Press of America, 1987); Gerald F. Hawthorne, *The Presence and the Power: The Significance of the Holy Spirit in the Life and Ministry of Jesus* (Dallas: Word, 1991); and Ralph del Colle, *Christ and the Spirit: Spirit-Christology in Trinitarian Perspective* (New York: Oxford University Press, 1994).

historic moment, Peter announces that this event signifies the beginning of the fulfillment of the words spoken through the prophet Joel:

> In the last days it will be, God declares,
> that I will pour out my Spirit upon all flesh,
> and your sons and your daughters shall prophesy,
> and your young men shall see visions,
> and your old men shall dream dreams.
> Even upon my slaves, both men and women,
> in those days I will pour out my Spirit;
> and they shall prophesy.
> And I will show portents in the heaven above
> and signs on the earth below,
> blood, and fire, and smoky mist.
> The sun shall be turned to darkness
> and the moon to blood,
> before the coming of the Lord's great and glorious day.
> Then everyone who calls on the name of the Lord shall be saved.
> (Acts 2:17–21, referencing Joel 2:28–32)

Two points deserve a bit more extended comment. First, this passage features the centrality of the Holy Spirit to the new work of God and clearly emphasizes the pneumatological character of the new covenant. What needs to be underscored is the extensiveness of the work of the Holy Spirit among the new people of God. At first glance, the text appears to limit the "effects" of the Spirit's work to that of prophecy, visions, and dreams. The divine objective expressed in Peter's sermon, however, is to prepare the way for the day of the Lord; more specifically, it is the full salvation of "everyone who calls on the name of the Lord" (Acts 2:21). As with the life of Jesus, this full salvation is a pneumatological work from start to finish. The Spirit is not only the sanctifier of those who are being saved, as it is commonly recognized, but also the one who actually brings about the new birth itself (Titus 3:5; John 3:3–7). More than that, it is the Spirit who is at work in the hearts and lives of individuals, preparing them for that new birth (John 16:8–11). Apart from that presence and activity of the Spirit of God, people would never be convicted about their sin or their need to repent and turn to God.

On one level, then, the "pentecostal" experience and event is an ecclesiological one: the work of the Holy Spirit in the present age is to birth and nurture Parthians, Medes, Elamites, and others in the body of Christ. On another level, however, Pentecost anticipates, as Peter clearly proclaims, the day of the Lord (Acts 2:17–21). This, along with the references to the many peoples present in Jerusalem, should caution us against reading the "all" of Acts 2:17 in an exclusively ecclesiological sense.[6] The Spirit's activity across the dimensions of both space—the Spirit's being poured out upon all people—and time—"in the last days," stretching from the Day of Pentecost to the coming of the kingdom of God—begs to be understood in a universal sense that transcends (at least the institutional boundaries of) the church. While I will return to develop this point later, it is important here to note that this universality is explicitly confirmed by Peter in his sermon to the household of Cornelius: "I truly understand that God shows no partiality, but in every nation anyone who fears him and does what is right is acceptable to him" (Acts 10:34b–35).

The Spirit of God in Final Creation

This leads to a second point regarding the events of Pentecost: the eschatological character of the Spirit's activity. The work of the Spirit of God covers not only original creation and re-creation (initial salvation), but extends also to final creation—the new heavens and the new earth. The diversity of peoples present in Jerusalem on the Day of Pentecost not only represents the configuration of the body of Christ but also anticipates the scope of the kingdom of God. The seer of the Apocalypse confirms that the saints are those from every tribe, language, people, and nation (Rev. 5:9; 7:9; 21:24). This testifies further to the universal presence and efficacious activity of the Spirit. Clearly, it is the Spirit who extends the divine invitation to the new heavens and new earth (Rev. 22:17) and also accomplishes the transition for the people of God. This is true not only in a symbolic sense (Rev. 4:1–2; 21:10), but also in the sense that it is the Spirit who is the power of resurrection life (Rom. 1:4; Ezek. 37:1–14).

6. Even the classical, exclusivist Pentecostal exegete Stanley M. Horton says that the "all" in this passage refers to "all mankind." See Horton's commentary on Acts 2:17 in *The Book of Acts* (Springfield, Mo.: Gospel Publishing House, 1981), 38; cf. Welker, *God the Spirit*, 228–78, for a much more extended argument for this interpretation.

Yet it is also important to note that the eschatological work of the Spirit of God involves not only the people of God but also the entirety of the creation itself. The Spirit is that power of God that both renews the face of the earth (Ps. 104:30) and also finally re-creates it. I refer here not so much to the emergence of the new heavens and new earth out of the fiery destruction of the initial created order (2 Pet. 3:12–13), even if the Spirit is symbolized throughout Scripture as God's purifying fire. Rather, I am thinking more specifically about the Spirit who groans in, with, and through us, in order to bring about the liberation of the creation itself (Rom. 8:18–27). This final creation will deliver the creation "from its bondage to decay and [bring it into] the freedom of the glory of the children of God" (Rom. 8:21). The Spirit, of course, is the Spirit of freedom, and life in the Spirit is salvation, deliverance, and liberation (Rom. 8:1–17).

The Spirit at work in original creation, re-creation and final creation thus highlights the dynamic character of the divine plan. It also explains the tension that exists in our time, one that is "between the times"—already but not yet, to use eschatological language. We not only eagerly anticipate the coming of the kingdom but also celebrate its presence in our midst (Luke 17:21), precisely because of the presence and activity of the Spirit (Luke 11:20).[7] The goal of the Spirit's activity, however, is not just a manifestation of what some call the *charismata*, but the establishment of righteousness, peace, and justice. In the words of the prophet Isaiah (32:15–17),

> . . . until a spirit from on high is poured out on us,
> and the wilderness becomes a fruitful field,
> and the fruitful field is deemed a forest.
> Then justice will dwell in the wilderness,
> and righteousness abide in the fruitful field.
> The effect of righteousness will be peace,
> and the result of righteousness, quietness and trust forever.

7. The NRSV reads Luke 11:20 as "the finger of God." Most scholars agree that Jesus' reference here to casting out demons by the "finger of God" refers to the Spirit of God, which is Matthew's language (Matt. 12:28); cf. the comments on these passages by D. A. Carson (on Matthew) and Walter Liefeld (on Luke) in vol. 8 of *The Expositor's Bible Commentary*, ed. Frank E. Gaebelein (Grand Rapids: Zondervan, 1984), 289 and 951 respectively.

The Spirit is thereby the universal presence and activity of God. He is a universality that permeates both the external structures of the natural and human world and the internal realms of human hearts. He is also a universality that spans the entirety of God's work from original creation, to re-creation, to final creation. Having established this pneumatological framework, the question that now needs to be asked is this: How does this pneumatological vision enable theological understanding of the phenomena we today call the diversity of religions?

The Theological Framework

Having laid the biblical foundations for a pneumatological approach to the religions, I now proceed to develop the theological framework for this project in three steps. First, the trinitarian character of this pneumatological theology will be made explicit. Second, the basic axioms of a pneumatological *theologia religionum* will be detailed. Finally, mention will be made of how this proposal is suggestive for advancing the contemporary discussion in Christian theology of religions.

Pneumatology and Trinitarian Theology

I see numerous advantages to a pneumatological approach to theology of religions. The most important of these is that such an approach is both motivated by and invigorates trinitarian theology. To put it bluntly, only a genuinely pneumatological theology is a fully trinitarian theology. This is in part because Christians cannot speak of the Holy Spirit apart from either the First or the Second Persons of the Triune God. The Spirit is the supremely mediational and relational symbol. Augustine, for example, understood the Spirit as the love that existed between Lover (Father) and Beloved (Son). For Barth, the Spirit reveals to us (i.e., is the "revealedness" of . . .) what the revealer (Father) has revealed (Son). Another trinitarian analogy sees the Spirit as the breath that mediates speaker (Father) and the spoken word (Son) (Gen. 1:1–3). Theological schemas that explicate this same idea present the Spirit as mediating between the mystery of the transcendent Father and the revelation of the immanent Son; between the primordial Alpha and the eschatological Omega; between creation and redemption; between world and church; between nature and the kingdom of God; and so on. Certainly, at any number of levels, one can easily succumb to an idolatrous exaltation of the Spirit to the neglect or subordination of the Word, even as another can succumb to a misguided Jesusology apart from Father or Spirit. However, I am convinced that serious theological reflection today has to capitalize on the relational and mediational resources of pneumatology rather than "forget" the "silent member" of the Trinity as previous generations have done.

I would suggest that one way to forge a robust trinitarianism is to revisit the patristic metaphor of Word and Spirit as "the two hands of the Father." The origins of this metaphor go back to Irenaeus.[8] Briefly stated, the Word represents concreteness—as in, for example, Jesus of Nazareth and the written Scriptures—historical particularity, and the human experience of objectivity; the Spirit represents the dynamism of the Anointed One—as in, for example, the Christ and the living, inspired, and illuminating word of God—cosmic relationality, and the human experience of subjectivity. I will later (in chapter 6) propose a metaphysical interpretation of the "two hands." For the moment, however, I understand these first and foremost as theological categories that function heuristically and metaphorically. They enable us to envision the truth that God works all things with the divine hands: by and through *both* Word and Spirit. This means *not* that some things are to be considered manifestations of Word and other things of Spirit, but that Word and Spirit are inseparable features of *all* things. Thus, there is the universality of Word (e.g., the cosmic Christ) as well as a particularity of Spirit (e.g., that accentuates and values the differentiated order of determinate things) precisely because both aspects inhere—as in the patristic notion of *circumincessio* and the Greek notion of *perichoresis*—and inform each other.[9] If

8. Irenaeus, *Against Heresies* 4, preface, 4. I prefer this trinitarian model over the communitarian model currently advocated by social trinitarians because it seems to me to be capable of preserving the centrality of the notion of community inherent in the social doctrine without the latter's tendencies toward tritheism. For elaboration of this theme, see my *Spirit-Word-Community: Theological Hermeneutics in Trinitarian Perspective*, New Critical Thinking in Theology and Biblical Studies (Aldershot, Hampshire, UK, and Burlington, Vt.: Ashgate, 2002), chaps. 2 and 3.

9. The notion of the particularity of Spirit is argued extensively by Welker in his *God the Spirit*. See also Colin Gunton, *The One, the Three, and the Many: God, Creation, and the Culture of Modernity* (Cambridge: Cambridge University Press, 1993), 180–209; David Cunningham, *These Three Are One: The Practice of Trinitarian Theology* (Malden, Mass., and Oxford: Blackwell, 1998), 205–7; and George Hendry, *Theology of Nature* (Philadelphia: Westminster, 1980), 169–70.

this is the case, then any assessment that neglects either aspect of what God does fails to capture the heart or essence of that work or reality.

This togetherness of Word and Spirit means that the advantages of a pneumatological approach to the theological task can be assessed from a number of angles. Theologically, it means that reflection should bring together the biblical context and horizon with the contemporary context and horizon. Doctrinally, it means that articles of faith should be articulated in terms of faithfulness to past witnesses and relevance to contemporary needs and concerns. Most important, however, are the methodological implications regarding the doing of theology as involving Scripture, tradition, reason, and experience, each considered as the conjunction of both Word and Spirit. Scripture, for example, is the Word of God even as it testifies to Christ as the Logos; at the same time, Scripture as a product is inspired and illuminated by the Spirit as well. Tradition is the interpreter of Scripture, even as it is led by the Spirit in that process of interpretation (e.g., as in the New Testament canonical process). Reason is both Logos (John 1) and Spirit as the mind and interpreter of God (1 Cor. 2:10b–11). Experience is both concrete—of Christ—and dynamic—of the Spirit—even while ultimately being of God (Christ as the representation of the Father and the Spirit as the presence of the Father). The point is that the dualism between Word and Spirit are bridged and relational connections seen and reasserted within a trinitarian framework.

Toward a Pneumatological Theologia Religionum: *The Basic Framework*

To better appreciate these aspects of a pneumatological approach to theology of religions, the following three controlling axioms need to be succinctly stated. *Axiom 1: God is universally present and active in the Spirit.* Articulating this universal presence and activity is the task of foundational pneumatology—the investigation of the pneumatological features of the entire created order. While I will return to explicate this notion in the next chapter, it is helpful here to note the kinds of questions it is designed to engage. Such include, but are not limited to, the following: In what ways is the Spirit identifiable in creation—in the cosmos, in nature, in human history, and human experience? If human society includes politics and economics, what is the Spirit doing in those arenas of human life? If human culture includes the arts and the religions, what are the purposes of the Spirit in those domains of human experience? How does the Spirit sustain these dimensions of human life, and how do these reflect the presence and activity of the Triune God? The trinitarian character of this pneumatological proposal that defines Spirit not only in relationship to God but also in relationship to the Word should not be underestimated. It is the trinitarian framework that makes this pneumatological theology of religions distinctively *Christian* and distinguishes it from a Hindu theology of religions, whereby all things are Atman vis-à-vis Brahman, or a Buddhist philosophy of religions, emphasizing the interdependence of all things, or a Neo-Confucian metaphysic of the 10,000 things derived from the Great Ultimate.

Axiom 2: God's Spirit is the life-breath of the imago Dei *in every human being and the presupposition of all human relationships and communities.* This means that there is a pneumatological dimension to each human individual that sustains intersubjective communication, interpersonal relationships, and intentional, rational, moral and spiritual life.[10] All human engagements with the "other"—whether that other be human others, the world, or the divine—are pneumatologically mediated. This is first and foremost an ontological claim (thus Gen. 2:7 regarding our breath of life and Acts 17:28 regarding our life together in God) rather than a soteriological one. As such, might it not also connect with the Johannine claim that the Logos is "the true light, which enlightens *everyone*" (John 1:9a, my italics)? Together, these considerations support my contention that human beings are individuals-in-communities and are enabled by the Spirit of God. In other words, we live, think, communicate, and relate as spirit-beings, and our quest for ultimate reality proceeds from our being-in-communities (all of us belonging to multiple communities with varying degrees of commitment).

10. This is the thesis of Steven G. Smith, *The Concept of the Spiritual: An Essay in First Philosophy* (Philadelphia: Temple University Press, 1988), who builds on the work of Buber. Smith argues from a philosophical perspective that spiritual activity consists precisely of the relationships that intentional beings have with one another. I would not, however, wish to limit the notion of spiritual only to intentional relationships as Smith does. My own view, to be developed below, is that the category of spirit should be more robust, able to account not only for personal intentionality but also for natural trajectories, as well as the demonic.

I will return later to the importance of understanding the communal context of all religious quests. For the present, however, what needs to be emphasized is the fundamental human commonality—as pneumatologically situated individuals-in-communities—that transcends human differences of gender, race, ethnicity, class, and, of course, religion. At the same time, the constitution of human beings by Word and Spirit points to the objective *and* the subjective nature of human being-in-the-world. This calls for a recognition of human fallibility, and for human openness to each other in humility, as seeing through a glass, dimly (1 Cor. 13:12).[11]

Axiom 3: The religions of the world, like everything else that exists, are providentially sustained by the Spirit of God for divine purposes.[12] While I will qualify this thesis in important ways later, it is important to state this boldly here. Unless one is prepared to say that all forms and expressions of human culture are antitheistic, one cannot arbitrarily separate out one dimension of culture—the religious aspect—and so label it, as previous generations of theologians have, as either solely human efforts to reach God or as demonic. Rather, all human endeavors reflect either God's permissive or active will toward ultimately divine purposes centered around the full revelation of Jesus Christ and the impending kingdom of God. This should be no different with regard to the religions. As Clark Pinnock has observed, "It would seem strange if the Spirit excused himself from the very arena of culture where people search for meaning. If God is reaching out to sinners, it is hard to comprehend why he would not do so in the sphere of religion."[13] In short, a pneumatological approach to the religions enables an inclusive methodology and hermeneutic rather than a monological one that assumes in an a priori sense that the religions lie beyond the pale of divine presence and activity.

11. James K. A. Smith, *The Fall of Interpretation: Philosophical Foundations for a Creational Hermeneutic* (Downers Grove, Ill.: InterVarsity, 2000), understands this epistemic dimness as connected to the distance between subject and object. His primary contribution, however, lies in his argument that this distance is inherent to creation itself—a creation pronounced good by the Creator—rather than being the result of the fall.

12. This is the proposal of Joseph A. DiNoia, *The Diversity of Religions: A Christian Perspective* (Washington: Catholic University of America Press, 1992), esp. 65–107.

13. Pinnock, *Flame of Love: A Theology of the Holy Spirit* (Downers Grove, Ill.: InterVarsity, 1996), 203.

A Pneumatological Paradigm: Advancing the Conversation

I submit that the foregoing represents the latent power of a pneumatological (read: trinitarian) theology to overcome the traditional impasses that have hindered developments in *theologia religionum*. Let me briefly identify three advantages to this approach. First, pneumatology is the key to overcoming the dualism between christological particularity and the cosmic Christ. When one recalls that the historical Jesus was who he was precisely because of the Spirit of God and that the risen Christ was resurrected by the power of the Spirit, then the either/or of particularity/universality dissolves. Rather, in consistent trinitarian fashion, all things have to be seen as the conjunction of Word and Spirit, including both the historical Jesus and the coming Christ, as well as the dynamic presence and activity of God in the world. In this framework, the Spirit is certainly the Spirit of Jesus, even as Jesus is the one anointed by the Spirit of God (Acts 10:38). Yet this mutuality should not obscure the broader trinitarian framework in the sense that the Spirit is also the Spirit of God even as Jesus is the Son of God.

Second, pneumatology is the key to understanding the tension between what has traditionally been termed specific and natural revelation—that is, between the sacred and the profane or the church and the world. These categories have previously been correlated with those who are saved and those who are lost—specific revelation being necessary for salvation, and natural theology being sufficient only for damnation. A pneumatological understanding of salvation, however, is dynamic, requiring triadic recategorization of "was saved," "am being saved," and "will be saved." (I leave aside the questions regarding the salvation of infants, the mentally incapacitated, and so forth.) In this framework, conversion itself needs to be understood as a multifaceted process involving cognitive, moral, affective, spiritual, sociopolitical, religious, and other dimensions of human experience.[14] My point is

14. It is arguable that my connecting a processive soteriology to a pneumatological *theologia religionum* was anticipated by Jonathan Edwards. Gerald McDermott suggests that the doctrines of original and progressive revelation (the *prisca theologia*), creation as typological or semiotic pointers to divinity, and salvation as dispositional were central to the Puritan theologian's eighteenth-century fascination with the non-Christian religions; see McDermott, *Jonathan Edwards Confronts the Gods: Christian Theology, Enlightenment Religion, and Non-Christian Faiths* (Oxford: Oxford University Press, 2000).

that with both revelation and salvation, a pneumatological perspective emphasizes dynamic process rather than intractable dualisms. This does not deny the value of understanding revelation as "natural" or "specific," nor does it reject the ancient *extra ecclesia nulla salus* ("no salvation outside the church") formula. It does relativize the meaning of theological categories vis-à-vis the historical frameworks within which they emerged, and demands a reassessment of their meanings within the wider contexts of Scripture, the entire historical and dimensional scope of human life and experience, and the eschatological horizon.

Last but not least, I need to return to the view of religion mentioned in the introductory chapter. Generally speaking, at least some forms of pietist and evangelical Christianity have been identified as the individual's cognitive awareness of a living relationship with Jesus (whether mediated sacramentally or otherwise). By implication, all other religions are false, being either failed human efforts to reach God or inspired by the devil and his demons. This disregards both the universality of Spirit and the dynamic nature of divine activity. With regard to the religions, this means that religious traditions are dynamic, evolving realities and that hard-and-fast lines between religion and culture and between one religious tradition and another are difficult to draw. Given this, it is better to see the diversity of religious traditions as serving divine purposes in greater or lesser degrees at each stage of their evolution. The Christian tradition, as Barth noted, also is not exempt from either the vicissitudes of history or the presence and activity of the Spirit of God. There is as much human frailty and demonic activity "within" Christianity as there is "without." Further, where "Judaism," for example, stops and where "Christianity" starts is difficult to determine in some respects—as, for example, in their monotheistic commitments or their ethical codes.[15] Pneumatology enables us to transcend the intellectual conundrums generated by these questions, even while recognizing their contextual rather than absolute validity.

15. Jews for Jesus, for example, highlights the complexity of lived religiosity. Members of Jews for Jesus would claim to be both Jews and Christians, yet their former claims are rejected by their fellow Jews, even while on a simplistic reading, their "Jewishness" might be said to be simply "cultural" expressions rather than inherently religious ones by fundamentalist Christians.

My point is that a pneumatological approach to the religions offers alternatives to the traditional impasses and offers new, relational categories to sustain further inquiry. It does this negatively and positively—the former by enabling the surmounting of static dualisms erected by traditional theological frameworks, and the latter by vitalizing and animating a robust trinitarian (read: relational, holistic) framework for theological reflection. Spirit is supremely mediational and relational.

Potential Objections to a Pneumatological Theology of Religions

It is important for any major research program to face squarely the objections that may be raised, especially by the constituency to whom the project advocate is appealing for support. I want to briefly raise and respond to three potential objections to a pneumatological approach to Christian theology of religions: that it is not distinctly *Christ*-ian, in the sense of subjecting Christ to the Spirit; that its evangelical credentials are suspect; and that it smacks of a more subtle form of theological imperialism that is anathema in our postmodern situation.

Pneumatological Theologia Religionum *as Sub-Christian*

In some respects, the project outlined in these pages is not new. I am thinking specifically about the spiritualist understandings of religious diversity characteristic of nineteenth-century American transcendentalism and the recent New Age movement. Influenced by the tradition of Western esoterica such as the Perennial Philosophy, Rosicrucianism, and Theosophy, as well as by Eastern traditions, the category of "spirit" has also been central to how spiritualists then and now think about religion. For them, Christ is certainly important but only as one of many religiously crucial personalities. He may be a master avatar, a profound teacher, or even a decisive spirit-guide, but he is understood, in effect, as having secondary importance in contrast to the transcendental unity all human beings enjoy through their spiritual connections. By virtue of the ever-present and active divine spirit, all authentic religious traditions point to the truth and are ultimately salvific.

I say this to caution us, and especially myself, against being deluded with euphoria about finding *the* resolution to the impasse posed by christological approaches to Christian theology of religions. Clearly, a pneumatological *theologia religionum* is susceptible, over time, to diminishing the centrality of Christ to Christian theological reflection; this tendency should be recognized and admitted. But it is also clear that an energetically pneumatological theology of religions will be nothing less than a fully trinitarian theology of religions. It is the vigorous trinitarian character of a pneumatological theology of religions that not only distinguishes this project from that proposed by spiritualist thinkers but also holds promise for the foreseeable future. To repeat, a Christian theology recognizes that God does all things through Word and Spirit and is therefore doubly armed for reflective engagement with the world's religions. Word and Spirit provide the two poles through which all orthodoxy must pass. How both poles relate to each other and how to keep either pole from subjugating the other is part of the dialectical task that pneumatologists of religion have to work out continuously.

But the question still remains: Does not a pneumatological approach to the religions effectively undermine the Christian conviction regarding the centrality of Christ? Does not the universality of Spirit have to be understood within the context of Jesus Christ as the way, the truth, and the life (John 14:6), the one apart from whom no one can be saved (Acts 4:12)? Does not Christian salvation depend on calling on the name of the Lord and confessing the lordship of Christ (cf. Rom. 10:9–15)?

I believe that Christians can affirm all of these truths within the contours of a pneumatological approach to the non-Christian faiths, since affirmation of these truths does not undermine the obligation that Christians have to engage religious otherness with respect and integrity. Here, the task of theology of religions—that of taking up the question concerning the relationship of the religions to divine providence—should be emphasized. Theologians of the religions are not called to check passports at heaven's gate. Certainly, to reflect on the religions with the proposed pneumatological categories raises questions about whether those in other faiths can be or perhaps even are saved. But pneumatologists of religion may be able to affirm the place of the religions in the divine providence even as they affirm the absolute centrality of Jesus Christ's life, death, and resurrection for salvation. I believe that the issue of the religions and the issue of the unevangelized should be recognized as distinct for the purposes of doing theology of religions. At the same time, of course, they are also connected, as any first-year student taking courses on Christian systematic theology understands. This leads to the more specific "evangelical" objection to the kind of pneumatological approach to the religions that I have sketched here.

Pneumatological Theologia Religionum *as Sub-evangelical*

Any attempt to define "evangelical" in the North American, much less global, context will inevitably impose a limited perspective on what is a diverse and pluralistic worldwide movement.[16] As a Pentecostal, however, I am concerned not so much with the formal or even institutional boundaries of "evangelicalism" per se but with the going forth of the evangel—the good news of Jesus Christ. How, it may be legitimately asked, is a pneumatological approach to the religions that emphasizes dialogue able to sustain the evangelical and missionary enterprise? Does not a theology that emphasizes the universality of the Spirit's presence and activity undercut the motivation for missions and proclamation? If in fact the Spirit is already at work in the religions, then why bother with conversion of non-Christians at all? What is the object of theology of religions after all?

These are valid questions that concern all Christians. My initial response is that those who insist theology of religions should motivate the mission of the church are presenting a primarily pragmatic rather than theological argument. While I am committed to the notion that all truth is pragmatic in one sense, I reject the idea that pragmatism should be the sole or even dominant criterion for theological truth. In other words, I think it a weak argument to reject a pneumatological *theologia religionum* simply because one feels that emphasis should be placed on preaching the gospel rather than dialoguing with religious others. And this is especially the case since nowhere in my reading of the New Testament is

16. On the complexity of evangelicalism, see, e.g., Donald W. Dayton and Robert K. Johnston, eds., *The Variety of American Evangelicalism* (Knoxville: University of Tennessee Press, 1991); and George A. Rawlyk and Mark A. Noll, eds., *Amazing Grace: Evangelicalism in Australia, Britain, Canada, and the United States* (Grand Rapids: Baker, 1993). More recently, see Jon R. Stone, *On the Boundaries of American Evangelicalism: The Postwar Evangelical Coalition* (New York: St. Martin's Press, 1999).

there a direct link made between missionary motivation and the fear of eternal damnation.

Second, however, it also should be made clear that dialogue and proclamation are not mutually exclusive but intrinsically connected.[17] Genuine dialogue proclaims truth, and effective proclamation engages with others at an interpersonal level. From a missiological perspective, many already agree that lasting conversions are achieved best through the establishment of one-on-one relationships. Dialogue, rather than proclamation, characterizes such relationships. More important, mutual vulnerability is a feature of such relationships rather than attitudes of superiority. A pneumatological approach to the non-Christian faiths supports and encourages precisely such dynamics and enables us to cultivate just such virtues. It opens up the Christian to whatever is true, good, beautiful, and holy in the other tradition, even while nurturing an environment in which the non-Christian can come to appreciate the same in Christian faith. What else is this besides grassroots "evangelism"?

Conservative Christians, however, might still be concerned that we are going too far. After all, "dialogue" seems too passive. Further, many would argue that the discontinuities between Christian faith and the world's religious traditions are much more profound than the continuities. For these people, engaging in the interfaith conversation might seem a betrayal of one's commitments to the exclusive claims of the gospel. Indeed, some conservative evangelicals do not even think that dialogue with Catholics, Orthodox, or non-evangelical Christians in general is all that valuable, much less dialogue with non-Christians or, more specifically, Jews, Muslims, Hindus, Buddhists, Confucianists, Taoists, practitioners of indigenous traditions, and the like.

These concerns, however, may also be approached from another direction—that of how deep inculturation of the gospel occurs. Does not the process of translating the message of the gospel require prolonged engagement and exposure to the "foreign" cultural and religious milieu? Rather than being afraid of diluting evangelical truth, should not Christians be confident that the advance of the gospel rests not so much in human hands but in its

17. See, e.g., Jürgen Moltmann, "Dialogue or Mission: Christianity and the Religions in an Endangered World," in his *God and Secular Society: The Public Relevance of Theology*, trans. Margaret Kohl (Minneapolis: Fortress, 1999), 226–44.

universal relevance as delivered by the power of the Spirit of God (cf. Acts 1:8)? There is always a fine line between syncretism and inculturation (or indigenization, contextualization, acculturation, etc.), but recognition of this fine line should not produce withdrawal; instead, it should translate into engagement through the discerning empowerment of the Holy Spirit. This kind of zeal, however, will no doubt raise the accusation that dialogue is actually motivated by polemical, apologetic, and expansionist concerns, all under the guise of taking the religious other seriously on his or her own terms. This, I think, is the most serious objection and requires somber reflection.

Pneumatological Theologia Religionum *as Modernist and Covertly Imperialistic*

Ours is a postmodern world. Whatever else postmodernity might mean, it means that ours is at least a postfoundationalist, post-Enlightenment, post-Western, postcolonial, and perhaps also post-Christian experience. It also means the emergence and empowerment of local languages, local rationalities, and local ways of being human. The language and concepts undergirding a pneumatological theology of religions—foundational pneumatology, divine presence and activity, universality, and so on—will rightly seem to many postmoderns to betray a hegemonistic impulse. They will point out that even the very use of the pneumatological categories themselves is an imposition of Christian notions on the practices and beliefs that religious others consider to be sacred and ultimate. How then can a pneumatological *theologia religionum* proceed without being imperialistic in the despised sense of that term in our time? While I will take up this question in greater detail in the next chapter, for the moment let me respond briefly here along three lines.

First, theological reflection today can only be postfoundationalistic if by this the Cartesian sense of foundationalism is meant.[18] The postmodern turn, I am convinced, is largely true. There is no neutral place from which unbiased engagement of the world's religious traditions can proceed. This is especially the case in theology, where words and concepts are ultimately symbols that enable truer and more meaningful engagement with the divine and with reality. Those who would advocate a pneumatological theology of religions should be cognizant of

18. On this, see part 1 of my "The Demise of Foundationalism and the Retention of Truth: What Evangelicals Can Learn from C. S. Peirce," *Christian Scholar's Review* 29 (2000): 563–89.

their sociohistorical location as interpreters, of the ambiguity of interpretation, of the polyvalence of reference, and of the subjectivity of interpersonal encounter. I would argue that such admission derives, at least in part, from the ambiguity of the core pneumatological symbols themselves—for example, wind, fire, or water, which are gentle, purifying, and life-giving on the one hand but are destructive in one way or other on the other hand.[19] Yet a pneumatological approach to the religions is also open to the Spirit and proceeds from the conviction that it is the Spirit who leads the quest for truth amidst all those who are searching for it (John 14:17; 16:13; 1 John 2:27). In the postmodern context, then, a pneumatological *theologia religionum* legitimates rather than undermines the interreligious dialogue as an appropriate arena for Christian inquiry after truth.

This means, second, that a pneumatological theology of religions is tentative and open to correction. In its overall framework, it can be understood as a large-scale theological hypothesis that must be tested. The tests are applied in the long-term, multi-disciplinary, and multiperspectival conversation in which theology engages. Criteria of truth based on correspondence, coherence, and pragmatism operate not only to transform the theory in its details as well as generally, but perhaps also to undermine the overall plausibility of the theory during the course of the dialogue. (This is what true fallibilism at an epistemic level has to mean.) My point is that a pneumatological *theologia religionum* is always *in via*, as is any pneumatological enterprise. It is always in quest, open to further investigation by continuously enlarging the borders of inquiry and by including in the conversation any and all interested in the subject matter. This proceeds, again, from the fundamental convictions undergirding a pneumatologically informed worldview: that the Spirit of God is universally present and active. No voices or perspectives can therefore be excluded in an a priori fashion from the conversation.[20]

The result, of course, is that a pneumatological theology of religions is a fully public enterprise.[21] Certainly, I agree that it should

19. I develop the theological implications of these root metaphors for the Spirit in *Spirit-Word-Community*, chap. 6.

20. For detailed arguments regarding notions of truth and epistemic fallibilism interjected here, see *Spirit-Word-Community*, part 2.

21. Here I follow David Tracy's proposal that theology is foundational in engaging the world, systematic for the church, and pragmatic for Christian life in the world; see his *The Analogical Imagination: Christian Theology and the Culture of Pluralism* (New York: Crossroad, 1981).

serve the church, as should all viable theology. But serving does not mean isolating or parochializing. Rather, part of the service rendered is energetic cultural and religious engagement wherever the Spirit blows (cf. John 3:8). Christians convinced of the importance and truth of Christian faith should not be hesitant to test even the most central of its claims against those of other religious traditions. This kind of fully public theology invites a pluralism of ideas, convictions, doctrines, claims, and even criteria—including the frameworks of interpretation and worldviews from which criteria derive—for testing such claims. And as Gavin D'Costa points out, such an authentic pluralism is not only sustainable but is actually the outgrowth of a pneumatological approach to the religions, because only the universality of pneumatology enables emphasis to be laid on the particularity and difference of all non-Christian others.[22] It is dialogue in the most comprehensive sense, including testimonials, arguments, and even apologetics.[23] And, if conducted sincerely as they should be, such dialogues result in conversions at various aesthetic, ethical-moral, cognitive, existential-spiritual, doctrinal/theological, and even religious levels as truth unfolds. Without the rationalistic kind of certainty engendered by Cartesian foundationalism, there is always the risk that such mutual transformation will result in conversion not only of the non-Christian, but also of the Christian, at any of these levels. Yet, while possible on the theoretical level, it is rare that committed interfaith dialogue partners ever existentially leave their home religious traditions; instead, their convictions are often deepened precisely because their core beliefs and practices are honed through the crucible of in-depth interpersonal encounter.[24] This said, however, from a Christian perspective, is it too much to hope for the "conversion"

22. Gavin D'Costa, "The Resurrection, the Holy Spirit and the World Religions," in *Resurrection Reconsidered*, ed. Gavin D'Costa (Oxford: Oneworld, 1996), 150–67. Interestingly, D'Costa comes to his conclusions as a Roman Catholic theologian by following the ecclesiological, evangelistic, missionary implications of the Paraclete pneumatology in John's Gospel.

23. See, e.g., Paul Griffiths, *An Apology for Apologetics: A Study in the Logic of Interreligious Dialogue* (Maryknoll, N.Y.: Orbis, 1991).

24. This is suggested also by William Placher, who writes that "to say that other folks are wrong about religion is not necessarily . . . to say that they are damned. . . . [Further,] even while arguing for the essential truth of one's own position, one can acknowledge [because of the fact that the divine mystery is beyond human comprehension and linguistic conceptuality] that the truth one holds is only partial, that others have hold of real truths too, and that one can learn from them in ways that will lead to correcting one's own position. . . . [In addition, as

of the non-Christian dialogue partner, due to the presence and activity of the Holy Spirit in the conversation?

This, I submit, is possible in large part because of the pneumatological assumptions that motivate this kind of theology of religions. A Spirit-inspired vision is evangelistic and missiological in the best—namely, relational—sense of those terms. More important, it is (as it should be) genuinely humble in its quest for truth, especially since Christians should be among the first to confess their finitude and sinful conditions. It is thereby open, honest, and sincere in engaging religious others precisely because it recognizes the *imago Dei* and the breath of life in each person, thereby enabling respectful listening, ongoing learning, and spiritual transformation. Christ is lifted up in this encounter precisely because it is the Spirit that accomplishes this through the human forms, rather than our taking on this task ourselves. And that, I would submit, is exactly what a Christianity that is evangelical should be about.

In this chapter, I have outlined the biblical and theological framework of a pneumatological approach to the religions and raised and attempted to respond to a few potential objections to the project as a whole. I will return to a number of these themes in the following pages. For the moment, however, I need to elaborate on the concept of foundational pneumatology, which I introduced earlier.

---

with, e.g., J. A. DiNoia, *The Diversity of Religions*] Christians might even hold that some non-Christians best serve the providence of God by continuing to live in their particular non-Christian faiths. . . . [Finally, the special case of Judaism allows us to] recognize that adherents of other religions may well be saved, may well have hold of partial truths on matters where our own truths are partial as well, and may well be serving God's providential purposes in pursuing the depths of their own faiths" (*Narratives of a Vulnerable God: Christ, Theology, and Scripture* [Louisville: Westminster John Knox, 1994], 123–25). Whatever else may be said about Placher's latter statements—which, incidentally, are ultimately eschatological claims—it is certainly the case that those seasoned in interreligious dialogue confirm my main point about what such dialogues have done for them as religious persons; see also the now-classic work by John B. Cobb Jr., *Beyond Dialogue: Toward a Mutual Transformation of Christianity and Buddhism* (Philadelphia: Fortress, 1982).

3

Foundational Pneumatology and Theology of Religions

Who or what is the Holy Spirit? What is the Holy Spirit saying and/or doing today? In what directions is the Holy Spirit leading? How is the Holy Spirit to be discerned? These are the kinds of questions that are at the heart of the contemporary renaissance in pneumatology. Resolutions to these questions are relatively easier to formulate within the confines of the church. The questions are often dismissed or not even seriously considered when relocated to the arena of the world at large. Even when they are seriously posed in this latter context, the answers are elusive. To articulate and respond to these questions about who the Holy Spirit is relative to the world as a whole and what the Spirit is doing in the world is to plunge into the subject matter of foundational pneumatology.

This chapter takes up three lines of questions. First, what is a foundational pneumatology? Second, why is this an important undertaking for contemporary Christian theology of religions? Third, how are the general features of foundational pneumatology specified with respect to the particularity that informs Christian theological reflection? The movement in this chapter will be from the foundational pneumatology as abstractly articulated to its application in *theologia religionum* to a case-specific discussion of its value and function with regard to modern Pentecostalism.

What Is Foundational Pneumatology?

Central to the pneumatological approach to theology of religions in this volume is the concept of foundational pneumatology. In what follows, I will clarify what I mean by foundational pneumatology in dialogue with the work of Donald L. Gelpi, S.J. My goal here is to continue to develop the interreligious and intercultural hermeneutic operative in this book.

The Foundational Pneumatology of Donald L. Gelpi, S.J.

One of the most ambitious efforts to develop a foundational pneumatology thus far is Donald Gelpi's book *The Divine Mother: A Trinitarian Theology of the Holy Spirit* (1984).[1] In order to briefly outline the task of foundational pneumatology and its inherent difficulties, two comments about Gelpi's book and work are in order. The first is his commitment to a nonfoundationalistic epistemology. This derives in part from his overall project of developing an inculturated theology in dialogue with the North American philosophic tradition stretching from Edwards and Emerson through Brownson, Abbott, and Santayana, to Peirce, Royce, James, and Dewey.[2] Under the tutelage especially of the pragmatism of C. S. Peirce and his successors, Gelpi came to question the transcendentalism and a priori methodologies of neo-Thomists such as Rahner and Lonergan, which he imbibed in his Jesuit training, and moved in the direction of a fallibilistic epistemology and empirical theology. Both moves are to be applauded. My own foundational pneumatology follows Gelpi in eschewing the strong Cartesian foundationalism that bases all beliefs ultimately on self-evident intuitions. It proceeds instead from what Peirce called a "contrite fallibilism," wherein all knowledge is

1. Donald L. Gelpi, S.J., *The Divine Mother: A Trinitarian Theology of the Holy Spirit* (Lanham, Md.: University Press of America, 1984). Gelpi has published extensively not only in pneumatology, trinitarian theology, and foundational theology but also in charismatic theology, theological anthropology, theology of conversion, christology, and theological method. For an overview of his work, see Amos Yong, "In Search of Foundations: The *Oeuvre* of Donald L. Gelpi, S.J., and Its Significance for Pentecostal Theology and Philosophy," *Journal of Pentecostal Theology* 11.1 (2002): 3–26.

2. Cf. Donald Gelpi, *Inculturating North American Theology: An Experiment in Foundational Method* (Atlanta: Scholars Press, 1988).

provisional, relative to the questions posed by the community of inquirers, and subject to the ongoing process of conversation and discovery.[3]

The *foundational* element in Gelpi's pneumatology, however, is methodological rather than specifically epistemological. Gelpi himself builds on the work of Lonergan, who argued for foundations as one of eight functional specialties intrinsic to theological method.[4] The details of Lonergan's work need not detain us here; what is of import for him and Gelpi is the role of conversion in providing theology with foundations. Conversion, whether limited to intellectual, moral, and religious dimensions (Lonergan) or taken to include affective and sociopolitical dimensions as well (Gelpi), both enlarges the horizons of one's ability to comprehend and integrate theological data and produces the transformation of soul needed to take responsibility for one's theologizing relative to oneself and one's religious community. In this way, conversion supplies the foundation or indispensable pathway through which theology must eventually proceed. It functions methodologically, in Lonergan's terms, as the "horizon within which the meaning of doctrines can be apprehended."[5] In its most basic form, for example, the idea of conversion suggests that one cannot theologize truthfully if one has never been disposed in any way to God to begin with.

Gelpi has, however, attempted to take Lonergan's notion of foundation even further in seeing conversion as a subset of the category of experience. His own appropriation of the North American philosophical tradition has allowed him to see the value in formulating a theory of experience that is potentially universal in scope and applicable not only to human beings but also to God.[6] The capability of such a theory to account for the experience of conversion generally and Christian conversion more specifically lies at the center of Gelpi's foundational pneumatology. "Foundational" is thus employed in Gelpi's pneumatology as suggestive of a fundamental category of reality, including God, as descriptive of

3. For my reading of the value of Peirce's method of inquiry for theology, see Yong, "The Demise of Foundationalism and the Retention of Truth: What Evangelicals Can Learn from C. S. Peirce," *Christian Scholar's Review* 29 (2000): 563–89.

4. Bernard Lonergan, *Method in Theology* (1972; reprint, Minneapolis: Winston and Seabury, 1979).

5. Ibid., 131.

6. Gelpi, *Divine Mother*, 82–102.

human experience, and as both prescriptive and normative for the ways in which Christians (and others) have experienced and should experience God. Yet more importantly, following Lonergan, Gelpi still holds that what is foundational here is primarily methodological and related to experiences that allow for specific kinds of theological reflection—in this case, pneumatology. Because Gelpi defines foundational theology itself as the attempt to "formulate a normative account of the conversion experience which ought to lie at the basis of a religious tradition," it is not surprising that he sees the task of foundational pneumatology as that of formulating a normative account of the Christian experience of the Holy Spirit.[7] This is borne out in the objectives that Gelpi itemizes for his version of foundational pneumatology: (1) to synthesize the experience of the Spirit with the biblical witness to the Spirit's presence and agency in the apostolic church; (2) to explore the practical consequences and moral demands of Spirit-inspired living; (3) to comprehend the relationship between the Second and Third Persons of the Trinity; (4) to probe into the soteriological implications of the charismatic work of the Spirit in the contemporary world; (5) to provide both prophetic challenge and words of wisdom for individuals, churches, and society; and (6) to connect affectivity and cognitivity in the Christian life of faith.[8]

Questions for Gelpi's Project

While I am sympathetic to Gelpi's efforts and see them as a stimulus to my own reflection as a theologian, I wish to raise one specific complex of questions and suggest one direction in which to further develop his idea of foundational pneumatology. The former concerns the methodological dependence of Gelpi's pneumatology on the functional role of conversion experiences. More specifically, I question the propriety of insisting, as Gelpi does, on Christian conversion as a prerequisite for pneumatological understanding. This might raise the suspicions of those who are convinced that the Holy Spirit is the property only of Christians and that non-Christians cannot possibly reflect on a reality (the Holy Spirit) whom they either have never experienced or, even if they have, do not recognize by that name. Yet ponder for a moment a fact Gelpi himself admits—that conversion is a process that

7. Ibid., 241.
8. Ibid., 7–9.

shapes the reflective capacities of *all* human beings, not only Christians and certainly not only Christian theologians.[9] He agrees, following Lonergan's delineation of theological method, that anyone, including those yet to experience Christian conversion, can participate in research, interpretation, history, and dialectics (the first four functional specialties). However, Gelpi then goes on to insist that only those who have experienced some level of Christian conversion (foundations, the fifth specialty) can adequately undertake the task of doing Christian theology.

That this is insufficiently dialectical should be clearly evident. Does not engagement in the process of research, interpretation, history, and dialectics itself inform the kinds of conversion that one experiences? Do not conversion experiences at all the levels Gelpi identifies, however inchoate, inform the kinds of activities connected with movement through the first four specialties? Gelpi himself is well aware that one cannot arbitrarily divide conversion experiences from dynamic life processes and that certain types of conversions both accompany and enable engagement with theological methodology. Conversion therefore extends through the entire process and is intrinsic to it. But because Gelpi (and Lonergan) connects "foundations" so closely to Christian conversion, he forfeits appeal to the breadth of human conversion experiences, which are complex and always *in via*. Instead, his methodologically constructed foundation turns out to be a rather limiting platform. By tying the idea of foundations to the experience of Christian conversion so explicitly, the kind of foundational pneumatology that emerges seems to be restricted to the Christian experience only and is therefore somewhat incapacitated outside of that environment.

I suggest that a better strategy for foundational pneumatology is to focus on the entirety of the epistemological and experiential spectrum of the human being-in-the-world rather than on the methodological or functional role of specific experiences, including that of Christian conversion. I think Gelpi has been extremely helpful in constructing a theory of experience that accounts not only for how human beings encounter and engage the world but also for how humans relate to God and vice versa. While there is

9. Cf. Gelpi, *The Conversion Experience: A Reflective Process for RCIA Participants and Others* (New York and Mahwah, N.J.: Paulist Press, 1998).

neither time nor space for an extended discussion of this notion, at the very least, experience as understood by Gelpi is what defines human and sentient beings.[10] People do not have experiences; rather, experiences are what people consist of. Used in this broad sense, experience refers to the complex integration of perception, mentality, affectivity, and volitionality involved in the human being-in-the-world. From this, what I wish to capitalize on is the fact that as a metaphysical construct, Gelpi's theory of experience is universally extensive to the human situation.

I wish to build on this toward a foundational pneumatology. If in fact Gelpi's metaphysics of experience is valid—and, for the record, I believe it to be essentially on the right track—the very idea of foundations connected to experience would resist its restriction to that of Christian conversion. Of course, certain aspects of Christian pneumatology undoubtedly make no sense apart from the experience of Christian conversion. That Gelpi seeks to clarify the normative elements of the *Christian* experience of the Holy Spirit, I wholeheartedly endorse. But are Christian experiences of the Holy Spirit exhaustive? As a Catholic theologian, Gelpi clearly recognizes that even non-Christians experience the Spirit. But what is (or should be) decisive for him is that the notion of foundation as he develops it itself requires an emphasis on the idea that the pneumatological categories to be developed are potentially universal in scope and application since they are derivative from such universal experiences in actuality. I recognize that there is a key step missing in the above equation—that of connecting the experiences of the Holy Spirit with human experiences in general—and promise to make this connection explicit in the following section. For the moment, however, it seems undeniable that Gelpi's doctrine of experience would itself extend the scope of the foundations for pneumatological reflection far beyond that derived by Christian conversion. Perhaps I am quibbling about what appears to me to be Gelpi's arbitrary and restrictive use of "foundational" in his pneumatology. I am simply pleading for the

10. For the details, see Gelpi, *Divine Mother*, 17–44. Since Gelpi draws from Alfred North Whitehead's cosmological categories, those who are convinced Whiteheadians will hold that experience applies equally to non-sentient realities. Gelpi himself is noncommittal about that specific thesis, preferring to focus his reflection more extensively on human experience. He notes the ambiguities surrounding the term in a later work (*The Turn to Experience in Contemporary Theology* [New York and Mahwah, N.J.: Paulist Press, 1994], 2–3) and therefore rightly cautions us to be wary about how it is used theologically.

recognition that Gelpi's idea of "foundational," connected intrinsically as it is with his theory of experience, requires such a wider framework.

Acknowledgment of this wider framework also flows in part from recognizing the public nature of truth. Here I draw from David Tracy's distinction between what he calls fundamental, systematic, and practical theologies and their publics.[11] For Tracy, fundamental theology is more philosophic in nature, is addressed principally but not exhaustively to the academy, and seeks to engage all who are willing to entertain the topic. Systematic theology is more confessional in nature, is addressed primarily but not exclusively to the church, and seeks to render Christian symbols and doctrines plausible to those within the Christian tradition. Practical theology is oriented toward liberative and transformative praxis and is addressed primarily to those engaged in correlating theological reflection with the doing of the work of the kingdom of God in the world. Each is clearly distinct from the other, yet none can ultimately be disconnected from the other two because of their inherent interrelatedness.

Foundational Pneumatology and the Pneumatological Imagination

What is foundational about the pneumatology being developed here charts a path forward from the crossroad where Gelpi's pneumatology and Tracy's fundamental theology meet. It seeks to build on Gelpi's understanding of experience but undertakes to articulate such within the largest framework possible. The public it is addressed to is surely academic. However, the experiences it attempts to comprehend are by no means limited to academics, or even Christians, but are rather common to all human beings. The public for a foundational pneumatology is therefore the universal *humanum* and properly includes any and all who are interested in the subject matter. Correlatively, the truth of the matter in foundational pneumatology cannot be parochial by virtue of the universal experiences of the Spirit (a point to be argued in the next section) and the universal scope of the public to which it is addressed. What is true of the Holy Spirit in a foundational pneumatology

11. Cf. David Tracy, *The Analogical Imagination: Christian Theology and the Culture of Pluralism* (New York: Crossroad, 1981), 54–82.

cannot be true only for Christians but has to be relevant to, and perhaps compelling for, all.

This is what lies behind Tracy's insistence that fundamental theology—or foundational pneumatology, what is attempted here—is inherently universal or universalizing in character. As a rationality that implicitly presupposes a universal experience and explicitly strives to engage a universal audience, it cannot avoid philosophic and metaphysical abstractions.[12] Such a rationality, however, is tempered by a fallibilistic epistemology, even while it emerges from the ongoing dialectical conversation between self- and what David Krieger calls "other-rationality."[13] This extension of Gelpi's notion of foundationalism allows a stronger theory of truth to be emphasized, one that is not relativized by cultural-linguistic worlds or perspectives. This is especially urgent given the claims and counterclaims of truth in the world of religions and in light of our postmodern situation.

What informs the foundationalism envisioned here is thus not so much conversion, even in its expanded sense, as it is a "pneumatological imagination"—a way of seeing God, self, and world that is inspired by the (Christian) experience of the Spirit.[14] It needs to be clearly acknowledged that the foundational categories presented here derive from the dialectical interplay between personal (including my own) experiences of the Holy Spirit and reflection on this experience from within the broader Christian community of faith. I therefore propose the metaphor of "shifting

12. Cf. Tracy, *Analogical Imagination*, esp. 56–64; cf. also 85 n. 31 and 89 n. 47.

13. David J. Krieger, *The New Universalism: Foundations for a Global Theology* (Maryknoll, N.Y.: Orbis, 1991), argues for the potential meaningfulness and truthfulness of theological truth claims across cultural-religious lines by means of a universal method of argumentation and a universal hermeneutics. He draws from Panikkar's diatopical hermeneutics, Karl-Otto Apel's ethics of discourse, Habermas's communicative action, Gadamer's philosophical hermeneutics, and even Gandhi's pragmatics of nonviolence, all in an effort to construct a theory of intercultural communication. The key for Krieger, however, is Wittgenstein's later notion of finding our own reasonableness via the confluence of *other-rationality*—a notion embedded in the windows of language games open toward a universal horizon, thus allowing and in fact actually inviting correction in order to maintain rationality. Gelpi would insist that rationality and experience not be understood dualistically, and I concur. I do, however, think that Gelpi's own emphasis on a broad construct of experience at times overwhelms the process and activity of cognition. A viable foundational pneumatology should be able to preserve both elements.

14. The term "imagination" has proliferated in recent literature. I elaborate on the concept of a "pneumatological imagination" at length in *Spirit-Word-Community: Theological Hermeneutics in Trinitarian Perspective*, New Critical Thinking in Theology and Biblical Studies (Aldershot, Hampshire, UK, and Burlington, Vt.: Ashgate, 2002), chap. 4.

foundations" to underscore the dialectic of Scripture and experience, of thought and praxis, of theology and doxology, of reason and narrative, of object and subject, of a priori rationality and a posteriori empiricism, of the self and its sociohistoric location in community, in all knowledge.[15] These are all elements that combine to inform the pneumatological imagination. As an epistemological and methodological construct, however, the pneumatological imagination in turn both envisions the foundational categories and is shaped by them. I suggest, on the one hand, that a theology of the Holy Spirit emerges out of Christian experience of God's presence and activity in the world, even while, on the other hand, it enables us to experience that presence and activity in more precise, intense, and true ways. Further, the flexibility and cogency of the foundational pneumatology for identifying the most basic features of the Holy Spirit as related to the world enable us to comprehend not only divine and human experience and reality but also that of the demonic and of nature.[16]

This brief sketch raises many more questions than it answers. The discussion in the following section should further clarify what is involved in a foundational pneumatology by elaborating on its relevance for contemporary Christian theology of religions.

Foundational Pneumatology and Contemporary Theology of Religions

Gelpi's foundational pneumatology is driven first and foremost by dogmatic considerations. His task in *Divine Mother* is to frame a comprehensive theology of the Holy Spirit for the Catholic charismatic renewal rather than to engage the problematic engendered by the contemporary encounter of religions. My own appropriation of foundational pneumatology, however, is motivated

15. On these dialectical issues in epistemology, see, e.g., Nicholas Lash, *Easter in Ordinary: Reflections on Human Experience and the Knowledge of God* (Charlottesville: University of Virginia Press 1981); Wayne Proudfoot, *Religious Experience* (Berkeley: University of California Press, 1985); and Caroline Franks Davis, *The Evidential Force of Religious Experience* (Oxford: Clarendon, 1989).

16. The concept of the demonic is a corollary to a fully biblical pneumatology as well as central to any *weltanschauung* oriented toward *pneuma*; I will return to this topic in chapters 6 and 7. At this juncture in world history, it is important for Christians to develop a systematic theology of nature. I sketch the beginnings of such a theology of nature in *Spirit-Word-Community*, chap. 6. A foundational pneumatology, I am confident, will provide resources for revisioning both of these theological loci within a trinitarian framework.

primarily by the latter considerations. I now want to make explicit the relevance of foundational pneumatology for Christian theology of religions. My goal here is to show the epistemological promise of a foundational pneumatology for engaging others in general and religious others in particular in our postmodern world. As such, the following takes up the problem of the meaningfulness of talking about pneumatology in light of the postmodern critique, further probes the epistemological and alethic questions related to the public (audience) of interreligious theological reflection and debate, and develops in greater detail the biblical and theological resources for the pneumatological paradigm being advanced by this project.

Foundational Pneumatology and the Postmodern Critique

The "object" of a foundational pneumatology is to provide theological reflection on the Holy Spirit. At the most basic level, the Holy Spirit symbolizes the presence and agency of God in the world. To say anything about the Holy Spirit is to venture an opinion about this presence and agency. This presupposes, however, that one has epistemic justification for such statements. It assumes that one has adequate "foundations" that secure the meaningfulness of such assertions. More challenging in today's intellectual climate, which despises the kind of Cartesian foundationalism undergirding the modern project, as theological discourse, it makes claims not only to meaningfulness but also to universal truthfulness. It suggests that divinity is present and active, not only in the world that Christians inhabit, but also on the cosmic or universal level. Such scandalous and appalling (for some postmoderns) discourse proceeds here from a cautious optimism regarding the possibility of a universal rationality and grammar.

What kind of optimism is this? It is not premodern, for the premoderns never even thought to question this possibility. It is not modern, for the moderns reveled in an unbridled sense of evolutionary progress and sanguinity. It is not postmodern, for the postmoderns have already decided that such an attitude is meaningless and implausible at worst, or only relative to specific cultural sites and discourses at best. Better to label this a "chastised optimism" that is painfully aware of the postmodern critique. It believes itself capable of making meaningful *and* truthful statements about the Holy Spirit—God's way of being in and transforming the world—that have application to the widest possible audience. At the very least, a foundational pneumatology takes up the challenge of engaging in theological conversation any person or public, regardless of cultural-linguistic-religious background, interested in reflecting on and discussing the notion of divine presence and agency.

But does this kind of engagement actually occur, and if so, how? Post-Wittgensteinians would be suspicious of claims to translate any theological concept emergent from a distinctive set of experiences and practices outside of that "language game."[17] They would point, for instance, to the fact that even my notions of foundational pneumatology and the pneumatological imagination have their origins in the Pentecostal Christianity in which I was raised (see below). Certainly, a pneumatological imagination derived from the Pentecostal-charismatic experience would have little difficulty in granting that the Holy Spirit is indicative of divine presence and agency in the world. Indeed, is it not coincidental that the one responsible for sensitizing the theological world to the need for a foundational pneumatology, Donald Gelpi, has himself been a participant in the Catholic charismatic renewal since its emergence in the late 1960s? Thus my conclusion that a pneumatological imagination—especially one cultivated within the Pentecostal-charismatic community—is uniquely suited to undertake the task of developing a foundational pneumatology is no more than an unsubstantiated claim that is incomprehensible to those whose imaginations have not been pneumatologically nurtured. In this way, the parochialism of building on such a "foundation" is assumed to be demonstrated. My own strategy, however, is to take this as a challenge to connect the theological articulation of our experience of the Holy Spirit with the experiences of others vastly different from ourselves in order to render claims of such experiences universally comprehensible (at least potentially) and to

17. This critique is best represented by George Lindbeck's cultural-linguistic theory of religion, summarized in his *The Nature of Doctrine: Religion and Theology in a Postliberal Age* (Philadelphia: Westminster, 1984). I summarize and raise a few critical questions about another version of the post-Wittgensteinian project in my "The 'Baptist Vision' of James William McClendon, Jr.: A Wesleyan-Pentecostal Response," *Wesleyan Theological Journal* 37.2 (2002): 32–57.

invite others toward deeper and more specifically understood experiences of the Spirit.

Before elaborating more concretely on the task before us, one comment regarding the concept of Spirit as symbolic of divine presence and agency in the world is in order. This notion of God being present and active in the world is surely problematic once we move from confessional and testimonial language to the making of theological claims in the public square.[18] There is no unanimity among Christian theologians about this transition from confessional theology to fully public discourse. The complexity and precariousness of the conversation multiplies exponentially the moment other publics are introduced into the dialogue. This is clearly evident, for example, in the theological engagement with modern science and with the other religions. These conversation partners bring contrasting methodologies, assumptions, and discourses to the table and pose different problems. Modern science, for example, demands of theology a vision of God as agent that is consonant with the world as we know it.[19] Any theological claims made in such discussions need to be empirically verifiable or falsifiable, at least in principle. A foundational pneumatology contributes to such a conversation by elaborating on the kind of God and the kind of world that allows for a relationship of (mutual) presence and (at least asymmetrical, from the divine to the world) agency. Such a pneumatology seeks and allows for theological claims consistent with the findings and ongoing inquiry of the natural sciences. In fact, I would go so far as to suggest that apart from a robust trinitarian pneumatology in the foundationalistic sense that I am urging here, it is inconceivable that a coherent theological response can be given to the questions raised by the religion-science dialogue.

18. See, e.g., Owen C. Thomas, ed., *God's Activity in the World: The Contemporary Problem* (Chico, Calif.: Scholars Press, 1983); Thomas V. Morris, ed., *Divine and Human Action: Essays in the Metaphysics of Theism* (Ithaca, N.Y.: Cornell University Press, 1988); Thomas F. Tracy, ed., *The God Who Acts: Philosophical and Theological Explorations* (University Park, Pa.: Pennsylvania State University Press, 1994); Keith Ward, *Divine Action* (London: Collins, 1990); and Paul Gwynne, *Special Divine Action: Key Issues in the Contemporary Debate (1965–1995)* (Rome: Pontificia Universita Gregoriana, 1996).

19. See, e.g., Robert John Russell, Nancey Murphy, and Arthur R. Peacocke, eds., *Chaos and Complexity: Scientific Perspectives on Divine Action* (Vatican City State: Vatican Observatory; Berkeley: Center for Theology and the Natural Sciences, 1995).

Foundational Pneumatology and Interreligious Engagement

The task before us, however, is to sketch how authentic engagement with religious others is possible in light of the postmodern (in general) and post-Wittgensteinian (in particular) critiques. To take up this question, consider the issues and problems that attend to the notion of divine presence and agency—pneumatology—in the context of the interreligious dialogue. Both world and indigenous religious traditions present contrasting visions of God or ultimate reality that are, at many places, contradictory.[20] Undoubtedly, diverse models of the God-world relationship flow from these diverse theological and philosophical convictions. The Buddhist doctrine of dependent origination, the emanation of the 10,000 things from Yin and Yang, which in turn derive from the Great Ultimate of Neo-Confucianism, and the contraction theory (*tsimtsum*) of Cabalist Judaism by which the "divine sparks" (*sefirot*) are released provide but three of the numerous religious visions available to those who ponder this matter. From these starting points, contrasting notions of religious experience follow, whether that be the Buddhist claim that enlightenment is the realization that *nirvana* (the religious ultimate) is *samsara* (the wheel of existence) and vice versa, or the Neo-Confucian vision of balancing the Yin and Yang in order to flow with the Tao, or the Jewish experience of the *Shekhinah* (the final *sefirot*), whereby God is both present and hidden at the same time. In contrast, *one* way in which the Christian tradition has attempted to understand the God-world relationship is expressed in the doctrine of God creating all things by Word and Spirit (Irenaeus's "two hands of the father") *ex nihilo*. As a corollary, Christians experience God graciously—as an undeserved gift of the Spirit—by way of the incarnation of the Logos in the historical Jesus of Nazareth and by way of encountering the Holy Spirit in the various dimensions of life.

My conviction is that a foundational pneumatology provides one possible avenue by which to explore, discuss, and perhaps adjudicate some of these differences. A pneumatological starting point furnishes the broadest of contexts for the interreligious encounter, both by beginning with the doctrine of creation (of the

20. In the following discussion, I use the word *God* in a sense inclusive of the signifier *ultimate reality* more common to the interreligious dialogue.

cosmos and of the *humanum*) and by supplying conceptual and linguistic resources by which to inquire into the divine presence and agency in the world. As the Catholic charismatic theologian Ralph del Colle suggests in his own argument for the viability of Spirit-Christology, such a point of entry allows the interreligious dialogue "to be focused at the point of inquiry where the dialogue will be most fruitful."[21] What this does is highlight the themes common to the human religious quest, even as it provides the kind of latitude for the emergence of comparative categories to facilitate further dialogue. In the process, theological nuances are established, problematic contrasts are located at the right places and in their proper respects, and genuine harmonies and differences between religious traditions are defined with greater clarity. This is part of the process by which competing claims to truth are adjudicated on this side of eternity. This is not only because a foundational pneumatology is motivated by the idea that God is the "object" of religious encounter regardless of one's traditional affiliation, but also because it trades on the most general or abstract categories drawn from our common human experience as mediated by the Spirit as divine presence and agent.

From this, it is clear that foundational pneumatology is *not* content with only systematic coherence or with ensuring that the biblical data be packaged so as to provide a meaningful symbolic world and fluid narrative. A foundational pneumatology recognizes the differences and connections between meaning and truth, between systematic coherence and referential correspondence. Any system whose internal parts relate consistently to each other is meaningful on its own terms. In Wittgensteinian terms, the Christian and Buddhist symbol systems, just to name two, are subspecies of the religious language game, and their "truths" are operative *only* within their respective frameworks and are meaningless without. In this connection, "systematic pneumatology" is important precisely because it orders the diversity of symbols of the Holy Spirit both within the biblical revelation and the historical Christian tradition into a coherent whole. "Truth" as coherence in systematic pneumatology, however, is thus relativized only to Christians and those within the Christian tradition because it is

21. Ralph del Colle, *Christ and the Spirit: Spirit-Christology in Trinitarian Perspective* (New York: Oxford University Press, 1994), 213.

unable on its own terms to adequately engage the question of whether or not there is a correspondence between its symbolic signifiers and reality "outside" the system.

Against this reductionism of the notion of truth to systemic coherence, however, biblical theism makes public claims to truth that resists regionality and ethnocentricity and strives toward universalism. To complete theological reflection on pneumatology therefore requires that the "system" (and all its parts) be tested against reality, and, as a religious and doctrinal system, against competing systems that also claim to interpret such reality correctly. To take this step is to move from truth as coherence to truth as correspondence, from systematic to foundational pneumatology. It is to extend reflection on divine presence and agency from its confines within the *ecclesia* to engagement with the world.[22]

This is the apologetic function of foundational pneumatology that is open to the world. Such openness entails vulnerability to criticism and correction from these other systems of thought and action. It is, in this sense, truly a "pneumatology of quest."[23] At the same time, foundational pneumatology is also, by its very nature, committed to truth in its strongest sense (truth as correspondence between sign and thing signified).[24] This commitment obliges defense against all potential critics and alternatives. In its aspiration to be globally accountable and applicable, it makes itself contextually particular to each religious-cultural-linguistic tradition. The result is a pneumatology that is universal, abstract, and metaphysical on the one hand and local, particular, and concrete on the other. A successful foundational pneumatology must be able to bring the broad scope of systematic pneumatology into dialogue

22. I have previously argued that systematic theology remains incomplete if it does not engage in foundational theology (or fundamental theology in Tracy's sense): "Whither Systematic Theology? A Systematician Chimes in on a Scandalous Conversation," *PNEUMA: The Journal of the Society for Pentecostal Studies* 20.1 (spring 1998): 85–93.

23. This is analogous to what is taking place under the rubric of "humility theology" in the science-religion dialogues; see, e.g., John M. Templeton, *The Humble Approach: Scientists Discover God*, 2d rev. ed. (New York: Continuum, 1995). The emphasis in my "pneumatology of quest" and in "humility theology" is on the fallible nature of all human knowledge since "now we see in a mirror, dimly" (1 Cor 13:12).

24. It should be clear that I am a committed metaphysical realist who endorses the thesis that things exist apart from any human mentality. At the same time, I would not go so far as to deny the claim of the theistic idealist that things are what they are ultimately because of God's thinking them. The latter claim, however, is a speculative metaphysical thesis located firmly in the arena of philosophical theology. The former is a far less controversial claim insofar as empirical warrants are concerned.

with any and all interested in the subject matter. In this sense, a foundational theology of the Holy Spirit, while nondogmatic, is contextual and missionary. It is thus a relevant pneumatology, unrestricted in terms of the scope of its audience even as it is universal in intent with regard to its applications and claims.

This leads to a consideration of the practical rationale for foundational pneumatology, some of which should have been evident in the preceding discussion. It should be clear that because foundational pneumatology is motivated by the conviction that divine presence and agency are universal in scope, a fully developed version demands that attention be given to discerning the ways such presence and activity are mediated by the Holy Spirit. As a corollary, a foundational pneumatology requires a theology of discernment in its widest and most robust sense since the Holy Spirit is not the only spiritual reality present and active in the world. A theology of *spirit* is thus in order, one that is metaphysically and theologically sophisticated enough to account for the diversity of spirits in the world—from human to cultural-religious, socio-structural, cosmic, and demonic, just to name a few—even while it provides some means by which to discern divine presence and activity in, through, and against them. A foundational pneumatology is eminently equipped for these tasks (theology of spirit and theology of discernment) given its nature and scope. I will return to this point later.

Again, the Pneumatological Imagination

Having said all of this, however, it is also important to admit that the speculative demands of foundational pneumatology are not empty abstractions but have been nurtured by what St. Paul calls "life in the Spirit." As such, foundational pneumatology and its attendant epistemology—the pneumatological imagination, I have called it—have emerged from a way of life that has been impacted by and is particularly attentive to the Spirit of God. In fact, the ecclesial people of God were founded by their one experience of the Spirit amidst the plurality and diversity of their particular tongues and languages on the Day of Pentecost (Acts 2). The same Spirit who enabled cross-cultural understanding and *koinonia* in the early church is the one in whom all humankind also lives, moves, and has its being (Acts 17:28). From this ecclesial reality that spans languages, cultures, space, and time comes the pneumatological imagination—the capacity to apprehend the Spirit, to speak the Spirit's languages, to experience the Spirit's reality, and to engage reality spiritually—which is thereby intrinsically one only in and through its plurality.[25]

My optimism that a truly transcultural and universal discourse and rationality is available to encultured human beings is finally founded, then, on the experiences of the ecclesial people, who participate in the kingdom of God even while anticipating its full realization. In that case, Christian engagement with non-Christians is always pneumatological or spiritual along two fronts. First, interpersonal human relationships are holistic, irreducible to their material, psychological, intellectual, affective, or sociopolitical dimensions, except when they have been destroyed by the effects of sin. Second, genuine spiritual and theological engagement is inevitably a gracious gift of the Spirit of God since "no one comprehends what is truly God's except the Spirit of God" (1 Cor. 2:11b). If the things of God are discerned only spiritually through the charismatic endowment of the Spirit's presence and activity (cf. 1 Cor. 2:9–16), then all authentic theological engagement that occurs in the interreligious dialogue is pneumatologically infused. The pneumatological imagination has to be recognized, therefore, as the lens through which we see, the context within which we engage religious others authentically. As Killian McDonnell puts it, just as we use "thinking in attempting to discover what the 'object' of thinking is, so in much the same way we must use the Spirit to understand the Spirit . . . because the Spirit is the universal comprehensive horizon within which any and all theological reflection is possible."[26]

The potential of this project, then, is predicated on the possibility of engaging others in truly authentic ways. This includes the possibility of learning another language; of developing an appreciation for and capacity to embrace radical difference, otherness, and alterity; of participating and sharing in a different way of life; of increasing in understanding of another world-and-life-view; of forging a cross-cultural hermeneutic; in short, of being transformed through interpersonal encounter. And, insofar as these are

25. See my "'As the Spirit Gives Utterenace . . .': Pentecost, Intra-Christian Ecumenism, and the Wider Oekumene," *International Review of Mission* (forthcoming).

26. Killian McDonnell, "A Trinitarian Theology of the Holy Spirit?" *Theological Studies* 46 (1985): 216.

actual possibilities resident in the gift of life, they are not restricted in any way except as we purposefully erect borders between ourselves and others in order to "keep the alien out." True openness, however, embraces the work of the Spirit wherever the Spirit may blow (cf. John 3:8). And this would include the possibility of a transformative encounter with those in other faiths.

Of course, these possibilities are part and parcel of a pneumatologically inspired imagination since those schooled in the ways of the Spirit will be alert to the Spirit's meeting us in unexpected places, at awkward times, and through unfamiliar media. Such a pneumatological imagination is properly humble in the face of the partiality, finitude, and perspectival character of all human knowledge.[27] As such, the pneumatological imagination is conducive to developing the kind of dynamic epistemology needed for sustained interaction and engagement with radical alterity. Since this is the kind of alterity encountered in and through engaging religious others and otherness, the pneumatological imagination serves as the epistemic precondition of genuine interreligious engagement, and foundational pneumatology refers to the ontological context that nurtures and transforms the engaging partners.

The brevity of these comments prevents a comprehensive argument for the importance of either foundational pneumatology or the pneumatological imagination for contemporary theology. Much more needs to be said. I wish to do so, however, in a more concrete way that spells out the value of both foundational pneumatology and the pneumatological imagination for the task of theology of religions. The final section of this chapter will demonstrate the promise of foundational pneumatology for interreligious dialogue as seen concretely in the case of global Pentecostalism.

Whither Foundational Pneumatology? The Case of Pentecostalism

Rather than providing additional reasons for engaging in foundational pneumatology that are materially different from those delineated above, I want instead to strengthen the argument by making concrete connections with a particular historical tradition. In what follows, I will examine the philosophical, theological, and practical rationale that motivates Pentecostals and charismatics

27. For detailed argument, see my *Spirit-Word-Community*, chap. 5.

(henceforth PCs) to engage in foundational pneumatology. I do so here in part because it is the Christian tradition I am most identified with and in part because it has nurtured my theological identity and inspired my theological journey. At the same time, what follows is only exemplary and should not be considered an exhaustive treatment.

Pentecostalism and Foundational Pneumatology

Those familiar with the PC movement are aware of its global significance.[28] Global presence requires global response and responsibility. PCs are still learning the ropes of ecumenical dialogue with other Christians. In this context, there is mutual understanding that takes place, as well as the development of a critical PC apologetics vis-à-vis historical and contemporary Christian theology. There is, however, a much larger theological public than that found among Christians, if theology is defined as critical thinking about God or things ultimate. To engage seriously, meaningfully, and truthfully in these broader conversations, PCs must further develop their conceptual, linguistic, and analytical apparatus.

As with any dialogue, understanding and apologetics are mutually informing and supporting objectives. Neither can take place without the other, and both are transformative for earnest dialogue participants. This is, in part, because new languages and perspectives are brought to bear in the process of reflection, conversation, and argument. This is part and parcel of relating one's own theological tradition and religious experiences to other audiences. The PC experience of the Holy Spirit, for example, begs for comparative analysis. Many PCs believe there is an intrinsic connection between this experience—what PCs call "baptism in the Holy Spirit"—and the phenomenon of speaking in tongues. The anthropologist Cyril Williams has called PC glossolalia a "mysticism of sound" that is phenomenologically similar, in its global forms, to shamanistic language, the repetitive Sufi *dhikr*, spontaneous Cabalist utterances, certain forms of Hindu mantras, and Tibetan tantrism. He concludes by calling for a multi-disciplinary approach to

28. Cf. e.g., Karla Poewe, ed., *Charismatic Christianity as Global Culture* (Columbia: University of South Carolina Press, 1994); Walter Hollenweger, *Pentecostalism: Its Origins and Development Worldwide* (Peabody, Mass.: Hendrickson, 1997); Murray W. Dempster, Byron D. Klaus, and Douglas Peterson, eds., *The Globalization of Pentecostalism: A Religion Made to Travel* (Oxford and Irvine, Calif.: Regnum International, 1999); and David Martin, *Pentecostalism: The World Their Parish* (Malden, Mass.: Blackwell, 2001).

the experience of glossolalia in its affective, cognitional, somatic, and other dimensions.[29] Such approaches to the entire phenomena of PC experience are still needed; that they should be conducted in a global, comparative context should go without saying. These kinds of investigations will surely be a catalyst for creative PC theology while serving apologetic ends, since they would require that PCs develop a coherent account of their experience related to commonalities and differences—both theologically and phenomenologically—with those of other traditions and defend the plausibility of their interpretations in dialogue with any and all parties interested in the subject matter.

The success of such endeavors, besides the number of converts to Christianity or the transformation of PC soul and tradition for the better, hinges in large part on the ability of PCs to communicate their experiences in the concepts and languages of another. For PCs, this raises in its sharpest form, epistemological, methodological, and philosophical questions. This arena of intellectual inquiry is one in which PCs have traditionally been weakest. My dialogue with Peirce, Gelpi, and others doing theology in conversation with the philosophic tradition may be a "turn-off" to some PCs who would be inclined to take scriptural texts like Col. 2:8 (Paul's warning against "deceptive philosophy" [NIV]) literally. A further complaint, articulated clearly by Henry Lederle, might be that Gelpi (and those doing philosophical theology) "employs such a wide range of philosophical approaches that he undercuts basic communication with most of those interested in a theology of the charismatic renewal."[30]

One's weaknesses are best handled, however, not by ignoring them but by addressing them. As PC scholarship has grown in sophistication, there is a greater openness today than in the 1970s and 1980s to seeing both the value and the need of rethinking not only theological but also philosophical categories for our experience of the Spirit. In fact, I am ready to argue that our pneumatological imagination, if severely criticized and applied, will result eventually in a revisioning of the primary philosophical and metaphysical categories themselves. At any rate, foundational theologies, targeted

29. Cyril Williams, *Tongues of the Spirit: A Study of Pentecostal Glossolalia and Related Phenomena* (Cardiff: University of Wales Press, 1981), 192–212.

30. Henry Lederle, *Treasures Old and New: Interpretations of "Spirit-Baptism" in the Charismatic Renewal Movement* (Peabody, Mass.: Hendrickson, 1988), 117.

as they are to the widest possible public, cannot escape the philosophical elements that are concerned with methodological and presuppositional issues. I am inclined to believe that many PCs are ready to enter not only these kinds of philosophical conversations but also others such as the interreligious dialogue and the dialogue between science and religion/theology that have far-reaching implications in our global context. This matter is especially urgent given the PC proclivity for personal testimony and witness. To present one's beliefs and practices to this larger public requires an interpretation of tongues and an argument for their truth. This in turn demands an enlargement of PC horizons of discourse.

Pentecostal Mission and Praxis

There is, however, at least one other important philosophic-theological reason for PCs to engage in foundational pneumatology. PCs are among the most convinced of Christians regarding the presence and activity of divinity (through the Holy Spirit) in the world. However, to claim that the Holy Spirit reproves the world of sin, righteousness, and judgment (John 16:8–11) without providing some explanation of how that happens is theologically vacuous. Aside from existential confirmations, translating this biblical and (for PCs) experiential truth into more general philosophic categories is *one* way to buttress its claims for the non-Christian public. To provide a plausible account for the Spirit's agency in the world in these matters is also to further legitimate the pneumatological vision that PCs claim to guide their experience and their being-in-the-world.

The close and complex relation between praxis and cognition is nowhere more evident than in PC orientation to the spirit world. PCs talk much about discernment in general and about the discernment of spirits in particular, and rightly so. The nature of PC phenomena and the diversity of spiritual manifestations require this. Yet, the pneumatological orientation among PCs has not led to the kind of reflection on a theology of spiritual discernment that differs substantively from that produced by non-PC Christians. In their concern to be biblical, PCs have failed to translate the norms of discernment given in Scripture into comparative categories that undergird all effective discernment. In their spiritual zeal, PCs have been rightly accused of a dangerous subjectivity regarding this matter.[31] The intent of these general criticisms is to spur PC thinking on this issue. PC praxis, as much as belief, is dependent on our engaging the task of foundational pneumatology.

Pentecostalism and the Pneumatological Imagination

Before concluding, it is imperative that something further be said about the pneumatological imagination that is connected to the project of foundational pneumatology pursued here. The underlying issue is the relation between PC theology and epistemology, or, alternatively, between specific and natural revelation, Scripture and experience, or faith and reason. In arguing for the necessity of translating the PC imagination-experience into more neutral categories amenable to a wider theological conversation, would that mean that the former experience has been forced into a foreign philosophical framework? If so, does the interpretive framework skew the explication of the experience so that its particularity is compromised? On the other hand, if it is said that the foundational pneumatology and its categories arise from the PC imaginative-experiential background, then the resulting foundational pneumatology runs the risk of being an imperialistic PC (Christian) imposition on other dialogue partners willing to be seated at the discussion table.

As previously indicated, I resist the dualism implied by these lines of reasoning. I do concede that the pneumatological imagination I am proposing arises out of a specific cluster of PC experiences—engagements of the Holy Spirit in the world. What I deny is that this imagination is insulated from outside criticism, whether such be biblically derived by those internal to the Christian tradition or whether they eventuate from secularists, non-Christians, or members of other faiths. A dialectical process is at work here, as there undoubtedly is in all questions of this sort. Experience and interpretation are mutually informing and correcting elements in

31. There are manuals aplenty on discernment produced for popular consumption. More critical material includes Walter Hollenweger's *Geist und Materie*, vol. 3: *Interkulturelle Theologie* (München: Kaiser, 1988); and Stephen E. Parker's *Led by the Spirit: Toward a Practical Theology of Pentecostal Discernment and Decision-Making*, Journal of Pentecostal Theology Supplement Series 2 (Sheffield: Sheffield Academic Press, 1996). Hollenweger, of course, has long been encouraging us Pentecostals to think critically for ourselves, while Parker's focus is more on what is identified in the subtitle to his book than the kind of broad theology of discernment I have in mind.

any community of knowers.[32] Further, what I am proposing here is put forward tentatively for reflection, discussion, and criticism. The theoretical and conceptual apparatus will always fall short of the richness of experience. The foundational pneumatology is both provisional and vulnerable to criticism, amplification, and adjustment. Our pneumatological imagination is being constantly challenged, enlarged, transformed, or exposed through our faithful attention to the Scriptures, participation in rituals of the Spirit, engagement in dialogue with an other, and obedience to the presence and agency of the divine Spirit in the world. I do, however, think that any foundational categories generated from our interpretation of the PC experience will be correct in their general features, in large part because they will be pneumatological features that are intrinsic to human processes of engaging divine presence and agency in the world. There is a hermeneutical spiral in this process whereby the Spirit illuminates our experiences, which in turn reveal to us more about who the Spirit is.

This is not to deny that the pneumatological imagination needs to be cultivated and that the PC experience fosters such cultivation. It only asserts what has long been affirmed by the traditional doctrine of common grace: that human life and experience is dependent only on the prevenient presence and activity of the Spirit of God, and that this should put us on the alert for possible experiences of the Spirit and alternative specifications of the pneumatological imagination outside of explicitly PC or even Christian contexts. Other pneumatological visions exist, both in Christian and non-Christian forms, and none can claim a monopoly on the Spirit's presence, work, and revelation.[33] I believe that dialogue on

32. I am not alone among Pentecostals and charismatics on this point. The same or similar epistemological thesis has been argued by others with regard to the hermeneutical issue, e.g., William W. Menzies, "Synoptic Theology: An Essay on Pentecostal Hermeneutics," *Paraclete: A Journal Concerning the Person and Work of the Holy Spirit* 13 (1979): 14–21; W. Randolph Tate, *Biblical Interpretation: An Integrated Approach* (Peabody, Mass.: Hendrickson, 1991); Roger Stronstad, *Spirit, Scripture, and Theology: A Pentecostal Perspective* (Baguio City, Philippines: Asia Pacific Theological Seminary, 1995); Scott A. Ellington, "Pentecostalism and the Authority of Scripture," *Journal of Pentecostal Theology* 9 (1996): 16–38; and Joel Shuman, "Toward a Cultural-Linguistic Account of the Pentecostal Doctrine of the Baptism in the Holy Spirit," *PNEUMA: The Journal of the Society for Pentecostal Studies* 19 (1997): 207–23. Cf. also the earlier observations of Walter Hollenweger, "*Creatur Spiritus*: The Challenge of Pentecostal Experience to Pentecostal Theology," *Theology* 81 (1978): 32–40.

33. Pentecostals and charismatics have a pneumatological imagination different from that exhibited by Reformed (see, e.g., Jürgen Moltmann, *The Spirit of Life: A Universal Affirmation*, trans. Margaret Kohl [London: SCM, 1992]; and Michael Welker, *God the Spirit*, trans.

this subject will bring about convergence that recognizes genuine differences while clarifying other problems. It needs to be emphasized that the more neutral language that emerges out of any such engagement, even as it translates what is meaningful for one religious tradition to other interested parties, must be able to preserve (or retain the capability of preserving) the deepest *truthful* convictions of the traditions in dialogue. Anything less than that would not be a foundational pneumatology in the sense envisioned here.

Acknowledging that the foundational pneumatology I am proposing arises from a particular pneumatological imagination requires at least one final comment relative to the issue of universality. As used here, "imagination" refers to the synthetic processes of world-making that bridge elemental perception and cognition in human experience. The imagination is what operates at the border of the finite and the infinite and forms the possibilities for both human worldviews and for our being-in-the-world.[34] The antifoundationalist critique therefore means only that classical foundationalism of the Cartesian type is dead; it does not mean that there are no "foundations" at all or that all knowledge sits on thin air. A truly foundational pneumatology will be open to insights and correction from the many perspectives that derive from humankind's historical encounter with the divine Spirit. From the PC perspective, all that emerges out of the ongoing conversation will be subject to the biblical revelation of the personal character, nature, and work of God the Spirit, even as it exposes and reveals the many ideological manipulations and sinful employments of the biblical data. The task of justifying any theological construct requires that the quest for the universal elements in human experience that make for meaning, knowledge, and truth be something other than social

---

John F. Hoffmeyer [Minneapolis: Fortress, 1994]) or Roman Catholic theologians (e.g., Gelpi). The interreligious dialogue is beginning to yield some understanding of similar imaginations in other traditions (see, e.g., Allan Anderson, *Moya: The Holy Spirit in an African Context* [Pretoria: University of South Africa Press, 1991], and Michael E. Lodahl, *Shekhinah/Spirit: Divine Presence in Jewish and Christian Religion* [New York: Paulist Press, 1992]). It is arguable that there is also a kind of pneumatological imagination at work in the reflections of non-Christian secularists (e.g., Joel Kovel, *History and Spirit: An Inquiry into the Philosophy of Liberation* [Boston: Beacon, 1991]).

34. I have learned a great deal about this from my teacher, Robert Cummings Neville; see his *Reconstruction of Thinking* (Albany: SUNY Press, 1981), part 2, and idem, *The Truth of Broken Symbols* (Albany: SUNY Press, 1996), esp. chaps. 2–3.

conventions or convenient fictions. As a Christian theologian, I proceed with some optimism that pneumatology, concerned as it is with explicating divine presence and agency in the world, provides the broadest framework for reflection, discussion, and debate about theological matters. The kind of universality I envision is therefore a posteriori in nature, building on the empirical findings of our engagement with the world and the convergences that emerge out of the ongoing theological dialogue. It is ultimately eschatological in realization, but such an orientation is not alien to the PC orientation.

In this chapter, I have attempted to lay out the epistemic, methodological, and philosophical framework for the pneumatological approach to theology of religions. I am urging that the paradigm shift to pneumatology is critical to advancing the discussion in Christian *theologia religionum.* It is now time to pull together the details of the proposal theologically. To do so, I propose to analyze previous efforts to develop a pneumatological theology of religions. Three preliminary cases from Orthodox, mainline Protestant, and Roman Catholic theology will be overviewed briefly (chapter 4) before a more intensive engagement with an evangelical theology of religions (chapter 5).

4

Pneumatological Approaches to the Religions

Description and Prospectus

Not long ago, Paul Knitter reported on the "turn to pneumatology" in Christian theology of religions taken by the Dialogue subunit of the World Council of Churches (WCC) at the Theological Consultation that met in January 1990 at Baar, Switzerland.[1] He observed that while the traditional emphasis on soteriology had produced almost unbearable tensions in *theologia religionum* as evidenced in the intense disputes between advocates of exclusivism, inclusivism, and pluralism, an emerging pneumatological paradigm was suggestive of a way forward in the debate. Central to the soteriological question, of course, was the uniqueness, absoluteness, and normativeness of Christ as mediator of salvation. Whereas traditional formulations had subjected the economy of the Spirit to that of the Son, perhaps in order to preserve the availability of salvation only under and through the name, person, and work of Jesus, a pneumatological approach that affirmed the

1. Paul F. Knitter, "A New Pentecost? A Pneumatological Theology of Religions," *Current Dialogue* 19 (1991): 32–41. The entirety of this issue of *Current Dialogue* was devoted to this meeting, which included the statement produced by the Baar Consultation: "Religious Plurality: Theological Perspectives and Affirmations," 47–51.

related but distinct economy of the Spirit seemed to make more readily accessible the saving grace of God to all persons, and especially those who had never had an opportunity to receive the gospel. As such, starting with pneumatology rather than with christology invited theological reflection on and exploration of the possibility of the Spirit's "saving presence" and "saving power" in the non-Christian faiths.

The corollary emphasis on the *relationes subsistentes* (subsistent relations) of the trinitarian Persons also led to a view of all religions as perhaps complementary and relational, leaving open to definition the exact relationship between the economy of the Word (incarnate in Jesus of Nazareth and in Christian faith in the church) and that of the Spirit (instantiated possibly, at least in part, in the religions). On the one hand, this allowed for the continued Christian insistence on the uniqueness of Jesus Christ, both (1) the emphasis on the universality of Jesus' saving work without insistence on either explicit knowledge of or confessed commitment to him as a prerequisite and (2) the requirement for a decisive Christian response as appropriate in the face of absolute relativism. On the other hand, it also enabled accentuation of the universal activity of the Spirit in the world—essentially related to but not exhaustively bound by the economy of the Word, thus requiring ongoing dialogue, interpretation, and clarification and resulting in a deepening awareness of new (unseen or unresponded to) facets of the mystery of salvation. A pneumatological approach to the religions would thus issue forth in an essential transformation of the theological landscape since the loci of theology would of necessity include themes, motifs, doctrines, and even the religious symbols of the non-Christian faiths. As Knitter put it, "Because the Holy Spirit is alive and well among those persons, ours must be a dialogical theology."[2]

As a veteran theologian of interreligious dialogue who had wrestled long and hard with the question of the religions during the previous two decades, Knitter's endorsement of the "pneumatological turn" seems initially assuring. For all its promise, however, this theme has remained surprisingly untapped in that a full treatment of the subject has yet to appear. While Knitter might have been expected to make much more of the pneumatological

2. Knitter, "A New Pentecost?" 41.

structure of salvation than he actually has given his movement toward liberation and eco-human soteriocentrism, he has actually returned to christology in his latest books and left the pneumatological insight largely undeveloped.[3] In fact, one detects a certain retreat on Knitter's part, especially in his discerning the greater extent to which the alleged independence of the economies of the Spirit and the Word need to be qualified. Rather than emphasizing the distinctiveness of the Spirit's economy, Knitter writes instead that "the Spirit exists within the Word, just as the Word exists also in the Spirit. Thus the genuine difference of the kingdom in other religions must be related, understood, and clarified within the Word incarnate in Christ and living in the church. As the Word and Spirit have their existence in each other, so does the kingdom within the church and the kingdom beyond it."[4] While an emphasis on the distinctive economy of the Spirit seems to initially inspire Christian theologizing on the religions, Knitter's work demonstrates that such attempts have not been able to proceed very far before re-encountering the christological question. There is an almost inseparable connection between Spirit and Word that reasserts itself in Christian theology whenever it has been suggested that the two economies are distinct and perhaps autonomous.

To further examine this connection, it may be instructive to review the fortunes of others who have proposed various beginnings toward a pneumatological theology of religions and, like Knitter, have not been able to take leave of christology. For this analysis, it is fortuitous that we have the efforts of theologians like Georg Khodr, Stanley Samartha, and Jacques Dupuis, all of whom made the turn to pneumatology in the early 1970s. The fact that they derive, respectively, from the diverse traditions of Eastern Orthodoxy, Protestantism, and Roman Catholicism will also enable a more comprehensive assessment of the viability of a pneumatological approach to the religions. Their attempts and partial successes may enable us to answer two related questions. First, is the pneumatological turn only a detour in Christian theology of

3. Paul F. Knitter, *Jesus and the Other Names: Christian Mission and Global Responsibility* (Maryknoll, N.Y.: Orbis, 1996), section entitled "The Spirit and the Church—Ecclesiology and Pneumatology," 111–14. Knitter's prior book, *One Earth, Many Religions: Multifaith Dialogue and Global Responsibility* (Maryknoll, N.Y.: Orbis, 1995), has four paragraphs on the Spirit and the religions (pp. 77–81). These appear to be practically inconsequential considering that the text of both volumes totals 348 pages.

4. Knitter, *Jesus and the Other Names*, 114.

religions that eventually returns us to christology? It appears to be the case that this turn generates new problems, the chief of which may be how the presence and activity of the Spirit in the religions is to be discerned. Since the criteria by which such discernment takes place has been primarily christological, Christian theology of religions cannot disconnect pneumatology entirely from christology. We can therefore perhaps also learn something from the efforts of Knitter and his predecessors on a second, related question—that of discerning the Spirit in the religions. Rather than taking a futile detour, I will seek to show that the turn to pneumatology by Knitter and company can be employed as a conduit for further reflection, for they have laid a sturdy foundation for an approach to the religions that does not displace but rather complements the christological.

An Eastern Orthodox Emphasis on the Distinct Economy of the Spirit

Orthodox Theology and the Work of Georg Khodr

Given the perennial Orthodox resistance to the *Filioque*, it is hardly surprising that one of the first attempts to address the twentieth-century consciousness of religious pluralism via an emphasis on the distinct economy of the Holy Spirit was by Georg Khodr, metropolitan of the Mount Lebanon Diocese of the Greek-Orthodox Patriarchate of Beirut, Lebanon. In his address to the Central Committee of the WCC at Addis Ababa in 1971, Khodr contrasted Western and Eastern soteriologies.[5] Whereas the Latin West had traditionally understood soteriology as a subdivision of ecclesiology—as evidenced by their *extra ecclesia nulla salus* position ("no salvation outside the church")[6]—Eastern Orthodoxy has preferred to emphasize the concept of *oikonomia* over that of "salvation history," and that in its trinitarian framework rather than solely in terms of the historical Christ and the visible church. The affirmations are then made, following Irenaeus, (1) of the hypostatic independence of both the Son and the Spirit (which

5. Georg Khodr, "Christianity in a Pluralistic World—The Economy of the Holy Spirit," *The Ecumenical Review* 23 (1971): 118–28.

6. On this doctrine, see Francis A. Sullivan, *Salvation outside the Church? Tracing the History of the Catholic Response* (New York: Paulist Press, 1992); and Molly Truman Marshall, *No Salvation outside the Church? A Critical Inquiry* (Lewiston, N.Y.: Edwin Mellen, 1993).

secures the distinction between the two) and (2) "that the advent of the Holy Spirit in the world is not subordinated to the Son, is not simply a function of the Word."[7] This, of course, serves to fortify the reconception of the divine missions to the world not simply as one *Heilsgeschichte* but in terms of differentiated *oikonomia.* What Khodr points out is that the *oikonomia* of the Son brings us to participation in the divine life itself and hence into the larger *oikonomia* of the Spirit. Khodr thus views Israel as a representative typological election out of the entire economy and, analogously, the church as the firstfruits of those called to salvation.

Khodr quotes the well-known Orthodox theologian, Vladimir Lossky, only once in his address. Yet the latter's exposition of the distinct divine economies as seen in his *Théologie mystique de l'Elise d'Orient* permeates Khodr's essay.[8] Lossky was also convinced that the *Filioque* was at the root of the barrier between the Eastern and Western churches, and it was he who was most responsible for the thesis that the dominance of ecclesiology in Latin theology and its ecclesiologically defined soteriology was to be traced to the *Filioque.* Briefly stated, the import of this perennial doctrinal problem restated in this context is this: If the Spirit is from the Father *and* or *through* the Son (as affirmed by the West in its addition of the *Filioque* to the Creed), it makes sense to think of the domain of the Spirit more as circumscribed by the domain of the the Son and his body, the church, than not. If, however, on the proposed alternative reading, which is being increasingly accepted by a wide spectrum of theologians, the Spirit is from the Father *of* the Son, then the economy of the Son in no way limits that of the Spirit.[9] It would be interesting to determine whether or

7. Khodr, "Christianity in a Pluralistic World," 126.

8. See Vladimir Lossky, *The Mystical Theology of the Eastern Church* (London: James Clarke, 1957), chaps. 6 and 7. For more on the Orthodox view of the relationship between the two economies, see Angelos J. Philippou, "The Mystery of Pentecost," in *The Orthodox Ethos: Essays in Honour of the Centenary of the Greek Orthodox Archdiocese of North and South America,* ed. A. J. Philippou (Oxford: Holywell, 1964), 70–97, esp. 79–91.

9. For the recent discussion, see *Spirit of God, Spirit of Christ: Ecumenical Reflections on the Filioque Controversy,* ed. Lukas Vischer (Geneva: World Council of Churches, 1981); Alisdair Heron, "The *Filioque* Clause," in *One God in Trinity,* ed. Peter Toon and James D. Spiceland (Westchester, Ill.: Cornerstone Books, 1980), 62–77; Jürgen Moltmann, *The Trinity and the Kingdom: The Doctrine of God,* trans. Margaret Kohl (San Francisco: Harper & Row, 1981), 178–88; Yves Congar, *The Word and the Spirit,* trans. David Smith (London: Geoffrey Chapman; San Francisco: Harper & Row, 1988), chap. 7; and Gary D. Badcock, *Light of Truth and Fire of Love: A Theology of the Holy Spirit* (Grand Rapids: Eerdmans, 1997), chap. 3.

not it was this conviction that led to Lossky's developing in greater detail the distinction of the economies of the Spirit and the Word, or if it was the other way around. Probably one would not be far off to posit a dialectical relationship between these two theological intuitions.

The Distinct Economies of the Word and the Spirit

Whatever Khodr's own view of Lossky's thesis regarding Latin Christianity, it is certainly the case that the Eastern Orthodox distinction between the two divine economies is central to his pneumatological account of religious pluralism. Since it is admitted that between the economies of the Son and the Spirit "there is a reciprocity and a mutual service" and that mutuality assumes some kind of distinction rather than identity, it is therefore possible to grant that "the Spirit operates and applies His energies in accordance with His own economy and we could, from this angle, regard the non-Christian religions as points where His inspiration is at work."[10]

Khodr recognizes that this acknowledgment demands a rethinking of Christian mission, and he proposes a fivefold response. First, he urges the acceptance of the various religious traditions as divinely ordained "training schools" of mercy, peace, and patience that gradually lead toward the eschatological consummation and recapitulation of all things in Jesus Christ. Second, non-Christian religious communities, experiences, and even scriptures should be received as realities that can enrich and enlighten the divine mystery revealed within the Christian tradition. Third, even if legalism prevails to a greater or lesser extent in all traditions, all genuine symbols in the various religions potentially mediate the divine to those who are able to see beyond the finite signs of their own faith. For this reason, it is incumbent upon Christians to "penetrate beyond the symbols and historical forms and discover the profound intention of religious men and to relate their apprehension of divinity to the object of our Christian hope."[11] This requires, fourth, a Christian approach to those of other faiths such that its missionary relations are conducted in the humility of Christ, free from confessional pride and cultural superiority. From this flows the fifth point: a transformed Christian mission wherein

10. Khodr, "Christianity in a Pluralistic World," 126.
11. Ibid., 127.

genuine two-way communion and communication is the *modus operandi*, and the supreme task of missions is not to enlarge the border of the church but to recognize the mystery of the church in its permeability and to "identify all the Christic values in other religions, to show them Christ as the bond which unites them and his love as their fulfilment."[12] Khodr's conclusion is that "true mission laughs at missionary activity. Our task is simply to follow the tracks of Christ perceptive in the shadows of other religions."[13]

While this is perhaps laudable in contrast to the traditional missionary objective of conversion to Christendom (note the noun, rather than my depicting Christian conversion as personal conversion to Jesus Christ), Khodr's presentation is nevertheless not free from tension. Theologizing as he does from within the framework of Orthodox trinitarianism, he sees the missions of the Son and the Spirit are much more interconnected than not. While the religions may be the working of the economy of the Spirit, yet they are at the same time in a very real sense connected to the economy of the Son. The keen reader would have observed in the fivefold program outlined above that Christ is very much at the center, not only of Khodr's Orthodox conception of other religious traditions but also, unbeknownst to these others, of their own faith as well. Thus Khodr can propose not only that non-Christian scriptures be read in the light of Christ—since it is "Christ alone who is received as light when grace visits a Brahmin, a Buddhist or a Muhammadan reading his own scriptures"—but also that "any reading of religions is a reading of Christ," and that "every martyr for the truth, every man persecuted for what he believes to be right, dies in communion with Christ."[14] Ultimately, "the task of the witness in a non-Christian context will be to name him whom others have already recognized as the Beloved. . . . The entire missionary activity of the Church will be directed towards awakening the Christ who sleeps in the night of the religions."[15] At least in this initial formulation of a pneumatological approach to the religions, it appears that there is, after all, no escape from christocentrism as

12. Ibid., 128.

13. Ibid.

14. Ibid., 125.

15. Ibid., 128. And, of course, this position of Khodr's sketched in 1971 is remarkably close to Karl Rahner's "anonymous Christianity" thesis, also propounded during the revolutionary second Vatican council. Raimon Panikkar argues similarly from this Rahnerian perspective in his *The Unknown Christ of Hinduism* (London: Darton, Longman & Todd, 1964).

traditionally conceived. What Khodr does manage to highlight is that since the Holy Spirit is recognized to be at work in the faith traditions of others, there remains no further room for Christian condescension toward them.

Later Developments?

I have been unable to locate developments in Khodr's thinking from the time of his 1971 address until a similar address given almost two decades later at the Baar Consultation. In fact, Knitter credits the pneumatological themes presented by Khodr and Françoise Smyth-Florentin with having inspired the Consultation after having retired from the previous day's discussion with a rather bleak outlook of the tensions christology posed for religious pluralism.[16] Khodr still talks about the hiddenness of Christ everywhere in the religions and says that "it is the Johannine agape that was experienced by those great witnesses of the crucified love lived by the muslim sufis."[17] He also seeks to avoid the language of inclusivism or exclusivism, preferring instead to speak of "the idea of affinity or similitude among religions." At the same time, however, "Christ, *[sic]* remains the typos par excellence of every being and dispensation."[18]

In this address, however, Khodr does push the distinctiveness of the pneumatological mission in an effort to overcome the possibility of misreading his earlier essay as subordinating pneumatology to christology. Wanting to resist the temptation to comprehend all other traditions within the horizons or framework of Christianity since that would be to dismiss the genuineness of their particularities, he now speaks of the various spheres of religions and the vast diversity of faiths as a seemingly "permanent oikonomia of God."[19] Christ is still to be found in all religions, but it is explicitly affirmed that "the economy of Christ is not understandable without the economy of the Spirit" while "the Spirit fills

16. Knitter, "A New Pentecost," 35, referring to Khodr, "An Orthodox Perspective of Inter-Religious Dialogue," *Current Dialogue* 19 (1991): 25–27, and Françoise Smyth-Florentin, "From Yes to Amen or 'The Unheard of' Gospel: Is There a Holy Spirit for Inter-religious Dialogue?" *Current Dialogue* (1991): 28–31. Smyth-Florentin does refer at the beginning of her talk to Khodr's discussion of "spiritual oikonomism" given at an address at St. Pölten in 1984. She comments only on its marking an epoch (which she does not define) and on its acceptance of the heritage of Barth. I have been unable to find that address in print.

17. Khodr, "An Orthodox Perspective," 27.

18. Ibid.

19. Ibid., 26.

everything in an economy distinct from that of the Son."[20] The purpose of the church is not to "read, through the mystery of which it is the sign, all other signs sent by God through all times and in the various religions in view of the full revelation at the end of history."[21] In fact, Khodr admits now that the religions are in touch with God even if the divine name of Christ is never confessed or disclosed. An important shift appears to have emerged in Khodr's thought in supposing the economy of the Spirit as in some way preceding and succeeding the Son (historically speaking) and being larger than that of the Son. If one were to diagram his proposal, it may consist of a smaller circle representing the economy of the Son within a larger circle representing the economy of the Spirit, with rays radiating from the smaller into the larger circle signifying the influence of Christ in the larger realms of the Spirit, such as poetry, art, and the religions.

What emerges from this brief review of Khodr's pneumatological approach to the religions is the all-encompassing trinitarianism of Eastern Orthodoxy. Within this framework, the economies of the Spirit and the Word are related but clearly distinct. When it is asked how the Spirit's presence and activity is discerned, we see the tendency to develop christological criteria by which to enable such discernment. Yet, to his credit, Khodr is aware of this potential lopsidedness in this approach and, consonant with the Orthodox tradition, attempts to avoid it when possible and redress the scales. Ultimately, however, when this is done, Khodr is left asserting the theme of *mysterion*, another hallmark of Orthodox theology. In short, while an emphasis on the distinctiveness of the economy of the Spirit appears to liberate Christian theology of religions, apart from christological criteria it is still difficult, if not almost impossible, to speak of divine presence and the salvific gospel apart from christological terms in the non-Christian faiths.

A Protestant View on the Spirit and the Religions

Stanley Samartha and the Protestant Paradigm

Protestant thinking on the question of the divine presence and activity in the world has been divided. While some have understood

20. Ibid., 27.
21. Ibid., 26.

the divine presence in the world in pneumatological terms, other more christocentric theologies have ascribed the work of God outside the church to the Logos. Over the centuries, of course, the paradigm of a "cosmic Christ" had periodically appeared. Justin Martyr's famous doctrine of *Logos spermatikos* (the seeds of the Logos) was one of the initial versions of cosmic christology built on the Johannine declaration that the Word of God was "the true light, which enlightens everyone" (John 1:9). And since the seeds of the Logos were sown "outside" (at least) the institutional boundaries of Israel and the church, a plausible explanation was therefore provided for how divine (at least general) revelation had reached those who have never heard.[22] Of course, given the further plausibility of understanding Protestantism itself as an expression of Christian faith built around the second article of the Nicene Creed—with its emphasis on the Second Triune Person, on the Word incarnate and proclaimed—that Protestant *theologia religionum* would be predominantly christocentric should come as no surprise. The turn to pneumatology in Protestant Christianity, however, was taking shape even in the 1950s and 1960s. Barth's recognition later in his life that there was a legitimate place for a pneumatological theology as well as Tillich's turn to pneumatology in volume 3 of his *Systematic Theology* are primary evidences of this shift.[23] It would be only a matter of time before Protestants would begin to raise the question about a pneumatological paradigm for theology of religions as well.

22. On the cosmic Christ thesis, see J. Bayart, "The Cosmic Christ and Other Religions," *Indian Journal of Theology* 15 (1966): 145–49. On Justin Martyr and the cosmic Christ in the early church, see Jacques Dupuis, S.J., *Toward a Christian Theology of Religious Pluralism* (Maryknoll, N.Y.: Orbis, 1997), chap. 2; cf. also Graham A. Keith, "Justin Martyr and Religious Exclusivism," in *One God, One Lord: Christianity in a World of Religious Pluralism*, ed. Andrew D. Clarke and Bruce W. Winter, 2d ed. (Grand Rapids: Baker, 1992), 161–85; and Chrys Saldanha, *Divine Pedagogy: A Patristic View of Non-Christian Religions* (Rome: LAS, 1984), chap. 2, esp. 52–62.

23. Barth said in an address given in 1957 that "there is certainly a place for legitimate Christian thinking starting from below and moving up, from man who is taken hold of by God to God who takes hold of man . . . one might well understand it as a theology of the third article. . . . Starting from below, as it were, with Christian man, it could and should have struggled its way upward to an authentic explication of the Christian faith" (see Barth's "Evangelical Theology in the 19th Century" in his *The Humanity of God* [Richmond, Va.: John Knox, 1972], 24–25; my thanks to Frank Macchia for this reference); cf. also, Philip Rosato, *The Spirit as Lord: The Pneumatology of Karl Barth* (Edinburgh: Clark, 1981). I discuss the role of pneumatology in Tillich's theology of religions in *Discerning the Spirit(s): A Pentecostal-Charismatic Contribution to Christian Theology of Religions*, Journal of Pentecostal Theology Supplement Series 20 (Sheffield: Sheffield Academic Press, 2000), chap. 3.

This occurred formally in an exploratory essay presented at the Fifth Oxford Institute on Methodist Theological Studies in the summer of 1973 by Stanley Samartha, the first director of the Dialogue Program of the WCC.[24] In this address, Samartha acknowledges that until recently, Christian theology had neglected any sustained reflection on the relation of the Holy Spirit to people of other faiths. Having also participated in the Addis Ababa Committee, Samartha quotes Khodr and speaks sympathetically of the Orthodox vision of divine presence. He insists that it was not so much a matter of extending the work of the Spirit "outside the hedges of the Church as a more inclusive doctrine of God himself."[25] He therefore encourages the larger Christian community to work on this vital issue not simply conceptually in the context of theological debate but in the relational ebb and flow of mutual dialogue, worship, and Christian service.

Yet, as a Protestant, Samartha has to face up to the Reformation motto of *sola Scriptura*. He thus cautions against drawing too many hasty conclusions regarding the divine mode of operation in the world from the scant scriptural evidence, especially when the biblical writers were concerned primarily with relating the person and work of the Spirit to Christ and the early Christian community, and less so or not at all with relating the same Spirit to other faith traditions. But he is also reluctant to either hide behind the *sola Scriptura* principle or allow it to hinder or dictate what the church should say. So even though the biblical witness is focused primarily on the Spirit's activity in the believing community, that does not necessarily deny his work in the secular world, nor "should [it] be regarded as negative judgment on Hindus, Buddhists, Muslims, and others today."[26] Further, however, when the category of religion is deconstructed, it becomes much easier to recognize that faith and piety are not abstract essences but rather the personal experiences, affiliations, and commitments of individual men and women.[27] As such, to deny that the Holy Spirit is at work in the lives of others in and

24. Stanley J. Samartha, "The Holy Spirit and People of Various Faiths, Cultures, and Ideologies," in *The Holy Spirit*, ed. Dow Kirkpatrick (Nashville: Tidings, 1974), 20–39.

25. Ibid., 21.

26. Ibid., 30.

27. Done most thoroughly by Wilfred Cantwell Smith, *The Meaning and End of Religion* (New York: Macmillan, 1962).

through their faith traditions is to run contrary to the assertions of Scripture itself regarding both the wedding of the spiritual and material dimensions of reality in creation and the divine drawing of all persons to salvation.

Discerning the Spirit and the Religions

Samartha, however, recognizes that to grant the possibility of the Spirit's presence and activity in other faith traditions is to automatically raise the question about the status of this relationship. To answer the question of whether the same Spirit who spoke through the prophets of old and descended upon Jesus also inspired Buddha, Mohammed, and perhaps Gandhi, Marx, and Mao Tse-Tung either in the affirmative or negative leads to the issue of criteria by which such judgment is rendered. He openly confesses that "the moment we talk about criteria to discern the activity of the Spirit we are in a dilemma."[28] However, he draws attention to the multilayered symbolism of the Spirit and points to the Spirit's activity in terms of life, order, and community in contrast to death, chaos, and separation or isolation as significant for discerning his presence. This leads to the assertion that when dealing with symbols of divine presence,

> we should probably look for existential rather than conceptual criteria. . . . Life may be recognized to be larger than logic; love may take precedence over truth; the neighbor as a person may become more important than his belief. Reflection on the work of the Spirit may be subordinated to a readiness to be led by the Spirit together with the partners into the depths of God's mystery.[29]

Samartha picks up on his exploratory work in a second essay written in preparation for the Seventh Assembly of the WCC, which met at Canberra, Australia, in 1991 under the theme "Come Holy Spirit, Renew the Whole Creation."[30] Samartha understands that it is the Spirit's work to renew the creation, which is not to say that such work is limited to being done only through Christians or the church. Being sensitive to the reluctance of many Christians to approve of all that occurs outside the church as

28. Samartha, "The Holy Spirit and People of Various Faiths, Cultures, and Ideologies," 33.
29. Ibid., 33–34.
30. Samartha, "The Holy Spirit and People of Other Faiths," *Ecumenical Review* 42 (1990): 250–63.

being of the Spirit,[31] Samartha notes several interconnected issues related to the arena of the Spirit's work. In the first place, Samartha approaches the fundamental theological issue of the *Filioque* by way of the question regarding the personhood of the Spirit. He opts to emphasize that the Holy Spirit is the Spirit of God and as such theologically justifies prayer to the person of the Spirit as prayer to God. This obviously leads him to favor understanding the procession of the Spirit in terms consonant with the Orthodox view of the Father being the sole source of the Spirit.[32] It may be significant that in this discussion Samartha nowhere mentions that the Christian Scriptures also identify the Spirit as the "Spirit of Christ," although he later says that "the Spirit is regarded as both relating and distinguishing the Father and the Son."[33]

Second, how is Pentecost to be understood relative to the divine mission, and what is the Spirit's relation to the church? Samartha thinks it important to see the church as co-instituted by the Son and the Spirit but without restricting the Spirit's work solely to this arena. This leads, in part, to a greater awareness of the Spirit's historical dealings in the world prior to Pentecost—and in fact also prior to the incarnation—such as in relation to the Hebrew prophets. This recognition perhaps in turn leads to the door being "a little more open for the prophets of other faiths to be smuggled into God's oikoumene."[34]

Third, how is baptism related to the Spirit? Samartha notes the biblical instance of the Spirit's being given prior to baptism in Acts 4:17; 10; and 19:1–7 and concludes that this clearly demonstrates the Spirit's activity outside the boundaries of the institutional ecclesia. The point he argues throughout his article is that the question no

31. Samartha mentions the obvious concerns regarding syncretism and the relativizing of divine revelation. He is careful to point out with regard to the former that the political and ideological valuation of differences in the contemporary world in effect blunts whatever forces there are toward syncretism. Regarding the latter, "pluralism does not relativize *Truth*. It relativizes different *responses* to Truth which are conditioned by history and culture" ("The Holy Spirit and People of Other Faiths," 253, italics in original).

32. Cf. Stanley Samartha, "The *Filioque* Clause in Ecumenical Perspective: Klingenthal Memorandum 1979," *Apostolic Faith Today: A Handbook for Study*, ed. Hans-Georg Link (Geneva: World Council of Churches, 1985), 243–45.

33. Samartha, "The Holy Spirit and People of Other Faiths," 261. This omission on Samartha's part is something that any investigation of the *Filioque* clause should not overlook and that any pneumatological approach to the religions must contend with. There will be more on this in the next chapter.

34. Ibid., 256.

longer relates to whether or not the Spirit is active outside the church but how this presence and activity is to be discerned: "Christians are called upon to *discern*, not to *control* the Spirit."[35]

This raises, of course, the by-now familiar question of how such discernment is to take place. Some of the characteristics delineated by Samartha by which the Spirit is discerned include freedom, spontaneity, unpredictability, boundlessness, and the power to create or bring about new relationships and communities, as well as the more traditional fruits of the Spirit. With regard to the last, his conclusion is revealing: "For Christians, these ethical fruits are rooted in their faith in God through Christ and in the power of the Spirit. Without being in God one cannot produce the fruits of the Spirit of God. For Christians, to be in Christ is indeed to be in God. But in a religiously plural world, to be in Christ is not the *only* way to be in God."[36]

Samartha does go on to admit that Christians cannot dispense with Christ in discerning the Spirit. However, drawing upon the work of Eduard Schweizer and Justin Upkong, he notes that the fruits of the Spirit (Gal. 5:22–23) are readily observable in all persons and cultures for those who have the eyes to see and that this should be acknowledged.[37] At the same time, while it is an important and perhaps the most visible of signs, ethics is by no means the only criterion for spiritual discernment. Added to this should be the spiritual marks of inwardness and interiority. Evidence of this should be taken as a sign not only of the Christian's abiding in Christ but also of the Spirit's presence and activity in those of other faith traditions. This is an important admission since "in all religious traditions the quality of inwardness, the marks of a life rooted in the depths of God, are self-authenticating and regarded as needing no proof."[38] It is this presence and activity of the Spirit that empowers people to relate to other people, to creation, and to God.

Pneumatology and Christology

Ultimately, however, Samartha is unconvinced that a pneumatological approach fully resolves the christological dilemma. He is

35. Ibid., 260; italics in original.

36. Ibid., 259, emphasis in original.

37. Cf. Eduard Schweizer, "On Distinguishing Between Spirits," *Ecumenical Review* 41.3 (1989): 406–15; and Justin Upkong, "Pluralism and the Problem of the Discernment of Spirits," ibid., 416–25.

38. Samartha, "The Holy Spirit and People of Other Faiths," 261.

concerned that a Christian theology of religions should be centered on the second article of the Nicene Creed—on christology—rather than the third and thus returns in *One Christ, Many Religions: Toward a Revised Christology* to the full force of the christological question.[39] Rather than developing his pneumatological insights, he proposes instead a theocentric and cosmic christology. This return to christology does not go unnoticed, being queried specifically by theologians such as Knitter.[40] Samartha's response is to caution against the temptation to follow after theological novelty or to be carried about from one theory to another, whether it be to the ecclesiocentrism of the traditionalist *extra ecclesia nulla salus* position, to the christocentrism of the cosmic Christ paradigm widespread during the post-Vatican II period, to the theocentrism of the emergent pluralist model, or now to his own sketch of a pneumatocentric approach.[41] Rather than regarding these as alternatives, he urges a more explicitly trinitarian approach with *Theos* as the foundation, *Christos* as the historical anchor, and *Pneuma* as the "guiding power for Christian life and witness in a pluralistic world . . . belong[ing] together in the diversified unity of God's life . . . the internal rhythm of the Trinity, symbolically pointing to the Ultimate Mystery, [which] should be retained for the sake of the integrity of Christian theology."[42]

Samartha's initial turn to pneumatology seems to have finally returned to the christological question. However, his turn is instructive for at least two reasons. First, when combined with the

39. Stanley J. Samartha, *One Christ, Many Religions: Toward a Revised Christology* (Maryknoll, N.Y.: Orbis, 1991).

40. Paul F. Knitter, "Stanley Samartha's *One Christ, Many Religions*: Plaudits and Problems," *Current Dialogue* 20 (1991): 28–29.

41. Note that Samartha penned these words during the heyday of the theocentric pluralist alternative, most definitively symbolized in the publication of *The Myth of Christian Uniqueness: Toward a Pluralistic Theology of Religions*, ed. John Hick and Paul F. Knitter (Maryknoll, N.Y.: Orbis, 1987), along with Hick's *An Interpretation of Religion: Human Responses to the Transcendent* (New Haven: Yale University Press, 1989).

42. Samartha, "In Search of a Revised Christology: A Response to Paul Knitter," *Current Dialogue* 20 (1991): 34. Samartha's concerns to further explore the pneumatological approach to the religions have not, however, completely abated. In a much more recent comment, he mentions this as a new question requiring "a new theological framework, new methodologies and new perceptions of the decisively changed historical context in which Christians live and work together with people of other faiths and ideological convictions in the world today," all of which in combination present a "difficult and hazardous task because one has to enter into almost uncharted territory which is liberally strewn with anti-heretic mines" (Stanley Samartha, *Between Two Cultures: Ecumenical Ministry in a Pluralist World* [Geneva: WCC Publications, 1996], 187).

work of Khodr, the emphasis on the economy of the Spirit as related to but distinct from the Word liberates Christian theology of religions from ecclesiocentrism. Second, Samartha identifies a number of criteria by which to discern the Spirit that remain to be developed. His own return to christology does not necessarily imply that the pneumatological turn is ultimately barren. Other ways forward remain possible, perhaps further defined in the work of Jacques Dupuis.

A Roman Catholic Pneumatological Approach to the Religions

Jacques Dupuis's "Turn to Pneumatology" after Vatican II

As a Jesuit, Jacques Dupuis has forged a theology of religions in dialogue with Vatican II. After a prolonged engagement with the cosmic-Christ approach favored by Catholic theologians in the period following the council, Dupuis took his own pneumatological turn in two essays that appeared in the mid-1970s: "The Cosmic Influence of the Holy Spirit and the Gospel Message" (1974) and "The Cosmic Economy of the Spirit and the Sacred Scriptures of Religious Traditions" (1975).[43] While he straightforwardly asserts near the beginning of the earlier article that "Christocentrism and Pneumatology are two inseparable aspects of the Christian mystery," he is also careful to say that "the influence of the Spirit reveals the action of Christ, not vice versa."[44] The central question for theology of religions is how the action of the Spirit is mediated to those of other faiths through their own traditions.

Dupuis first presents the biblical data regarding the universal action of the Spirit, delineates the personalizing function of the Spirit in all human relationality and spirituality, and summarizes the dogmatic pronouncements of Vatican II on the Spirit and non-Christians before focusing explicitly on the central question: How do non-Christian scriptures, practices, and rites convey the witness of the Spirit, or how do they induce or sustain in those of other faiths

43. The first appeared in *God's Word among Men*, ed. G. Gispert-Sauch (Delhi: Vidyajyoti, 1974), 117–38, and the second in *Research Seminar on Non-biblical Scriptures*, ed. D. S. Amalorpavadass (Bangalore: NBCLC, 1975), 117–35; both are minimally revised and republished in Dupuis, *Jesus Christ and His Spirit: Theological Approaches* (Bangalore: Theological Publications in India, 1977), 181–210 and 211–28. My quotations are from the latter source.

44. Dupuis, *Jesus Christ and His Spirit*, 184.

personal experiences of the divine? Dupuis does not at this time respond specifically to this question since "their true significance as possible channels of salvation for non-Christians cannot be decided by a theological evaluation of their content; it can only be surmised by the impact they make on their religious life, wherever this religious life bears the seal of an authentic openness to the Spirit of God."[45] He thus turns his attention instead to deciphering the form of the impact made on religious life. Anticipating Samartha's emphasis on inwardness, Dupuis identifies as concrete signs of the Spirit's presence in any person that "self-possession and self-respect springing from an awareness of the divine mystery, joy and peace experienced in a mature disinterested self-gift to others."[46] This openness to God in all genuine encounters with the divine produces in turn an openness to others. Once again, we see the emphasis on both ethics and interiority.

Because he had dodged the more specific question of how the constitutive elements of religious traditions—sacred scriptures and sacramental practices—actually mediate the action of the Spirit, Dupuis focused his 1975 essay on developing a pneumatology of non-Christian scriptures. Can Christian theology acknowledge divine revelation in other canonical texts and scriptural traditions? If so, in what sense or to what degree, and what would that mean for the traditional doctrine of divine inspiration? Dupuis proceeds by way of recapitulating the conclusions of the previous essay as the definitive theological presuppositions necessary for an affirmative response: that the Holy Spirit mediates any genuine experience of and encounter with God and that the Spirit is everywhere operative in the economy of salvation. What this means is that whenever Christians encounter traces of the mystery of God in the lives and experiences of non-Christians, they can then admit the active presence of the Spirit and are free to ponder how this presence "reaches the men of other faiths through the channels available to his divine operation, namely the sacred scriptures and the sacramental practices which together constitute their religious traditions."[47]

This leads to what Vatican II, following the early church fathers, expressed as "seeds of the Word."[48] Applying this to the sacred

45. Ibid., 206.
46. Ibid., 203.
47. Ibid., 219.
48. *Ad Gentes*, art. 11.

scriptures of other traditions raises a further question: What constitutes sacredness in other scriptures? The Christian response historically is that sacred Scriptures are a "record of divine revelation in such a way that God himself is their author."[49] The doctrine of biblical inspiration, however, does not assert a complete suspension of human faculties in the process of authorship but rather preserves human authenticity in the mysterious conjunction of the divine and the mundane, analogous to the incarnation of the Word. Does this interpretation of sacredness, however, imply that revelation can only be understood as a word of God to humankind, or can it perhaps be stretched to include human words to or about God? Further, even if, as Dupuis suggests, the former be acknowledged of non-Christian scriptures, what is the relation of the content of such relative to "the decisive word spoken by [God] to men in Jesus Christ, of which the Christian Scriptures contains the official record?"[50]

Dupuis's own position as evidenced in this last quote is clearly in line with the inclusivism of Vatican II. Nothing can be added to the revelation of God in Christ. At the same time, a pneumatological approach to the religions allows him to affirm other scriptures as initial revelations of the divine that necessarily precede and prepare the way for the definitive word of God in Jesus Christ. Thus, "the personal experience of the Spirit by the rishis [sages and holy persons of other traditions], inasmuch as it is in God's providence a first personal breakthrough of God to the nations, and in so far as it has been authentically recorded in their sacred scriptures, is a personal word of God addressed to them through intermediaries of his choice."[51] This is therefore an acceptance of the religious experiences of others and openness in dialogue. Because the non-Christian is unaware that this Spirit of God is also the Spirit of Christ, it is the responsibility of Christian witness to the gospel to prophetically interpret the *sui generis* character of the other's experience in a way that preserves its integrity even as Christ is brought to conscious recognition. In this sense, the religious experience is both the starting and ending point of dialogue. The Spirit is, after all, the meeting point between Christian and non-Christian, and between both and God.

49. Dupuis, *Jesus Christ and His Spirit*, 220.
50. Ibid., 223.
51. Ibid., 224.

Return to Christology?

Like Samartha, however, Dupuis also has failed to develop substantively the arguments advanced in these early essays. He does devote one chapter of his later volume, *Jésus-Christ à la recontre des religions* (1989), to a discussion of the "Economy of the Spirit, Word of God, and Holy Scriptures," but no new insights are to be found there.[52] Because he wants to be cautious about too hastily accepting all the sacred books of other traditions as divine revelation, he adds a rather conventional discussion of revelation as differentiated and progressive. There are various degrees to which the human authors grasped and communicated the divine truths and to that extent were under the inspiration of the Spirit, and because of this there is difficulty in sorting out the intrusion of merely human representations and words concerning the divine. However, he continues to understand the sacred books of the religions merely as *praeparatio evangelica* for the Christian revelation and resorts in the end to the more traditional classification of these stages as the cosmic, the Israelite, and the Christian.

The focus of this book therefore remains instead on the breadth of salvation history in light of the various covenants struck by God with all peoples and nations and culminating in the decisive covenant in Christ. Dupuis makes clear that "the decisive question that governs everything else is whether a theology of religions that means to be Christian has any real choice between a christocentric perspective, which acknowledges the Jesus Christ event as constitutive of universal salvation, and a theocentric perspective, which, in one fashion or another, places in doubt or explicitly rejects this central datum of traditional faith."[53] He therefore examines the entire cluster of issues related to this inclusivistic thesis—the problem of the particularity of the historical Jesus and the corollary of the universality of the Christ, and the tension between interreligious dialogue and the church's evangelistic mission—and leaves undeveloped the implications of the economy of the Spirit relative to this question. Throughout, pneumatological concerns are raised only within the larger christological framework that motivates his *theologia religionum*. The economy of the Spirit is,

52. Jacques Dupuis, *Jesus Christ at the Encounter of World Religions*, trans. Robert R. Barr (Maryknoll, N.Y.: Orbis, 1991), 152–77.

53. Ibid., 110.

after all, only that which is the point of contact between the human and the divine. The function of the Spirit is "to center, by its immanent presence, the human being—and the church—on Christ, whom God has personally established as mediator and as the way leading to God. The Spirit is not at the center."[54]

The State of the Question

This basic perspective is repeated in Dupuis's latest (and magisterial) book, *Toward a Christian Theology of Religious Pluralism.*[55] In some respects, this volume provides a *status quaestionis* on the discussion of Christian *theologia religionum* at the end of the twentieth century. Central to the constructive proposals of this magnum opus, however, is Christ and Christian faith. The key to seeing how Dupuis manages to understand the diversity of religious traditions as significant in the divine providence even while maintaining the centrality of Christ lies, perhaps, in his use of John 1:9—"The true light, which enlightens everyone, was coming into the world"—the most oft-quoted and referenced verse in this book. Dupuis's conclusions are therefore as follows. First, God speaks fully through the Son but in other places and times (Heb. 1:1) through other ways that include the religions. Second, the truths of the mystery of Christ and of Christian faith are therefore intrinsically related to truths found everywhere, including those in other faiths. Finally, the universality of divine revelation and salvation history means that there is a genuine, mutual (rather than one-sided) complementarity that demands reciprocal convergence between the religions in the eschatological reign of God. The religions are diverse even if unequal historical venues through which God has sought out human beings through Word and Spirit.

Dupuis thus works throughout this book with what he calls a "trinitarian christology" over and against a "christomonism." In this way, the relationship between the particularity of the Christ event with the universality of the Logos and of the Spirit is held together. Insightful discussions of pneumatology vis-à-vis the religions are found throughout this volume. Yet nowhere does Dupuis develop fully his earlier efforts to understand the religions through

54. Ibid., 153.

55. Some of the following comments derive from my extended review of this book in *Buddhist-Christian Studies* 21 (2001): 157–61; my thanks to the editors of *BCS* for permission to use this material.

a trinitarian *pneumatology*. To repeat, the strength of this book is its high—what Dupuis calls "constitutive"—christology. One is led to wonder, however, why Dupuis does not apply the dialectical method he employs so skillfully in his discussions of christology to the doctrine of God and of the Trinity itself. To have done so would have allowed an equally vigorous pneumatology to emerge as well, which when combined with Dupuis's high christology, would result in a robustly trinitarian theology of religions. Arguably, developing the pneumatology would have supplemented his constructive argument since both christological and pneumatological approaches to theology of religions are required to allow for the kind of mutuality, complementarity, and convergence that Christians in general and Dupuis in particular hope for eschatologically.

My goal in this chapter has been to follow the treks of those who have preceded me in the conviction that the Spirit blows wherever the Spirit wills (John 3:8). I have assessed the recent efforts of representatives of the three dominant Christian traditions in order to discern the viability of the turn to pneumatology in theology of religions. A pneumatological approach to theology of religions initially appears promising in that the emphasis on the related yet distinct economies of the Spirit and the Son allows for an understanding of the religions as perhaps having their own distinct existential function even if finally related to Christianity. Yet upon further reflection, such distinctiveness cannot be understood as absolute. Because of the relationality between Spirit and Son, any Christian theology of religions that begins pneumatologically must ultimately include and confront the christological moment. Thus the turn toward pneumatology as seen in the work of the Orthodox Khodr, the Protestant Samartha, and the Catholic Dupuis can be seen as one that both holds promise and yet remains somewhat ambiguous. The most crucial question that has emerged so far is how the christological criterion informs the discernment of the Spirit's presence and activity in the world of the religions. To insist on a robust christological criterion is to mute the identity of the other and to act imperialistically toward other faiths; to loosen the christological criterion is to risk the loss of Christian identity in the interreligious encounter. In order to take up this set of questions in greater detail, I propose to take a look at the evangelical *theologia religionum* proposed by the Canadian Baptist theologian Clark Pinnock.

5

Pneumatology and an Evangelical Theology of Religions

The question of the religions has become in the past decade a live one within evangelicalism. This debate can best be characterized as that between the *exclusivists* and the *inclusivists*. The exclusivists, in accord with traditional evangelical thinking on the subject, have generally followed Calvin, Edwards, and the Princeton theologians in denying that the unevangelized—including all adherents of non-Christian religions—have much hope of salvation. Its advocates have insisted on the particularity of salvation through belief in and confession of Jesus Christ (Rom. 10:4–13; Acts 16:30–31; Matt. 10:32–33), and thus on the importance of missionary and evangelistic proclamation of the gospel.[1] Inclusivists, however, have retrieved from such figures as Wesley and C. S. Lewis a less stringent approach regarding the salvation of those

1. In evangelical circles, exclusivists are known also as traditionalists, particularists (focused on the soteriological particularity of Christ), and restrictivists (emphasizing the narrowness of the gate that leads to salvation; cf. Matt. 7:13–14). In this chapter, I will use these terms synonymously to refer to evangelical exclusivists. Representative of this group of thinkers is Harold Netland, *Dissonant Voices: Religious Pluralism and the Question of Truth* (Grand Rapids: Eerdmans, 1991); idem, *Encountering Religious Pluralism: The Challenge to Christian Faith and Mission* (Downers Grove, Ill.: InterVarsity, 2001); Ajith Fernando, *The Christian's*

who have never heard the gospel. The recent efforts of Norman Anderson, John Sanders, Stanley Grenz, Gerald McDermott, and the more extensive contributions of Clark Pinnock have focused on the argument that salvation, while founded upon and made available only in Christ, is universally accessible to all, including those adherents of non-Christian religions who have no knowledge of the gospel.[2]

While there are many facets to this debate, the focus has been on the question of which approach is more faithful to Scripture. While advocates of inclusivism have recognized that their argument needs to pass muster biblically in order for the evangelical community to even seriously consider its merits, exclusivist critics remain unconvinced. At the same time, however, exclusivists have also raised other concerns about the inclusivist project regarding practical, ecclesial, and missiological issues: How does theological inclusivism work in the real world of the religions? Does moving from exclusivism to inclusivism demand a reevaluation of the notion of religion itself, conceiving it not so much as the failed human enterprise to know God or as of demonic origin but rather as the possible mediator of truth and salvation within the broader scope of divine *Heilsgeschichte*? In opening the door to the possibility

---

Attitude toward World Religions (Wheaton, Ill.: Tyndale, 1987); idem, *Sharing the Truth in Love: How to Relate to People of Other Faiths* (Grand Rapids and Uhrichsville, Ohio: Discovery House, 2001); R. Douglas Geivett and W. Gary Phillips, "A Particularist View: An Evidentialist Approach," in *More Than One Way? Four Views on Salvation in a Pluralistic World*, ed. Dennis L. Ockholm and Timothy R. Phillips (Grand Rapids: Zondervan, 1995), 211–45; Vinoth Ramachandra, *Faiths in Conflict: Christian Integrity in a Multicultural World* (Downers Grove, Ill.: InterVarsity, 1999); and Bruce J. Nicholls, ed., *The Unique Christ in Our Pluralist World* (Grand Rapids: Baker, 1994), part 1.

2. See, e.g., Norman Anderson, *Christianity and World Religions: The Challenge of Pluralism* (Leicester, England: InterVarsity, 1984); Stanley Grenz, "Toward an Evangelical Theology of the Religions," *Journal of Ecumenical Studies* 31.1–2 (1994): 49–65; John Sanders, *No Other Name: An Investigation into the Destiny of the Unevangelized* (Grand Rapids: Eerdmans, 1992); idem, "Inclusivism," in *What about Those Who Have Never Heard? Three Views on the Destiny of the Unevangelized*, ed. John Sanders (Downers Grove, Ill.: InterVarsity, 1995), 21–55; Gerald McDermott, *Can Evangelicals Learn from World Religions? Jesus, Revelation, and Religious Traditions* (Downers Grove, Ill.: InterVarsity, 2000); and idem, *Jonathan Edwards Confronts the Gods: Christian Theology, Enlightenment Religion, and Non-Christian Faiths* (Oxford: Oxford University Press, 2000). Cf. also Evert D. Osburn, "Those Who Have Never Heard: Have They No Hope?" *Journal of the Evangelical Theological Society* 32 (1989): 367–72; Ken R. Gnanakan, *Proclaiming Christ in a Pluralistic Context* (Bangalore: Theological Book Trust, 2000); and my discussion of other inclusivists in *Discerning the Spirit(s): A Pentecostal-Charismatic Contribution to Christian Theology of Religions*, Journal of Pentecostal Theology Supplement Series 20 (Sheffield: Sheffield Academic Press, 2000), chap. 6.

that the religions are mediators of truth, goodness, and perhaps even salvation, the fundamental anxiety may be exposed: how are such to be discerned? Would it be possible to discern the Holy Spirit from other spirits, the true from the false, the good from the bad, that which is salvific from that which is damning, in the religions? In the light of these issues, it may well be that underneath the concern for biblical faithfulness lie even more difficult and troubling issues related to the discernment of the religions.

I will argue here that the biblical, historical, and systematic foundations of an inclusivistic theology of religions, no matter how rigorously constructed, will always be less than plausible to traditionalists if inclusivists fail to test their claims or make provision for the testing of their claims against the empirical reality of the historical religions. One of the controlling questions that will continue to press itself upon us throughout this chapter is whether or not it is the lack of either a comparative methodology or a proper criteriology (or both) enabling discernment of falsehood, the demonic, and the idolatrous that renders theological inclusivism suspect to traditionalists. To get at this problem, I will review the work of Clark Pinnock, who has been one of evangelical inclusivism's most ardent and persuasive advocates. Part of the burden of this chapter will be to show that the inclusivists have labored exegetically and theologically to make their case for inclusivism, and to that extent the primary objective will be to delineate the development of Pinnock's theology, including his turn to pneumatology. But I will argue that inclusivists have in the process paid insufficient attention to the corollary questions of discernment. When applied to the religions, Pinnock's argument that the Spirit is at work in the non-Christian faiths raises many unanswered questions that have not escaped the exclusivist critique. My purpose is to nudge inclusivism forward from abstract theological theory to more concrete empirical analysis and engagement with the world of the religions.

Pinnock and the Development of Evangelical Inclusivism

Toward an Evangelical Inclusivism

Not many evangelical theologians have given the kind of sustained systematic reflection to the question of the salvation of persons in the non-Christian faiths as has Clark Pinnock over the last decade and a half.[3] Reviewing the growth of his inclusivistic theology of religions will allow an assessment of its strengths and weaknesses. His accomplishments demonstrate his evangelical commitment to Scripture and his systematic argumentation in laying out a comprehensive theological vision for inclusivism. Yet they also reveal the ambiguities that give exclusivist critics pause for concern. I will examine his writings on salvation and the non-Christian religions in terms of two stages of development: the earlier systematic presentation, culminating in *A Wideness in God's Mercy* (1992), and the more prominent pneumatological approach in his recent works. Throughout, I want to query Pinnock about whether his inclusivism is equipped to make discerning judgments about the religions and if so, how.

Throughout his career, it has been precisely Pinnock's willingness to attend to the human condition that has motivated him to reassess traditional evangelical thinking on soteriology, first regarding the salvation of Christians and then later of those in other religious traditions who have never heard the gospel. In an essay written in 1988, he confesses that he was led to reexamine the question of the religions because of his concern to relate scriptural truth to the emerging global religious consciousness. Recognizing this problem as a "first class hermeneutical challenge," Pinnock noted the following tension posed by the modern realization of religious pluralism:

> On the one hand, there is the strong desire to affirm in no uncertain terms the uniqueness and finality of Jesus Christ and to regard as heretical any attempt to reduce or water down this conviction. On the other hand, there is the belief in God's universal salvific will and

3. Representative are "The Finality of Jesus Christ in a World of Religions," in *Christian Faith and Practice in the Modern World: Theology from an Evangelical Point of View*, ed. Mark A. Noll and David F. Wells (Grand Rapids: Eerdmans, 1988), 152–68; "Toward an Evangelical Theology of Religions," *Journal of the Evangelical Theological Society* 33.3 (1990): 359–68; "Acts 4:12—No Other Name under Heaven," in *Through No Fault of Their Own: The Fate of Those Who Have Never Heard*, ed. William V. Crockett and James G. Sigountos (Grand Rapids: Baker, 1991), 107–16; *A Wideness in God's Mercy: The Finality of Jesus Christ in a World of Religions* (Grand Rapids: Zondervan, 1992); "Evangelism and Other Living Faiths: An Evangelical Charismatic Perspective," in *All Together in One Place: Theological Papers from the Brighton Conference on World Evangelism*, ed. Peter Hocken and Harold D. Hunter (Sheffield: Sheffield Academic Press, 1993), 208–18; "An Inclusivist View," in *More Than One Way?* 93–148; and *Flame of Love: A Theology of the Holy Spirit* (Downers Grove, Ill.: InterVarsity, 1996), esp. chap. 7: "Spirit and Universality."

> feelings welling up from within that God is not one to cast off millions who through no fault of their own lacked an opportunity to embrace Christ's salvation. How shall I correlate in my own mind the demands that come from my Christian tradition and my experience of life in the eighties?[4]

Elements of an Inclusivistic Theology of Religions

A follow-up article two years later both clarifies and extends the initial proposal.[5] In this piece, Pinnock sets forth an evangelical theology of religions as founded on the two axioms previously discussed, although appropriately fine-tuned at this stage: the universal and global reach of God's salvation and the particular salvation through Jesus Christ. Whereas the first axiom is calculated to combat the soteriological exclusivism of the traditional *extra ecclesia nulla salus* position ("no salvation outside the church"), the second opposes the theological relativism (of that time, although now in retreat) of pluralists such as John Hick and Paul Knitter.

With these two central axioms in hand, Pinnock proceeds to outline a theology of religions. First, the religions should be assessed as structures of human life analogous to cultural or political systems, all of which are marked by the tension of historical reality awaiting eschatological consummation. Because the religions exist within the scope of God's providence, they are therefore an expression of the presence and activity of divine grace. Pinnock thus understands the approach of Paul at Mars Hill (Acts 17:16–34) to be a dialectical and well-balanced one, worthy of emulation. At the same time, even if the religions are not, as the early Barth insisted, unbelief as such, Pinnock recognizes that they "may sometimes be unbelief or even worse."[6] They are therefore a mixed bag, containing both good that can be appreciated and evil that needs to be discerned and confronted. Pinnock does not, however, within the scope of this essay, attempt to deal with the question of how such discernment is to occur, outside of saying that "only as they [the religions] claim ultimacy for themselves are they demonic"; yet, he does hint that the task is an arduous one: "there can be no *aprioris* in this area, no shortcuts to dialogue and to discernment through the Spirit. We do not know what we may find

4. Pinnock, "The Finality of Jesus Christ," 152–53.
5. Pinnock, "Toward an Evangelical Theology of Religions."
6. Pinnock, "Toward an Evangelical Theology of Religions," 365.

when we encounter other faiths, whether good or ill. This can even be true with Christian faith."[7]

However, even if religions may be historically ambiguous, they are also dynamic, changing realities that are open to the process of eschatological transformation by Christ and the Spirit. As historical realities, the religions "are all being affected by the Spirit who is moving everything toward consummation."[8] Pinnock is wary that he might be misunderstood as predicting too rosy a picture; yet because God has provided salvation in Jesus Christ, he believes there is good reason for cautious optimism, which in turn calls for a greater exercise of responsibility on the part of the church. Rather than just thinking that all things will work out in the end, "Christianity is in a situation of conflict and contest with competitive religious truth claims. This means dialogue at the round table and engagement on all fronts. It means rational contests and spiritual encounters (like Acts 17:2–4 and 19:17). We are pluralists and not relativists, and therefore we want to engage the various truth claims openly and hopefully."[9]

The Systematic Argument for Evangelical Inclusivism

The sketch of Pinnock's inclusive theology of religions in his early articles received more extensive treatment and systematic elaboration in *A Wideness in God's Mercy* (1992). Pinnock begins with the axiom of God's universal salvific will by outlining a "hermeneutic of hopefulness." This he finds established in the Old Testament, disclosed first in the global covenants of Genesis 1–11 and then in God's concerns for the nations as expressed in the prophets. He then discerns an extension of this hermeneutic in the New Testament. This "wider hope" is central to Jesus' proclamation of the kingdom of God, highlighted in the epistolary discussions of universal atonement, integral to the doctrine

7. Ibid., 364–65.

8. Ibid., 367.

9. Ibid., 366. Pinnock is here contrasting his own "pluralism" with that of the self-avowed pluralists. The latter's "pluralism," which ignores the deep-seated differences between the religions, is actually more akin to "relativism." Pinnock, on the other hand, does not want to overlook fundamental and distinguishing features of the various religions and therefore considers his own model to be, in fact, more "pluralistic" than those in company with Hick and Knitter. To be fair, more recently, pluralists have taken heed of criticisms of their relativism and made adjustments so as not to simplistically overlook differences between the religions (e.g., Paul F. Knitter, *One Earth, Many Religions: Multifaith Dialogue and Global Responsibility* [Maryknoll, N.Y.: Orbis, 1995], 38–53).

of recapitulation based on the resurrection of Jesus, and evident throughout the eschatological images of the Apocalypse. He concludes that "salvation is going to be extensive in number and comprehensive in scope. The Bible itself closes with an eloquently portrayed optimism of salvation, including the renewal of all things and the salvation of all peoples."[10]

In defense of the second axiom—the particularity of Christian salvation—Pinnock asserts that the biblical evidence necessitates a normative christology so that even if one were to attempt to reinterpret the doctrine of the incarnation, one would nevertheless still have to deal with the finality of Christ. That being said, however, he insists that there are both logical/epistemological and theological reasons why a high christology does not entail a narrowness of salvation. With regard to the former, Pinnock follows the Second Vatican Council in distinguishing between "the ontological necessity of Christ's work of redemption from the epistemological situation of sinners."[11] Regarding the latter, Pinnock insists on the inseparability of christology from the doctrine of the triune God and God's prevenient grace. Briefly stated, Christians confess God the Father almighty, the creator of the world, in whom we live, move and have our being (Acts 17:28). The confession of Christ is simply the recognition that in the man Jesus, God has revealed himself; at the same time, the Logos who became flesh in the historical Jesus is "present in the entire world and in the whole of human history"; finally, the Spirit is confessed as "the mysterious presence, the breath and vitality of God in the world."[12] Pinnock considers following the Eastern churches in rejecting the *Filioque* as an important move for a contemporary theology of religions. In an important passage that prefigures the direction to come, he observes that

> according to the Eastern view, the Spirit is not tied to the Christ-event exclusively but rather can operate in the whole world, which is the Father's domain. This provides another way of thinking about God being active in the world at large. God is active by his Spirit in

10. Pinnock, *Wideness*, 35.

11. Ibid., 75. Pinnock generally feels that Vatican II did the right thing in repudiating the doctrine of *extra ecclesia nulla salus*, but he asserts that post-conciliar Catholic theologians have gone too far in seeing that which is good, holy, and true in the historical religions without discerning their darker side.

12. Ibid., 77–78.

> the structures of creation, in the whole of history, even in the sphere of the religions. The breath of God is free to blow wherever it wills (Jn 3:8). The economy of the Spirit is not under our control, and certainly it is not limited to the church. . . . There is no hint of the grace of God being limited to a single thread of human history.[13]

He concludes that the particularity axiom founded on a trinitarian christology goes hand in hand with the universality of the divine salvific will.[14]

Pinnock realizes, however, that the two central axioms serve only to lay a soteriological foundation for the salvation of the unevangelized and that a great deal more work needs to be done on the religions themselves in order for a theology of religions to emerge. What is now needed is a biblical and phenomenological investigation of religion. Appropriately, he pauses to define *religion* and does so by distinguishing between its subjective and objective aspects, adopting in some instances the language of *faith* and the *cumulative traditions* first utilized by the historian of religion, Wilfred Cantwell Smith.[15] Whereas the cumulative traditions are the institutions, teachings, rituals, symbols, and the like, which constitute the historical religions, faith is that personal response to what is considered the ultimate religious object. The Bible, Pinnock proffers, is concerned primarily with religion in the subjective sense as the proper heart response to God.

In surveying Scripture on the objective aspects of religion, Pinnock is surprised by the biblical data. To be sure, false religion is exposed by the biblical writers, whether it be Canaanite or Israelite idolatry, Jewish religious hypocrisy, or the corrupted

13. Ibid., 78. I take up the question of the *Filioque* in some detail in my *Spirit-Word-Community: Theological Hermeneutics in Trinitarian Perspective*, New Critical Thinking in Theology and Biblical Studies (Aldershot, Hampshire, UK, and Burlington, Vt.: Ashgate, 2002), chap. 2.

14. Space considerations preclude any extensive treatment of Pinnock's discussion of the historical response of the church to religious plurality. Suffice it to say that in resurveying the history of Christian thought, Pinnock finds an optimism of salvation supported by church fathers such as Irenaeus, Justin Martyr, Clement of Alexandria, Origen, Theophilus of Antioch, and Athenagoras. John Sanders adds substantially to this list in his *No Other Name*, 267–80.

15. See Wilfred Cantwell Smith, *The Meaning and End of Religion* (New York: Macmillan, 1962); *The Faith of Other Men* (New York: New American Library, 1963); *Belief and History* (Charlottesville, Va.: University of Virginia Press, 1977); and *Faith and Belief* (Princeton: Princeton University Press, 1979).

religious practices confronted by the early Christians. The Bible is clear that "religion may be dark, deceptive, and cruel. It harbors ugliness, pride, error, hypocrisy, darkness, cruelty, demons, hardheartedness, blindness, fanaticism, and deception. The idea that world religions ordinarily function as paths to salvation is dangerous nonsense and wishful thinking."[16] But Pinnock also finds in Scripture forms of noble religion and religiousness outside the traditionally demarcated history-of-salvation lines. Drawing from the "holy pagan tradition" in Scripture, he mentions numerous believing men and women, including Abel, Enoch, Noah, Job, Daniel (from Ezek. 14:14, not to be confused with the biblical author), Melchizedek, Lot, Abimelech, Jethro, Rahab, Ruth, Naaman, the Queen of Sheba, the Magi from the East, Cornelius, and others, "who enjoyed a right relationship with God and lived saintly lives, under the terms of the wider covenant God made with Noah."[17] In many of these instances, the relationship of these "pagan saints" was mediated to God by means of their own local religious customs and practices. This can be explained either anthropologically or theologically. On the one hand, the openness of the human spirit to God allows the development of the religions out of human aspirations; on the other hand, the non-Christian religions can be understood in some sense to reflect both general revelation and the prevenient grace of the Triune God.

The question of general revelation, however, does not receive adequate treatment in *Wideness*. Pinnock argues later that the "faith principle" of Hebrews 11 is what makes salvation universally accessible. Along with the fathers mentioned earlier, he cites others, such as Zwingli, A. H. Strong, and the contemporary evangelical apologist Stuart Hackett, in support of the argument that all who are saved—from Old Testament non-Israelite saints and intertestamental individuals to the unevangelized who are judged on the basis of their works (Matt. 25:40; Acts 10:34–35) to babies who die in infancy and the mentally handicapped—are accepted

16. Pinnock, *Wideness*, 90. For this and other reasons, Pinnock forthrightly rejects as "naïve speculation" Rahner's theory that the historical religions are the divinely appointed sociocultural means by which God has always been sought and found (ibid., 91). Whether or not Rahner is as naïve as Pinnock believes him to be is itself a valid question, but one that is beyond the scope of this book.

17. Ibid., 92; Pinnock acknowledges here his dependence on Jean Danielou, *Holy Pagans of the Old Testament* (London: Longmans, Green, 1957).

because of their faith response to God.[18] Yet nowhere does Pinnock explicate the notion or the content of general revelation.

For Pinnock, then, the biblical evidence not only allows that "religious experience may be valid outside Judaism and Christianity," but also that "there are positive features in other religions due to God's presence and revelation."[19] He concludes that there is a *via media* that avoids Barth's blanket chastisement of the religions and Rahner's rosy-eyed optimism but that it is a path that requires discernment to determine whether truth or falsity is at work, whether any individual is exercising subjective faith in God or remains under fleshly or demonic delusions, or whether the cumulative tradition (objective religion) helps or hinders personal faith. The import of discernment thus appears:

> Spiritual discernment in the context of the believing community is what is critical in these areas. As John says, "Dear friends, do not believe every spirit, but test the spirits to see whether they are from God, because many false prophets have gone out into the world" (1 Jn 4:1). There must be a testing in the Spirit, a weighing of all utterances. The spiritually gifted need to judge whether a person is moving in the direction of faith or not. Is the will of the Lord being heard and done here? Is God at work here, or is this another spirit? Such questions cannot be answered on the basis of reason or exegesis alone. The community taught by God through the Spirit must exercise critical judgment in the realm of prophecy and all other such matters.[20]

This is an important admonition, but it is fraught with difficulties. Rather than retreating into the safe haven of Christian orthodoxy, Pinnock sees the call to dialogue and confrontation as all the more urgent in this situation. Because the religions are a mixture of good and bad, truth and falsity, the divine and the demonic, they should be continually confronted by the gospel in a variety of encounters. On the one hand, there is the encounter between the Holy Spirit and the demonic, resulting in the gradual transformation of the religions (Pinnock cites as instances the triumph over Canaanite religion by the

18. Hackett's laconic remarks oppose the traditional evangelical understanding of general revelation as having only the negative function of ensuring the damnation of sinners; see Stuart C. Hackett, *The Reconstruction of the Christian Revelation Claim* (Grand Rapids: Baker, 1984).

19. Pinnock, *Wideness*, 94, 106.

20. Ibid., 110.

worshipers of YHWH and the demise of the quasi-religion, Marxism). On the other hand, there is the interchange of ideas in dialogue and in the intense competition of intellectual life. The question, however, persists: how are conflicting truth claims to be adjudicated? Pinnock urges an inclusivistic theology of religions on to participation in the interreligious dialogue, which includes the willingness to (1) listen to and appreciate other religions, (2) live and think globally rather than parochially, and (3) exchange critical questions about truth claims. From this, Pinnock envisions the transformation of both persons and cumulative traditions as the Holy Spirit works to bring about recognition of the gospel. However, there is not much suggested as to how this transformation comes about or how conflicting truth claims are to be adjudicated. Although he eschews both relativism and fideism since neither position enables the quest for truth, he goes so far as to admit that "truth will be resolved eschatologically. This means we will never fully resolve the conversation but patiently await the arrival of full knowledge from God."[21]

The book ends with a consideration of the implications of inclusivism for missions. Given Pinnock's arguments that God desires to save everyone, that Christ's life, death, and resurrection have ontic rather than epistemic implications for soteriology; that the unevangelized are saved by their faith response to general revelation; and that the cumulative traditions are providentially ordained by God with a role to play in the eschatological formation of the kingdom, the motivation for missions, while not completely detached from the very real threat of judgment and damnation, is no longer to be driven by the pessimistic "fewness" doctrine. Rather, as reconstructed by Pinnock, Christian motives for missions need to move away from the pronouncement of the escape of wrath and terror to the announcement of the *evangelion*, from impending hellfire and damnation to the dawning of the kingdom of God, from solely proclamation and evangelism to a multiplicity of activities including dialogue and Christian service. There is, after all, "a wideness in God's mercy" that extends even to those who have not heard.

21. Ibid., 146. This admission, along with his caution against sole reliance on reason and exegesis in discerning truth claims (see previous quote), is bound to be troubling for conservative evangelicals, especially those aligned with the Princeton theology. Pinnock's bold embrace of the contingencies of history and a non-foundationalist epistemology is unlikely to win over many from the traditionalist camp. See his earlier defense of a narrative approach to theology in *Tracking the Maze: Finding Our Way through Modern Theology from an Evangelical Perspective* (San Francisco: Harper & Row, 1990), 153–87.

An Emergent Pneumatological Approach to the Religions

The Turn to Pneumatology

With the appearance of *A Wideness in God's Mercy,* an inclusivistic option was made available to evangelicals that did not sacrifice convictions about biblical authority or a high christology.[22] Yet the last word has by no means been uttered. The nagging questions that remain, along with the inevitable resistance set forth by evangelical exclusivists, demand that proponents of inclusivism continue to refine and, if possible, develop their own proposal. The direction for possible development, however, had already been hinted at in *Wideness* in the suggestion that an inclusivistic doctrine of Christ must necessarily be a trinitarian christology. This required, therefore, not only an overall doctrine of God but also an equally robust doctrine of the Holy Spirit. Since *Wideness* was focused on christology and not pneumatology, not much was said about the Spirit. Yet what little was said would prove to be integral to the theology of religions. Pinnock had already seen that within the trinitarian framework,

> God the Spirit also [along with the Son] proceeds from the Father and is present in the whole world. God's breath flows in the world at large, not just within the confines of Christian movements. The Spirit of Jesus is at the same time a cosmic force hovering over the waters and giving life to every creature (Ge 1:2; Ps 104:30). The Spirit is the overflow of God's love. We see his activity in human culture and even in the religions of the humanity. The doctrine of the Trinity means that God, far from being difficult to locate in the world, can be encountered everywhere in it. One needs to take pains and be very adept at hiding *not* to encounter God.[23]

Questions, however, remained. If indeed the Spirit is both present and at work on a cosmic scale, is not the urgency of missions undermined? Does not the doctrine of the Spirit's universality have eschatological implications? And, of course, the underlying

22. John Sanders's *No Other Name* also appeared in 1992. He added to the inclusivistic argument in two ways: first, by contrasting inclusivism with the two other models (exclusivism or restrictivism, and pluralism or universalism); second, with more thorough excursions into historical theology to establish its evangelical lineage.

23. Pinnock, *Wideness*, 104, italics in original.

question of discerning the Spirit becomes all the more important in this context.

The Charismatic and Pneumatological Dimension

Perhaps in part for these reasons, Pinnock chose to advance by focusing on the topic of an evangelical-charismatic approach to missions and the religions in his contribution to an international conference on world evangelism. In this short paper, Pinnock builds on Pope John Paul II's major encyclical *Redemptoris Missio* (1990) to add to the argument for global missions and evangelization from the standpoint of the charismatic experience of Pentecost. He emphasizes that because the Spirit is at work in the world "creating a profounder grasp of who the God revealed in Jesus Christ is, the Spirit is thus present before any evangelist arrives and prepares the world for Jesus to come. The experience of Pentecost accentuates this confidence in the Spirit's freedom and kindles a desire in us to meet the Spirit wherever it has gone among men and women."[24] This reinforces conclusions in *Wideness* regarding "pagan saints" and the necessity for both evangelism and dialogue. Here, the charismatic-Pentecostal experience of the Spirit "intensifies our capacity to believe and hope all things for these pagans who love God and are loved by him" and "encourages dialogue by creating greater love in us for others and quickening faith in us about the possibilities of God's grace at work in their lives."[25]

What appears to be at work at the foundations of Pinnock's inclusivism is a shift from an emphasis on christology to a trinitarian pneumatology. This shift is more evident in his contribution to a round-table discussion with representatives of pluralism and exclusivism published in the volume *More Than One Way? Four Views on Salvation in a Pluralistic World*. In this essay, the exclusion of the *Filioque* is here taken for granted, and Pinnock forthrightly admits that "the Holy Spirit plays a prominent role in my understanding of inclusivism."[26] The economy of the Spirit in the world is understood not as completely disconnected but as identifiably distinct from that of the Son. Pinnock locates the weakness of traditional

24. Pinnock, "Evangelism and Other Living Faiths," 211.

25. Ibid., 212.

26. Pinnock, "An Inclusivist View," 106. Pinnock's inclusivistic theology of religions takes advantage of the latitude that is granted by the gradually emerging consensus to remove the *Filioque*.

pneumatology as being almost exclusively bound to ecclesiology. He chides evangelicals for having "stressed so strongly the Spirit's role in bringing people to faith in Christ that we have neglected the salvific presence of the Spirit in humanity's search for meaning generally."[27] Thus there is a restoration of the link between creation and redemption since the Spirit is active in both arenas.

As always, Pinnock is careful to admonish that this move by no means implies that the religions are vehicles of salvation. The Spirit, after all, "is the power of God unto salvation, not to religion."[28] Because of this, discernment is imperative. And because the Spirit is both the Spirit of God *and* the Spirit of Jesus, the primary (if not only) Christian criterion for the discernment of the Spirit is christological. In an important paragraph, Pinnock writes:

> Christians must not believe every prophet or go with every flow, because not every spirit has a valid claim to be heard. As omnipresent, the Spirit is in everything but not as everything. Certainly God is present outside the symbolic world of Christianity, and his life-giving activity is not restricted to one segment of history. Nevertheless, not everything in the world, not everything in religion, can be attributed to the Spirit. The Paraclete is the Spirit of Jesus, and we orient ourselves by this insight. When we see Jesus' path, we know that the Spirit is near. As Lord of all, Jesus is the criterion of truth in religion, including the Christian religion.[29]

In this way, christology and pneumatology now act as complementary doctrines, just as the two axioms of universality and particularity functioned previously.

The Systematic Pneumatological Theology

What appears next from Pinnock is a comprehensive vision of the Spirit in the form of an impressive systematic theology. In *Flame of Love: A Theology of the Holy Spirit* (1996), pneumatology is the central motif by which Pinnock approaches the doctrines of God, creation, Christology, ecclesiology, soteriology, the religions, revelation, and truth. What is latent in "An Inclusivist View" is proclaimed in *Flame of Love*: "Christ, the only mediator, sustains particularity, while Spirit, the presence of God everywhere, safeguards

27. Pinnock, "An Inclusivist View," 105.

28. Ibid., 116; cf. also *Wideness*, 10, and *Flame of Love*, 207.

29. Pinnock, "An Inclusivist View," 114.

universality."[30] While there is not much that is distinctly new in this volume relative to Pinnock's inclusivism, it is possible to read *Flame of Love* as an extended and systematic argument for inclusivism, founded as it is upon the Trinity, connecting with the entire range of classical theological doctrines and bringing them to bear on the explication of a theology of religions. Several pertinent themes are given further attention, such as the connection between Spirit and creation, the interconnection and distinction between the economies of the Son and the Spirit, the salvific process of recapitulation by which the Spirit both applies the work of Christ to us and by which we are incorporated via participation into the divine reality, the relationship between the Holy Spirit and the human spirit, and mission as an activity and event of the Spirit *par excellence*. Because of the systematic coherence by which all the doctrines are unified around the pneumatological theme, there is much greater depth to the assertion of the ubiquitous presence and activity of the Spirit than before.

Having a renewed confidence, Pinnock is now able to state unequivocally that the Spirit is at work in the religions, and that divine truths have therefore been deposited in them: "Though Jesus is not named in other faiths, Spirit is present and may be experienced."[31] Pinnock is still reticent to sanction the view of Rahner and others that the religions are vehicles of grace, but he insists on being "sensitive to the Spirit among people of other faiths without minimizing real and crucial differences between them."[32] The possibility of revelation is affirmed, in fact welcomed, in the religions without displacing the centrality of Christ. This, of course, places the Christian under obligation to learn from the religions:

> Because truths are embedded in various religious traditions, we ought to seek redemptive bridges to other traditions and inquire if God's word has been heard by their adherents. We ought to look at other traditions with empathic understanding—and at our own religion with a critical eye. If we did so, we might be enriched and be moved to do our theology less in the "Christian ghetto" and more globally.[33]

30. Pinnock, *Flame of Love*, 192.

31. Ibid., 204.

32. Ibid., 207.

33. Ibid., 201. He further reasons that since religion is an important element, if not the most important segment of culture, "it would be strange if the Spirit excused himself from the very arena of culture where people search for meaning" (ibid., 203).

But how is the Spirit's presence and activity in the world of religions discerned, and how do we confront and pronounce judgment on that which is not of God? Pinnock devotes one section to this issue, where he elaborates further on the christological criterion from biblical texts (1 John 4:2–3; John 16:13–14; 14:26). Traces of Jesus that reveal the presence of the Spirit include "self-sacrificing love, care about community, longings for justice, wherever people love one another, care for the sick, make peace not war, wherever there is beauty and concord, generosity and forgiveness, [and] the cup of cold water."[34] These criteria, however, give the appearance of a natural morality that can be substantiated apart from biblical Christianity. Further, they suggest that praxis be accentuated in the encounter with the religions to the neglect of addressing conflicting doctrinal beliefs and truth claims, both of which are normally propositional and linguistic in form.

To assist in the discernment of truth, Pinnock notes other aids that have been divinely provided: the apostolic tradition, the Scriptures as the norm of truth, a prayerful and worshiping community, charismatic gifts such as the discernment of spirits, and the ecclesial offices of oversight. The Spirit relates the Christian tradition, the truth of Scripture, and the believing Christian community meaningfully to the world and vice versa, and in so leavening the world allows it to move in such a direction that it can come to realize the truth of Jesus Christ. In a short article written later in response to my raising this question of discerning the religions, Pinnock adds that in his own attempts to discern the religions, he is always looking for redemptive bridges that will enrich his understanding.[35] In a paragraph that deserves to be quoted at length, he points out that Jesus himself indicated that

> inasmuch as they [persons in general and people of other faith in particular] gave a cup of cold water to the thirsty they showed where they stood with respect to the kingdom and that they were positively oriented to Jesus himself, even though they did not know

34. Ibid., 209–10. Pinnock notes that these are the criteria used by Jesus himself in Matt. 25:35.

35. An earlier version of this chapter was published as "Whither Evangelical Inclusivism? The Development and Critique of an Evangelical Theology of Religions," *Evangelical Quarterly* 71.4 (1999): 327–48, along with another article representing an exclusivist critique. Pinnock's "Response to Daniel Strange and Amos Yong" appeared in the same issue on pages 349–57, esp. (vis-à-vis Yong) 354–57.

> him. The good Samaritan too had a heart for God's kingdom as revealed in his acts of compassion, and the inadequacies of his theology as a Samaritan did not worry Jesus, because evidently for Jesus the issue was the direction of his life toward the kingdom, not theological correctness. I believe that Jesus is the criterion of salvation both ethically and theologically, and that it is possible for those who have not known him to do the works of love which correspond to God's kingdom and participate in salvation at the last judgment.[36]

But, of course, Pinnock acknowledges that discerning the presence and activity of the Spirit in the religions nevertheless remains "a tall order."[37] Further, as Victor Pfitzner queries, if, following Pinnock, "a central test of Spirit possession is ethical . . . , can we speak of the Spirit's activity in the world only in christological terms. Is there not a priority of the Spirit *of God* before the incarnation which allows us to search for and attempt to enunciate the activity of the Spirit also in the created order and in the community of humankind *extra ecclesiam*?"[38] So the question remains: does Pinnock succeed in demonstrating the capacity to discern the Spirit in the religions in particular and in convincing evangelicals of the plausibility of theological inclusivism regarding the religions in general?

The Exclusivist Critique of Evangelical Inclusivism

In spite of the impressive work done by Pinnock, evangelicals are still troubled. Quite naturally, he has come under fire from the defenders of exclusivistic orthodoxy. Ronald Nash has charged evangelical inclusivists like John Sanders and Pinnock with fostering an unrealistic and unbiblical romanticism based on feeling and emotion, promoting a dangerously lax attitude toward missions

36. Pinnock, "Response to Daniel Strange and Amos Yong," 356–57. See also the criteriology of the Roman Catholic Federation of Asian Bishops' Conferences, which includes the fruits of the Spirit, the values of the kingdom, the church's confession of faith, a listening attitude, and the presence of qualities such as love, harmony, and unity ("The Spirit at Work in Asia Today: A Document of the Office of Theological Concerns of the Federation of Asian Bishops' Conferences," FABC Paper no. 81 [http://www.ucanews.com/html/fabc-papers/fabc-81.htm] 1998: §3.10.2).

37. Ibid., 355.

38. Victor Pfitzner, "'The Spirit of the Lord': The Christological Focus of Pauline Pneumatology," in *Starting with the Spirit*, ed. Stephen Pickard and Gordon Preece, Task of Theology Today 2 (Hindmarsh, Australia: Australian Theological Forum; Adelaide, Australia: Openbook, 2001), 113–32; quotations from 130–31, italics in original.

and evangelism, and implicitly affirming a salvation by human works.[39] Others have taken Pinnock to task by questioning how an evangelical confession of the finality of Christ can cohere with an openness to the truth and goodness in the experiences of religious others; whether or not the religions are being affected and transformed by Christ to the degree that the inclusivists say they are; what the vagueness of inclusivistic arguments proves; and to what extent their presumption about the Holy Spirit's operation in the religions can be justified.[40] These questions highlight some of the unresolved issues in inclusivism and intimate that inclusivism may raise more questions than it answers. Inclusivists have to further explicate how discerning their theological vision actually is, both as to the religions and as to the question of the Spirit's presence and activity.

Discerning the Religions

One of the concerns of exclusivists is that inclusivism floats on theological generalizations that assert the possibility of salvation for those in other religious traditions but does not specify when and how some can be either saved or damned in these traditions. Representative of those who remain unconvinced are the exclusivists Geivett and Phillips. They insist that the inclusivistic argument that reasons from the universal divine presence to the universal operation of divine grace in the religions is vague to the point of rendering Christians impotent against idolatry, false truth claims, and perverse systems of thought. Non-Christian religions are at least misleading and at worst distortions of general revelation that have abandoned the truth for a lie (they reference Rom. 1:22–25; 1 Cor. 8:4–7; 1 John 5:19–21). They conclude that "even the pervasiveness of God's grace does not entail that God is somehow soteriologically present within alternative religious traditions."[41]

As previously noted, however, Pinnock has consistently denied (especially against the inclusivism of Rahner) that the religions are divinely appointed ways of salvation. An evangelical inclusivism

39. Ronald Nash, *Is Jesus the Only Savior?* (Grand Rapids: Zondervan, 1994), 148.

40. For these criticisms of Pinnock, see Ramesh P. Richard, *The Population of Heaven: A Biblical Response to the Inclusivist Position on Who Will Be Saved* (Chicago: Moody, 1994), 72–95, and R. Douglas Geivett and W. Gary Phillips, "Response to Clark H. Pinnock," in *More Than One Way?* 133–40.

41. Geivett and Phillips, "Response to Clark H. Pinnock," 134.

does not propagate the notion that the religions themselves save as such but only opens up the possibility that sufficient general revelation may predispose non-Christians toward the salvation that has been secured by Christ. Pinnock and the other inclusivists, it must be remembered, are also very concerned with the relativism and the universalism of pluralists like Hick and Knitter. It is for this reason that the evangelical inclusivists are careful to insist on the importance of dialogue and the need for discernment with regard to competing and contradicting truth claims.

But how is general revelation related, if at all, to the religions, and is it saving? On these matters, inclusivists have to shoulder the responsibility for this ambiguity. Pinnock himself admitted early in *Wideness* that "optimism of salvation has much to contribute to our attitude regarding other religions in general, though only a little in the way of specific detail."[42] Even when specific criteria are provided to distinguish between the saved and the damned, Pinnock takes away with one hand what the other hand grants. This is evident in his discussion of how holy pagans are recognized. In referring to the narrative of Cornelius, Pinnock notes that Peter provides both a cognitive ("one who fears God") and an ethical ("one who does what is right") criterion (Acts 10:34–35). Yet no sooner is this done than in the ensuing pages Pinnock seems to eliminate or at least play down the role of the former. He first considers the case of Jews, Muslims, and even African traditionalists who all adhere to a supreme being: "We may assume that they are intending to worship the one Creator God that we also serve."[43] In his later discussion of the "faith principle," he asserts that "according to the Bible, people are saved by faith, not by the content of their theology."[44] The fact that this cognitive criterion is often left unsatisfied may have led Pinnock to ask if the ethical criterion alone may suffice in bringing an individual into divine favor. Quoting Jeremiah 22:16—"He defended the cause of the poor and needy, and so all went well. Is that not what it means to know me?" (NIV)—Pinnock concludes that "a person may know God without it coming to verbal expression."[45] It is no wonder, given Pinnock's use of the faith principle, that exclusivists like Millard Erickson ask "whether

42. Pinnock, *Wideness*, 46.
43. Ibid., 97.
44. Ibid., 157.
45. Ibid., 98.

sufficient elements are built into his [Pinnock's] theology to prevent it from slipping into . . . subjectivism."[46]

This indecisiveness regarding criteriology shows forth in Pinnock's references to Buddhism. On the one hand, he denies that Buddhism, especially of the Zen variety, satisfies the cognitive criterion since it proclaims an agnosticism of the void, if not an explicit atheism with regard to a personal deity; yet on the other hand, an individual like the Buddha himself seems to have satisfied the ethical criterion. He asks, "How can one fail to appreciate the noble aspects of the Buddha, whose ethical direction, compassion, and concern for others is so moving that it appears God is at work in his life?"[47] He then goes on to ponder whether the *dharma* "promotes redemption and salvation" and whether *nirvana* can be interpreted in a way that is "suggestive of revelation."[48] In doing so, however, Pinnock in practice seems to have disregarded the cognitive criterion. If the *dharma* and *nirvana* can both be understood in the way he suggests, why not the Zen doctrine of the void? While there are distinct and vast differences between Zen and Christian mysticism, is it not also possible to see analogues such as that between *sunyata* (emptiness and nothingness) in Zen experience and the "God beyond God" reality of the Christian apophatic tradition? By saying this, I am neither insisting that Zen mysticism is entirely compatible with Christian contemplation nor trying to devalue Pinnock's musings. I am simply pointing out that his criteria, both few and inconsistently applied, result in unsubstantiated generalizations regarding the religions.

It should not be surprising, then, to see an exclusivist like Ramesh Richard charge Pinnock with being guilty of hasty generalizations, simplistic reductionisms, question-begging, ambiguities, and equivocations.[49] This is the case because Pinnock's success in finding parallels and resemblances is obtained in part by disregarding the unique cultural-linguistic frameworks that undergird the various religious traditions. Rather than presuming the god of African traditional religion to be the biblical creator, Richard thinks

46. Millard J. Erickson, *How Shall They Be Saved? The Destiny of Those Who Do Not Hear of Jesus* (Grand Rapids: Baker, 1996), 187.

47. Pinnock, *Wideness*, 100.

48. Ibid.

49. Richard, *The Population of Heaven*, 81–85.

otherwise. For him, it is more in accord with empirical reality to say that this "animistic high-god seems closer to the Muslim Satan than to the biblical God."[50] Richard raises a good point that Pinnock is aware of: how can comparative theology of religions maintain Christian normativeness while at the same time avoid theological imperialism, and how can adequate or deep (rather than superficial) comparisons be made that heed the empirical differences between diverse and conflicting traditions? The problem for inclusivists, of course, is the argument that grace may be present even in the non-Christian religions. It can be identified either in Christian terms or according to the concepts and categories of the particular religions. To do the former is to appear to revert to an anathematized form of intellectual imperialism, to arbitrarily strip the other religions of their own particularities, and to risk reducing the otherness and alterity of the other to the familiarity of the self. To do the latter is to risk that which is distinctively Christian; worse yet, it is to suggest that not only goodness, truth, and nobility inhere in other religions, but that such may also either be preparatory for or somehow mediate salvation. Is it possible to assert the Spirit's presence while denying that saving grace is active throughout the world of the religions?

Discerning the Spirit

The problem is further compounded when Pinnock and the inclusivists resort to the pneumatological argument. Discernment in this case seems to be rendered even more difficult. The pneumatological approach is fraught with ambiguities and frequently labors under the burden of subjectivity. Imagine the concerns of the exclusivists when they read:

> While acknowledging the gracious presence of the Spirit in human life and culture, I am not dogmatic about how that hidden grace is present exactly. Whether a religion serves as a means of grace remains an open question, needing more study and always careful discernment. We do not know exactly what role, if any, a given religion plays in the divine economy. We are simply confident that the Spirit is operating in every sphere to draw people to God, using religion when and where it is possible and appropriate.[51]

50. Ibid., 83.
51. Pinnock, "An Inclusivist View," 106.

It is no surprise that Geivett and Phillips demand clarification of Pinnock since "to say that God's grace may be encountered through other religions is vague. Which other religions? And what elements?"[52] Alister McGrath asks an almost identical question. While he commends Pinnock for seeing in the religions both "noble truths" and "terrible errors," he queries, "How do we know which beliefs are 'truths' and which are 'errors'? There is a need for an evaluative framework, an interpretive grid, that allows us to criticize the religions."[53]

Pinnock does not quell the misgivings of exclusivists when he speaks of the Spirit as the "empirical power that breaks forth in perceptible ways" without providing assistance for an investigation of this empirical reality.[54] They are not comforted when they read, "We do not claim to know how the Spirit works among non-Christians, but only that he is active."[55] He inevitably returns to the christological criterion: "The ways of God are admittedly hard to track, but movements of the Spirit in history can be seen because they are movements of the Spirit of Jesus. . . . The truth of it [the *Filioque*] is precisely the point about Christ's being the criterion of Spirit activity."[56] But even such assertions, critics feel, remain at the level of a theological abstraction that does not provide the assurance of discriminating discernment. In short, without more concrete guidelines as to what is and is not salvific in the other religions, inclusivism's granting even the theological possibility of salvation in the non-Christian traditions is tantamount to a declaration of both the existential reality of this salvation outside of Christianity and the overall goodness, general truthfulness, and salvific potency of the non-Christian faiths. When Pinnock lists only the most obvious examples of falsity and the demonic in the religions (such as his mention of the religious practices of the Aztec child sacrifices, Haitian voodoo, the caste system of popular Hinduism, and Muslim fundamentalism),[57] he does not boost the confidence of traditionalists that he is able to discern boldly what appear to be the more ambiguous, borderline cases.

52. Geivett and Phillips, "Response to Clark H. Pinnock," 140.
53. Alister McGrath, "Response to Clark H. Pinnock," in *More Than One Way?* 131.
54. Pinnock, *Flame of Love*, 195.
55. Ibid., 207.
56. Ibid., 211.
57. Pinnock, *Wideness*, 91.

An All-Too-Rosy-Eyed Optimism?

I am arguing that undeveloped criteria for discerning the religions by inclusivists have contributed to exclusivist complaints of an unwarranted optimism. While this objection may never be decisively answered, I do think that satisfactory criteriology of discernment can, in principle, be given but only, as Pinnock has repeatedly pointed out, through the extended process of dialogue and empirical investigation. Thus, Pinnock says, "The purpose of dialogue is in part testing . . . truth claims. We enter into dialogue from a Christian commitment, accepting that all claims, including our own, are provisional, and we seek to show that the revelation of God in Jesus Christ is best able to illumine human life and pass the other tests for truth."[58] Clearly, Pinnock's inclusivism forestalls dogmatic pronouncements on the religions in favor of an open-ended conversation, both with fellow Christians and with those of other religions. In a very real sense, an inclusivistic theology of religions not only opens the door to interreligious dialogue but also requires that process to run its course. But here again, the red flags of traditionalists spring up since interreligious dialogue, in order to be genuine, has to be approached with a sincerity that not only listens to the other but also is willing to be transformed by any truth discovered in the other's position.

To compound things, Pinnock has yet to establish that such dialogue is not susceptible to theological confusion or that it is able to adjudicate the conflicting truth claims of the various religions. Exclusivists fear that inclusivism inculcates in Christians an uncritical acceptance of the validity of religious and spiritual experiences of other traditions. Further, since inclusivism recognizes other religious traditions and their sacred books as possibly even mediating salvation in some way, this dilutes the venerable Christian distinction between general and special revelation. If, in fact, biblical revelation is not absolutely required for salvation, are the pluralists not correct in their assertion of the fundamental compatibility of all religions, that "all roads lead to Rome"? Inclusivists would therefore become practical relativists or, worse, liberal-pluralist wolves masquerading in evangelical-inclusivist

58. Pinnock, "An Inclusivist View," 114. Pinnock's non-foundationalist epistemology is here evident again.

clothing.[59] Most importantly, to grant to adherents of the other faiths even the possibility of salvation within the parameters of their traditions is, from the restrictivist perspective, to sound the death knell of Christian evangelism and missions. In short, the exclusivistic concerns are that central Christian convictions as traditionally understood, such as revelation, the church, and missions, would no longer hold within an inclusivistic framework. An inclusivist optimism runs the risk of eventually betraying the *raison d'être* of evangelicalism. It seems that inclusivism will remain less than convincing as long as it cannot be more specific about how truth is to be argued or how the Spirit is to be discerned in the concrete world of the religions. The secure confines of evangelical exclusivism will remain appealing so long as evangelical optimism fails to fully, truthfully, and discerningly engage the historical religions.[60]

This chapter has focused on the evangelical reflections of Clark Pinnock, who has developed one of the most comprehensive evangelical theologies of religions to date. In assessing the strengths and weaknesses of Pinnock's inclusivist theology of religions, I have argued that underlying the exclusivist critique of Pinnock and his inclusivist colleagues is the concern that evangelical inclusivism lays itself open to the charge of relativism because the possibility of divine presence and activity is allowed in the non-Christian religions without any substantive (cognitive) criteria being developed for discerning when this is or is not the case. In this and the previous two chapters, this question about discernment has come up repeatedly and emerged as the potential Achilles' heel of any pneumatological theology of religions. It is time to engage the task of developing a theoretical and practical theology of discernment in general (chapter 6), and of the religions in particular (chapter 7).

59. Inclusivism as a halfway house toward pluralism is the concern of many traditionalists; cf. Nash, *Is Jesus the Only Savior?* 172; and also Millard Erickson, *The Evangelical Left: Encountering Postconservative Evangelical Theology* (Grand Rapids: Baker, 1997), 131–47.

60. Space constraints do not allow me to review the arguments of other inclusivists. Suffice it to say that either the framework of interpretation and comparison are simplistically moralistic (Stanley Grenz, "Toward an Evangelical Theology of the Religions"), too vague (John Sanders, *No Other Name*), or decidedly one-sided in terms of the criteria employed (Norman Anderson, *Christianity and World Religions*). Hence we turn to the arguments in the next two chapters.

6

Toward a Pneumatological Theology of Spiritual Discernment

The argument of this chapter may be underestimated on a first reading since I do not take up the question of discerning the religions specifically. I want to alert the reader, however, to my own sense that what is presented here may be the key to defending the pneumatological theology of religions in this book. It is certainly presumed in my discussion of discernment as applied to the world of the religions in the next chapter. What I attempt here is a systematic reconception of the nature of spiritual discernment. Properly understood, spiritual discernment is much more than the charismatic gift of discernment of spirits. Rather, in its broadest sense, it should be understood as a hermeneutics of life that is both a divine gift and a human activity aimed at reading correctly the inner processes of all things—persons, institutions, events, rites, experiences, and so on.

My argument, which is developed in three stages, involves three specific theses—the first metaphysical, the second biblical, and the third theological and practical. Thesis 1: All determinate things consist of both *logos* and *pneuma*, metaphysically understood—having both forms of concretions and dynamic vectoral trajectories. The *pneuma*, or spirit, of any "thing" is the complex of habits, tendencies, and laws that shape, guide, and in some way manifest and/or determine its phenomenal or concrete behavior. Thesis 2: The biblical authors understand discernment as the cultivation of human perceptual and cognitive senses that enables one to pierce the concrete forms of things to their inner spirits. Thesis 3: Spiritual discernment in its broadest sense includes, but is not exhausted by, the charismatic gift of the discerning of spirits. Instead, in this broad sense, spiritual discernment should be understood as a hermeneutics of life that is both a divine gift and a human activity aimed at reading correctly the inner processes of all things. The three major sections of this chapter will elaborate on and defend these theses in order.

The Metaphysics of Discernment: Spiritual Reality and Foundational Pneumatology

Foundational Pneumatology: A Review and Expansion

What follows builds on the earlier discussion of Word and Spirit as the "two hands of the Father" (chapter 2) vis-à-vis foundational pneumatology (chapter 3). To recapitulate, the former was proposed as a theological category for understanding Word and Spirit as, respectively, the concreteness and dynamism of all things, while the latter is an effort to articulate a fully public account of spiritual reality in general and of the Holy Spirit in particular. This leads to the metaphysical thesis I will be developing in this section, namely, that all determinate things consist of both *logos* and *pneuma*, the former being a thing's concrete forms, and the latter being the thing's inner habits, tendencies, and laws. Before plunging into the details of this thesis, however, I want to elaborate on two distinct aspects of the foundational pneumatology that undergird this project.

First, the "foundational" component that the following pneumatology highlights is its character as a public topic that strives to engage any and all interested parties regardless of their faith affiliation. There are two related reasons for this public character. The first is that, from a confessional perspective, the Christian doctrine of the Holy Spirit—pneumatology—draws on the conviction that God is present and active in the world and that such presence and activity is understood through the symbol of the Holy Spirit. Pneumatology thereby attempts to account for divine presence and agency in the world, understood comprehensively to include its natural, cultural, social, institutional, and interpersonal dimensions. The Christian belief that God is no respecter of persons (Acts 10:34)—regardless of race or ethnicity, gender, social standing, religious affiliation, or geographical location—and that the Holy Spirit is being poured out universally (Acts 2:17) means that whatever else we as human beings might be up to, we do not live apart from the Spirit of God nor can we escape the Spirit's presence and activity (cf. Ps. 139:7–12).

A second reason for understanding foundational pneumatology to be a fully public enterprise is that according to the Christian theological tradition, the *imago Dei* in human beings derives in part from our having received the divine breath of life. This breath sets us apart from other creatures. We are distinguished from them by our rational, volitional, moral, and interpersonal and relational capacities. Because human beings subsist through the expression of these capacities, we are all, in the words of Lyle Dabney, "otherwise engaged in the Spirit" (cf. Acts 17:28).[1] To choose freely, to act morally, to relate to others intentionally, to experience interpersonal subjectivity—these are the pneumatological features of human living in the world. Thinking itself, in this fundamental sense, is thus intrinsically pneumatological. Our processes of reasoning, whether in terms of imagining, hypothesizing, deducing, inferring, and so on, constitute, in part, our life in the Spirit. From this perspective, the Spirit is the means of thought in general and perhaps the object of thought when focus is placed specifically upon the Spirit's presence and activity. Any and all who think are therefore potentially addressed when discussing pneumatology; they become an actual part of the conversation when they accept our invitation to theologize about the Spirit or about human life and spirituality. In this sense, foundational pneumatology, by nature of its content, requires a universal horizon and potentially involves a universal audience as well.

1. D. Lyle Dabney, "Otherwise Engaged in the Spirit: A First Theology for the Twenty-First Century," in *The Future of Theology: Essays in Honor of Jürgen Moltmann*, ed. Miroslav Volf, Carmen Krieg, and Thomas Kucharz (Grand Rapids: Eerdmans, 1996), 154–63.

Usually Christians instinctively begin their pneumatologies by connecting the Spirit to the Son, and from the Christian perspective, there may be no other starting point. However, by assuming that all people experience the Holy Spirit in some fundamental way, foundational pneumatology is obligated to inquire into the most abstract or general features of this experience. Whether one begins or ends with the particularity of christology, foundational pneumatology requires that one pay close attention along the way to the universal features of the Spirit's reality. A public experience requires nothing less than a public language. Previous forays into foundational pneumatology have shown the appropriateness of metaphysics for providing such a common language.[2] As a philosophical enterprise concerned in a general sense with what the world is and how it functions, metaphysics provides a means of inquiry ideally suited to the project of foundational pneumatology. In what follows, I develop what might be called the ontological component of foundational pneumatology by presenting a metaphysical sketch of the concept of "spirit."

A Metaphysics of Spirit

What is "spirit"?[3] Historically, spirit has been contrasted with matter. Within the framework of the dipolar metaphysics of process philosophy, this contrast suffices to call attention to the concrete and dynamic poles of experience, to materiality and energy,

2. This is especially true of the Jesuit theologian, Donald Gelpi (see chap. 3). Gelpi, in turn, has been inspired by the metaphysics of C. S. Peirce, especially the latter's triadic doctrine of reality. The foundational pneumatology sketched here is Peircean in that sense, as mediated by both Gelpi and my teacher, Robert Cummings Neville. Those interested in the details of where I extend the insights of these thinkers and where I differ from them can see my *Discerning the Spirit(s): A Pentecostal–Charismatic Contribution to Christian Theology of Religions*, Journal of Pentecostal Theology Supplement Series 20 (Sheffield: Sheffield Academic Press, 2000), esp. chap. 4; and *Spirit-Word-Community: Theological Hermeneutics in Trinitarian Perspective*, New Critical Thinking in Theology and Biblical Studies (Aldershot, Hampshire, UK, and Burlington, Vt.: Ashgate, 2002).

3. For lucid historical overviews of the history of the notion of "spirit," see Steven G. Smith, *The Concept of the Spiritual: An Essay in First Philosophy* (Philadelphia: Temple University Press, 1988), 9–48; and Richard H. Killough, "A Reexamination of the Concept of Spirit in Christian Theology," *American Journal of Theology and Philosophy* 6.2–3 (1985): 140–46. To see how the biblical doctrine of spirit is both continuous with and discontinuous from historical conceptions, see Marie E. Isaacs, *The Concept of Spirit: A Study of PNEUMA in Hellenistic Judaism and Its Bearing on the New Testament* (London: Heythrop College, 1976); and Pamela M. Binyon, *The Concepts of "Spirit" and "Demon": A Study on the Use of Different Languages Describing the Same Phenomena*, Studies in the Intercultural History of Christianity 8 (Frankfurt: Peter Lang, 1977).

to being and becoming. Theologically, this dipolarity finds partial analogy in the patristic metaphor of the Word and the Spirit as the "two hands of the Father." What it fails to explicate, however, is the trinitarian character—Spirit, Son, *and* Father—at the heart of the Christian faith. The triadic metaphysics of the founder of the pragmatist tradition in American philosophy, C. S. Peirce, is much more suited for this task.[4]

For Peirce, all reality exhibits phenomenological features of *firstness*, *secondness*, and *thirdness*. *Firstness* is pure potentiality, the simple quality of feeling, that which makes a thing what it is in itself and impresses itself as itself upon our perception. What we perceive directly, for instance, are greens as greens, chairs as chairs, persons as persons, or buildings as buildings. These are each encountered at the various levels of reality as we engage them. *Secondness* is the element of struggle or of brute, resistant fact. It is that by which a thing is related to others. Greens are greens and not whites; chairs support sitting; parents nurture children; buildings structure habitation and movement, and so on. *Thirdness* is what mediates between firstness and secondness on the one hand, and between that and others on the other. Thirdness is the universals, laws, generalities, or habits that ensure the continuity of the process of reality. In less abstract terms, "green" is a generality with many shades instantiated in many things; the concept "chair" is a general that does not determine its color, its height, it weight, its function, its location, who sits on it, or other particularities; parents are constituted by the many features relating them and their activities to children, and these are general enough to include your parents, my parents, and so on; buildings also come in many shapes and sizes, each symbolizing and sustaining functions, ideologies, and activities. In sum, firstness is the simple quality of things in themselves at their various levels of aggregation; secondness is the brute factness of things—their actualities and particularities; thirdness is the general laws, habits, and tendencies that shape the temporal modality and relationality of things.[5]

4. On my initial appropriation of Peirce, see my article, "The Demise of Foundationalism and the Retention of Truth: What Evangelicals Can Learn from C. S. Peirce," *Christian Scholar's Review* 29 (2000): 563–89.

5. "Habits" is a Peircean term that calls attention to any thing's tendencies and ways of expected behavior. My use here includes the parallel Hegelian sense of *Gewohnheit*: "being-with" and "living-with" in such a way as to determine character; see Alan M. Olson, *Hegel and the Spirit: Philosophy as Pneumatology* (Princeton: Princeton University Press, 1992), 101–3.

Because of my overall objective in this chapter, I will comment less on the category of firstness in what follows and focus instead on the secondness and thirdness of things. In theological terms, all things in their suchness (firstness) consist of both Word and Spirit, or *logos* and *pneuma*. By "thing," I am referring to the essential complex determinations of being of which all reality consists. By virtue of being a determinate reality, each thing—whether a person, an event, an institution, an organization, a symbol, a ritual, or a natural or material fact—has both concrete form and inner spirit. A thing's concrete form is that which is manipulable, sensible, perceptible, and phenomenologically encounterable. A thing's inner spirit is the laws, habits, tendencies, and energetic force that shape its processive actuality and direct its temporal trajectory. My proposal is that any reality is what it is by virtue of having both form and spirit and that nothing can be apart from having both form and spirit (in addition, of course, to its simple felt qualities, its firstness).[6] In order to flesh this out, I will explore this thesis in three directions: the notion of personhood, the forms of community, and, most importantly for purposes of a pneumatological theology of religions, the idea of the demonic.

Rather than discussing personhood in the abstract, let me focus specifically on the person central to Christian faith: Jesus the Christ. In classical Christian theology, the person of Jesus has been understood in terms of the Logos, the Second Person of the Trinity. Spirit, in this framework, is the one who proceeds from the Father (and the Son, in the West) as the Third Trinitarian Person. Often, these categories lead to separate discussions of christology and pneumatology. More recently, however, the ancient model of Spirit-christology has been revived, and there has been fresh impetus to

6. An earlier formulation of this relationship between spirit and the forms of concreteness is the Russian theologian and philosopher, Nicholas Berdyaev: "Flesh is the incarnation and symbol of spirit. The spiritual life is the historical life, for the latter is concrete in character. . . . Everything without is but the symbol of that which is within. Matter itself is only the 'symbolization' of the inner states of the spiritual world." (*Freedom and the Spirit*, trans. Oliver Fielding Clarke, 4th ed. [London: Geoffrey Bles/Centenary, 1948], 18; cf. also Berdyaev's more extensive discussion of the "exteriorization," "objectification," and "realization" of spirit in the world in *Spirit and Reality*, trans. George Reavey [London: Geoffrey Bles/Centenary, 1946], 49–68 and 147–78). More recently, the philosopher Steven Smith also comes to a very similar place in his discussion of the spiritual as the "materialization of intention" (*Concept of the Spiritual*, 225–33). For Smith, we are made aware of intentions only as they confront us materially; unexpressed intentions are, in a sense, potentials only and never achieve full reality. I would prefer to say that these are underdeveloped spiritual realities struggling to achieve full materialization.

rethink christology in light of pneumatology and vice versa. Along these lines, as previously discussed (in chapter 2), Jesus the Christ is the full revelation of God precisely as borne by the Spirit: conceived, birthed, anointed, and raised from the dead by the power of the Spirit. The Spirit is concretely manifest and revealed as the power of God in the person and work of Jesus Christ. Apart from the inner dynamic of the Spirit, Jesus is not the Christ. Apart from the concrete form of the "Word made flesh," the Spirit remains hidden, ambiguous, ineffectual, and ultimately irrelevant. My point is that the person of Jesus of Nazareth himself is the Christ or Messiah, the Anointed One, pneumatologically defined. As such, Jesus the Christ is both the incarnate *logos* (or concrete form) and the anointed *pneuma* (inner dynamic field of force).[7]

This categorical reformulation is also generalizable. We are all who we are precisely as felt emotive qualities (firstness) and bodies (secondness) integrated by that inner, spiritual aspect of our being (thirdness). We are particular actualities, as well as legal, habitual, and intentional vectors or fields of force. The latter draws from our concrete forms—our biological genes, as the case may be—as well as our social environments and experiences. The difference between us and Jesus is, of course, qualitative: he was the full realization of the power and Spirit of God, while we struggle to align our own trajectories of being with that of the Spirit of God.[8]

What then about corporate forms such as communities, organizations, agencies, institutions, social groups, political and national entities, and the like? Followers of the modern German idealistic philosophical tradition, like Hegel, Herder, and Schelling, we may recall, spoke of *Geist* in terms of the inner characteristic features

7. Of course, the firstness of the man from Nazareth can also be explicated theologically in terms of his being the definitive revelation of the Father (Heb. 1:3). In addition, however, a proper conception of pneumatology—the doctrine of the Holy Spirit—emphasizes all three dimensions as well: the Spirit is who he is precisely because he mediates the revelation of the Father in the concrete personality of Jesus the Christ. In that sense, of course, the New Testament authors were right to recognize the divine Spirit as both the "Spirit of God" and the "Spirit of Jesus."

8. I should also distinguish my conception from Apollinarianism, whereby the spirit of Jesus is understood to be the Logos, and from some contemporary versions of Spirit-christology that are practically unitarian in character in denying the *hypostasis* of the Logos. As I hope is clear from the above discussion, my argument requires the Logos as *hypostasis* but not as independent from *pneuma*. Both, it seems to me, are absolutely necessary to the other. In these senses, I see the trinitarian model I am developing as congruent with classical as well as modern categories.

of nations and civilizations. Is that not, however, what the biblical conception of the Spirit as the life force of the church, the body of Christ, is all about? Further, we also find that Paul's language about governments is suggestive of both outward institutional structures and spiritual authorities (Rom. 13:1–6), and there are other references in Scripture to regional dominions of the "Sons of God" (Deut. 32:8–9; Job 1:6; 2:1; Ps. 82:1) or to the inner spiritual forces of nations (the "prince of Persia" of Dan. 10:13) and geographic regions (cf. Legion's domain in the country of the Gerasenes in Mark 5:10). The point I am making here is that corporate forms come in various aggregate arrangements, but each aggregate at various levels can and should be understood in terms of firstness—its simple, felt qualities of suchness, function, and appearance; secondness—its concrete particularities and actualities; and thirdness—its spiritual vectors or fields of force.[9]

What is important for our analysis is that we engage corporate realities on both the concrete and spiritual levels. Governments, for instance, are represented by buildings, political parties, police officers, security agents, and so on. These are the brute actualities of government in their phenomenological manifestation. But governments also consist of traditions, values, and visions for the way things ought to be, which are symbolized in their constitutions, flags, political offices, legal systems, and so on. It is evident that any attempt to understand government apart from both outer form and inner dynamic is fruitless, just as it is a hopeless task to attempt to accomplish political reform from only one rather than from both angles. Of course, each corporate entity is composed of a smaller nexus of aggregates and these, in turn, are ultimately reducible to individuals—whether persons in terms of human social aggregates or things in terms of natural aggregates. In that sense, to return to our previous example, governmental reform at some

9. The reconception of pneumatology in terms of vectoral powers or fields of force has been urged by a wide range of theologians including Donald Gelpi, *Experiencing God: A Theology of Human Emergence* (New York: Paulist Press, 1978), 178; idem, *The Divine Mother: A Trinitarian Theology of the Holy Spirit* (Lanham, Md.: University Press of America, 1984); Wolfhart Pannenberg, *Systematic Theology*, trans. Geoffrey W. Bromiley (Grand Rapids: Eerdmans, 1991), 1:382–84; Jürgen Moltmann, *The Spirit of Life: A Universal Affirmation*, trans. Margaret Kohl (London: SCM, 1992), 195–97; Michael Welker, "The Holy Spirit," *Theology Today* 46 (1989): 5–20; idem, *God the Spirit*, trans. John F. Hoffmeyer (Minneapolis: Fortress, 1994), 235–48; and, most recently, Lee Snook, *What in the World Is God Doing? Re-imagining Spirit and Power* (Minneapolis: Fortress, 1999).

level attends to particular persons in particular offices, representing particular values and visions. My point, however, is that the inner spirit or force field of any corporate entity is what determines its shape, personality, and activity vis-à-vis its relationship with other things and entities.[10]

A Metaphysics of the Demonic

Finally, it is especially important when attempting to understand spiritual discernment in general and discernment of the spirits of the religions more specifically to say something about how the foundational pneumatological framework operative here relates to the demonic.[11] As is the case with any other metaphysical reality, demonic realities feature the triadic categories of firstness, secondness, and thirdness. In its essential suchness, the demonic is a destructive reality that opposes the goodness and purposes of God. As such, the demonic is manifest in concrete forms and particular actualities and sustained as fields of force with destructive capacities. Most often, we conceive of the demonic in the category of thirdness, its immaterial field of power. I submit, however, that

10. Those familiar with the work of Walter Wink will note the obvious similarities between his proposals and what I am suggesting here and in the following subsection; see especially Wink's *The Powers* trilogy: *Naming the Powers: The Language of Power in the New Testament*; *Unmasking the Powers: The Invisible Forces that Determine Human Existence*; and *Engaging the Powers: Discernment and Resistance in a World of Domination* (Philadelphia: Fortress, 1984, 1986, 1992). I should point out, however, two crucial areas where my own work differs from Wink's. First, Wink relies on process-relational categories; and while I am also partial to such categories given the pneumatological framework of my own theological vision, I reject the dipolar doctrine of God in process theology. Second, Wink seems ultimately to reduce the demonic to social, institutional, or organizational realities, whereas I hope to show that it is important to emphasize the multidimensionality of the demonic in the various aggregates at natural, personal, and social levels.

11. The scholarly literature on the demonic is immense. For historical overviews, see Christopher Nugent, *Masks of Satan: The Demonic in History* (Westminster, Md.: Christian Classics, 1983); and Jeffrey Burton Russell, *The Prince of Darkness: Radical Evil and the Power of Good in History* (Ithaca, N.Y.: Cornell University Press, 1988). Other helpful discussions include: Alan M. Olson, ed., *Disguises of the Demonic: Contemporary Perspectives on the Power of Evil* (New York: Association, 1975); Michael Green, *I Believe in Satan's Downfall* (Grand Rapids: Eerdmans, 1981); Marguerite Shuster, *Power, Pathology, Paradox: The Dynamics of Good and Evil* (Grand Rapids: Zondervan, 1987); Daniel Day Williams, *The Demonic and the Divine* (Minneapolis: Fortress, 1990); Anthony N. S. Lane, ed., *The Unseen World: Christian Reflections on Angels, Demons, and the Heavenly Realm* (Grand Rapids: Baker; Carlisle, UK: Paternoster, 1996); Stephen F. Noll, *Angels of Light, Powers of Darkness: Thinking Biblically about Angels, Satan, and Principalities* (Downers Grove, Ill.: InterVarsity, 1998); cf. also John Bolt, "Satan Is Alive and Well in Contemporary Imagination: A Bibliographic Essay with Notes on 'Hell' and 'Spiritual Warfare,'" *Calvin Theological Journal* 29 (1996): 497–506.

any notion of the demonic that is incapable of recognizing its forms of secondness is inadequate. A demonic spirit, for instance, is nothing if not personally incarnate in demoniacs and is irrelevant if not manifest concretely in space and time. We can therefore talk meaningfully of the spirit of lust, or the spirit of murder, or the spirit of alcoholism, only because we see its effects in ruined relationships, tragic homicides, civil wars, malfunctional kidneys, or successive generations of families inflicted by habitually destructive patterns of activity. In the same way, what is demonic about the Crusades, the Holocaust, or apartheid racism is not any host of demonic spirits in the abstract but the very concrete events of "holy war," taking the form of knights, swords, the putrid gas chambers of Auschwitz, Boeing 747s used as missiles of mass destruction, and the socio-economic and political segregation and discrimination of peoples based on the color of their skin.

I am not here denying the idea of a personal devil and his demons. I am simply denying the claim that such realities can be conceived only in a spiritual sense apart from concrete forms. Even in the case of the satanic, the triadic symbolism of evil in the Apocalypse—the dragon, the beast, and the false prophet—suggests that real evil ultimately cannot be understood as being ontologically separable from its determinate and particular incarnations. My point, therefore, is to emphasize the reality of the demonic as consisting of both outer forms and inner dynamics. Both, it seems to me, are crucial, not only for understanding the demonic but also for discerning and engaging it.

But, the question arises that if all things have inner, vectoral, aspects—thirdness—what distinguishes demonic spirits from non-demonic—human, institutional—spirits? While I will expand on this further in my discussion of criteria for discernment, I will briefly delineate three characteristic features of the demonic at this juncture. First, the demonic is a destructive field of force. It attempts to influence the course of things and events so that destructive outcomes ensue. Second, the means of destruction characteristic of the demonic is that of developing inauthentic relationships between things. Rather than harmoniously connecting with others, demonic entities reject the divinely constituted relationality of things, resulting in strife, violence, isolation, and desolation. Finally, the demonic is ultimately destructive in that it inspires any thing to overreach its divinely appointed reason for being. The demonic perverts the divine intentions for things and moves them to claim more for themselves than appropriate. These features there-by define the demonic relative to the triadic categories.

One final word is needed before moving to the exegetical section of this chapter. It should be clear that mine is an ontological and metaphysical conception of Word and Spirit rather than just a hermeneutical one. Concerning the latter, Word and Spirit refer to the objective and subjective moments of engaging the truth. The objective aspect—the Word—is featured primarily in the biblical text and perhaps, for some, secondarily in the historical person of Jesus the Christ. The subjective aspect—the Spirit—is featured primarily in the illumination of the Word to the reader(s)-in-community and to the process of engaging and applying the Word to the contemporary context.[12] As I have argued elsewhere, however, the subjectivism that has been a constant threat to the church—witness, for example, the Montanist movement, the Reformation *Schwärmerei*, or the prophetic movements of our time like the Toronto Blessing and the Pensacola revivals—has led, effectively, to a subordination of the Spirit to the Word, even if we may have verbally denied such subordination. I am thereby convinced that we succumb to this temptation on the hermeneutical level in part because we do not have an adequate ontological or metaphysical conception of the "two hands of the Father." In short, my sense is that ours is not a sufficiently robust trinitarianism, and my commitment to pushing this issue includes filling out our theology and christology (the latter being our doctrine of the Word) with a more vigorous pneumatological account of divine and created reality.

The Hermeneutics of Discernment: The Biblical Materials

Introductory Remarks

If my first thesis, which reconceives the patristic doctrine of the "two hands of the Father" within the framework of foundational

12. For an excellent restatement of this dialectic of Word and Spirit in the contemporary theological scene, see Donald G. Bloesch, *A Theology of Word and Spirit: Authority and Method in Theology* (Downers Grove, Ill.: InterVarsity, 1992). Bloesch, of course, is building on the Reformation emphasis on Word and Spirit as well; cf., e.g., Luther's doctrine of revelation in Regin Prenter, *The Word and the Spirit: Essays on Inspiration of the Scriptures*, trans. Harris E. Kaasa (Minneapolis: Augsburg, 1965), and Calvin's methodological emphases in H. Jackson Forstman, *Word and Spirit: Calvin's Doctrine of Biblical Authority* (Stanford: Stanford University Press, 1962).

pneumatology, is true, then discernment has both a spiritual and a material component to it. Further, it should also mean that discernment is not only about identifying demonic spirits over and against the Holy Spirit, even if that may be important. Rather, spiritual discernment may be as much, if not more, concerned with recognizing the basic features of the world in which we live—its persons, institutions, circumstances, and so on—in order to get at the inner habits, tendencies, laws, and vectoral forces that dictate the processes of things. It may behoove us then to begin with the hypothesis that spiritual discernment is a complex activity that operates at many levels relative to the various dimensions of life in which human beings exist. The question immediately before us is whether or not there is ample biblical evidence to warrant an understanding of discernment that involves spiritual and material components and is attuned to the many faces of the world in which we traffic. To get at this question in some detail, I propose an investigation of the biblical terms related to the topic. Because spiritual discernment is a clearly delineated activity in the New Testament, I will begin there.[13]

Discernment in the New Testament

There are a number of words used in the New Testament whose root words can be variously translated "to discern."[14] I will limit my discussion to two terms and their cognates: *krinō* (to judge, select, decide, assess), and *dokimazō* (to test). The most obvious place to begin any scriptural investigation of spiritual discernment is the didactic or epistolary discussion in the New Testament. In Paul's discussion of the charismata, the gift we call discernment of spirits is *diakriseis pneumatōn* (1 Cor. 12:10). The root *krisis* is the noun form of *krinō* and has led translators to render *diakriseis* variously as "discerning" (KJV), "distinguishing" (NIV, NASB, cf. NEB), "discriminating" (PHILLIPS), the "ability to tell the difference"

13. With regard to what follows, I am aware of James Barr's warning that we do not conclude too much from lexicographical studies of biblical terms (see his *Biblical Words for Time* [London: SCM; Naperville, Ill.: Allenson, 1962]). I am, however, a systematic theologian. I leave the reader to judge whether or not the connections I am drawing from the biblical materials are either antithetical to, consonant with, supportive of, or perhaps just inconclusive regarding the theological and metaphysical vision expressed.

14. The literature here is vast. Two helpful overviews include John H. Wright, "Discernment of Spirits in the New Testament," *Communio* 1.2 (1974): 115–27; and James D. G. Dunn, "Discernment of Spirits—A Neglected Gift," in Dunn, *The Christ and the Spirit*, vol. 2: *Pneumatology* (Grand Rapids: Eerdmans, 1998), 311–28.

(TEV), or the ability to "know the difference" (NEW CENTURY VERSION) or "to recognize" (JB). For the author of Hebrews, *pros diakrisin* in Hebrews 5:14 literally means "toward a discerning" or "to discern."[15] Whereas the Holy Spirit is clearly the source of the charismatic gift of discerning of spirits in Paul, our familiarization with, reliance upon, constant use of, and disciplined training under the Word of God enables our discernment of good and evil in Hebrews (5:11–14).[16] Whether anointed or empowered by the Spirit or equipped with the Word, the nature of spiritual discernment does not bypass but involves the human faculties of judgment, discrimination, differentiation, and recognition.

Clearly, however, most of us understand the discernment of spirits as a spiritual exercise rather than in terms of our human faculties, and rightly so perhaps. This tendency no doubt derives from passages such as 1 Corinthians 2:14–15, where Paul uses the related verb, *anakrinō*, to discuss the capacity for spiritual discernment. The prefixed preposition *ana* ("up" or "through") might emphasize the clarity of the judgment, discrimination, or discernment called for. Paul then goes on to state in no uncertain terms that such discernment is available only to the spiritual person—one who has received the Spirit of God. The "natural person" (*psychikos anthrōpos*) is unable to discern the things of the Spirit of God. At this point, I leave aside the question of who the "natural person" refers to.[17] It is implied that this person is able to discern at least the things of this world. More important is the fact that the

15. *Diakriseis dialogismōn* in Rom. 14:1 is the only other occurrence of this term in the New Testament. Its meaning is also much more obscure. I therefore focus my discussion on the other passages.

16. The author of the Epistle to the Hebrews earlier used the adjectival form, *kritikos*, in describing Scripture's ability to discern the heart's thoughts and intents (Heb. 4:12).

17. The difficulties in interpreting this passage extend to the question of how Paul sees the distinction between the divine and the human spirit. Apart from this issue, however, most commentators think that the "natural person" in this passage refers to non-believers. Yet is it not also possible that it refers to a less mature group of Christians? Russell Spittler has noted that in this letter, Paul calls the Corinthian believers *sarkikos* ("carnal," 1 Cor. 3:1–3; cf. Spittler, *The Corinthian Correspondence: An Interpretive Look at St. Paul's Letters to the Church at Corinth* [Springfield, Mo.: Gospel Publishing House and Radiant Books, 1976], 24). While there is clearly a difference between Paul's use of *psychikos* and *sarkikos* in both passages, this should at least alert us to the ambiguity of the former term. *Psychikos* in 1 Cor. 2 may be a rhetorical device on Paul's behalf that sets the stage for his disciplining the Corinthian believers for their remaining fleshly or merely on the human level. On this, see Hans Conzelman, *1 Corinthians: A Commentary on the First Epistle to the Corinthians*, trans. James W. Leitch, Hermeneia (Philadelphia: Fortress, 1975), 67–69.

contrasting spiritual person in this passage is able to discern *all* things—whether of the world or of the Spirit. This reading would seem to be confirmed later in the epistle when Paul uses *anakrinō* to downplay the value of human judgment in comparison with the accurate judgment of God (1 Cor. 4:3–4).

But while this reading of *anakrinō* and that of the *diakriseis pneumatōn* in the later discussion of the charismatic gifts dominate our thinking about discernment, this is so perhaps only because of their being devoted specifically to the topic of spiritual discernment in this and the latter passages.[18] In point of fact, there are other usages of *anakrinō* in the New Testament that demand a broader understanding of the human faculty of discernment than this one suggests. Paul himself employs it in the sense of "to investigate," "to examine," "to inquire," and "to ask questions" (1 Cor. 9:3; 10:25, 27), as well as in a much looser sense of being judged, convicted, or called into personal account by prophetic utterances in congregational worship (1 Cor. 14:24–25).[19] The ambiguity found in these passages actually derives from the more common usages of the term in antiquity. Luke uses *anakrinō* and its cognates to describe the activities of questioning and cross-examination (Luke 23:14; Acts 12:19; 24:8; 25:26; 28:18), the disciples' being called to account for the healing of the cripple at the Gate Beautiful (Acts 4:9), and the Bereans' diligence in systematically studying and researching the Scriptures (Acts 17:11). The variety of translations appropriate to *anakrinō* can, however, be summarized as "to discern" or, better, "to investigate." The activity of discernment in these texts would therefore include questioning, examining, and scrutinizing whatever the object of inquiry may be.[20]

18. We should also not underestimate the history of the commentarial tradition in influencing our received understanding of spiritual discernment. As Joseph Lienhard has shown, the early church fathers' remarks on the "discernment of spirits" occur almost solely in either exegetical works—primarily when discussing 1 Cor. 12—or ascetical manuals or biographies focused on the impact of the charismatic gift of discernment on the personal battle against the flesh and the demonic; see Lienhard, "On 'Discernment of Spirits' in the Early Church," *Theological Studies* 41 (1980): 505–29.

19. Note that *anakrinetai* in 1 Cor. 14:24 should be read both as an expansion on and as an aspect of the other results of prophesy on unbelievers: being convicted, having the secrets of one's heart exposed, and being led to worship God; cf. William F. Orr and James Arthur Walther, *1 Corinthians: A New Translation*, Anchor Bible (Garden City, N.Y.: Doubleday, 1976), 304.

20. A synonym is *ereunaō*, "to search out" or "to examine." This term, however, is never used in the context of spiritual discernment (cf. 1 Cor. 2:10; Rom. 8:27; 1 Pet. 1:10–11; John 5:39; 7:52; and Rev. 2:23).

This broader meaning inherent in the discerning process is also pronounced in the verb *diakrinō*. Interspersed through the New Testament, *diakrinō* is a stronger form of *krinō* and means "to separate in order to make a distinction," "to discriminate," "to interpret," or "to discern."[21] Note, however, the variety of phenomena that call for discernment: the weather patterns and "signs of the times" (Matt. 16:3), legal and personal matters associated with human relationships (1 Cor. 6:5), physical, social, and economic conditions of others in the body of Christ (1 Cor. 11:29, 31), and prophetic utterances (1 Cor. 14:29). To be discerning in each of these situations is to be alert to the features of the natural, social, ecclesial, spiritual, semiotic, and semantic worlds in which we traffic. Undoubtedly, it can be argued that in each of these cases the biblical authors do not suppose that such discernment is a purely naturalistic physiological and cognitional activity. At the same time, however, it is arguable that they presuppose at least as much, even if it is perhaps noteworthy to point out that the biblical writers also recognized the possibility that the human faculties may intrude so negatively into the process of discernment as to effectively sabotage them (cf. *diakrinei* in 1 Cor. 4:7 and *diakrithēte* in James 2:4).

Another term used by the Christian authors that may be germane to our understanding of spiritual discernment is the verb *dokimazō* (to prove, test, approve, or examine; cf. 1 Cor. 11:28; 2 Cor. 13:5; Gal. 6:4). Whereas Matthew uses *diakrinein* in his pericope on discerning the signs of the times (Matt. 16:3), Luke's version reads as follows: "You know how to interpret (*dokimazein*) the appearance of the earth and the sky. How is it that you don't know how to interpret (*dokimazein*) this present time?" (Luke 12:56 NIV). The synonymous character of the verbs is clearly evident here. Whereas *diakrinein* may focus on specific situations or events calling for discernment, *dokimazō* tends to lay emphasis on the *process* of inquiry. At times it implies examination by trial and error (as in the trying out of oxen in Luke 14:19) or the application of various methods of testing (cf. 1 Tim. 3:10). At other times discernment may be a process of more or less passive discovery—the unveiling, as the Petrine community was advised, of a faith tried by fire (1 Pet. 1:7).

21. *Diakrinomai* means "to doubt" (e.g., Mark 11:23; Matt. 21:21; James 1:6; Rom. 4:20; and 14:23). This is related to the wavering between two or more discernable alternatives or positions.

Paul uses *dokimazō* and its cognates to exhort the Romans to discern, by way of testing and proving, the more excellent will and things of God (Rom. 2:18; cf. Eph. 5:10). In this connection, he explicitly says that approving the things that are excellent involves an extended process of being continuously transformed by the renewing of our minds (Rom. 12:2). Not insignificantly, at another place he indicates that the test for the earnestness and sincerity of the Corinthians' love for Christ is their visible and concrete generosity (2 Cor. 8:8). For Paul, the discernment of Christian character was a spiritual activity intricately connected with the manifestation of external phenomena over time (see also 2 Cor. 8:22, where demonstration of benevolence enables the discernment of inward character). Paul did not talk about spiritual discernment in these broader senses apart from consideration of the ongoing demonstration of the fruits of Christian life and faith.

Against this background, John's admonition to "test the spirits" (*dokimazete ta pneumata*, 1 John 4:1) acquires richer connotation. Clearly, the author here expects members of the Johannine community to observe rigorous processes of testing or discerning all claims regarding the gospel. Central to the criteria to be employed in spiritual discernment is the verbal confession of Jesus Christ as coming in the flesh, clearly designed to sift out gnostic views of the person of Christ. Other clues include whether or not those who claim to be within the fold actually remain therein (2:19), whether or not these accept apostolic authority (4:6), whether or not these claim to be without sin on the one hand (1:8–10) or continue in sin on the other (5:18), and whether or not they love those in the body of Christ (2:9–11; 3:14–23; 4:19–21).[22] These evidences derive from the entire spectrum of the Christian existence in the world. It is strongly implied that the testing or discerning of spirits cannot be divorced from steadfast attention to all the features of life's existence. Note that Paul also follows up his exhortation to the Thessalonians to quench not the Spirit and to despise not prophecies by demanding that they test *all* things (*panta de dokimazete*, 1 Thess. 5:21). For the authors of the New Testament, then, discerning the Holy Spirit—as well as discerning other spirits—requires observation of the broad range of the phenomenology of human behavior and experience.

22. See the more extensive discussion of James D. Hernando, "Discerning of Spirits," *Paraclete: A Journal Concerning the Person and Work of the Holy Spirit* 26.2 (1992): 6–9.

Dokimazein does occur in one other location in the New Testament, where Paul talks about discerning what is best for purity and blamelessness as derivative from one's growth in love, knowledge, and all judgment, or *aisthēsei* (Phil. 1:9–10). This latter term appears only in this place in the New Testament and is translated variously as "discernment" (NASB, RSV, ASV), "judgment" (KJV, TEV), "depth of insight" (NIV), "understanding" (NCV), "perception" (JB), and "true discrimination" (NEB). The related verb, *aisthanomai*, is prevalent in the Septuagint, where it ranges from a sense of moral and ethical discrimination to the kind of judgment that is derived from the physical senses.[23] Paul in effect prays that the Philippians will grow in love, knowledge, and (moral and perceptual) discernment (*aisthēsei*) so that they will be discerning (*dokimazein*) about the things that are more or less ambiguous or that have been differently understood (*ta diapheronta*). Christian discernment in this text is thus intricately tied to moral discernment as well as to the development of the human faculties of perception, understanding, and judgment in their broad senses. Growth in love and knowledge is inseparable from the acquisition of deep moral and perceptual insight, and all contribute to the continuing increase in the capacity of the Christian to accomplish moral and spiritual discernment.

Discernment in the Old Testament

How is the idea of spiritual discernment communicated in the Hebrew Bible? Is it as wide-ranging and as complex as we have found exhibited in the New Testament? Perhaps even more so. I will focus my inquiry here on two complexes of word-groups in the Old Testament: that of *nākar* and of *bînâ*.

The verb *nākar* occurs over fifty times in the Hebrew Bible. In many of these instances, it is translated as either "discern" or "recognize." Such discernment or recognition, however, occurs in a variety of ways. Most often, it is connected to the visual sense (Gen. 31:32; 38:25; 1 Kings 18:7; 20:41).[24] However, auditory discernment

23. *Aisthētērion* is an "organ of sense" in Philo and the LXX. It denotes "perception" in general (Job 23:5) leading to understanding, judgment, and decision (Prov. 17:10; Isa. 49:26). Cf. Gerhard Kittel and Gerhard Friedrich, eds., *Theological Dictionary of the New Testament*, abridged ed., trans. Geoffrey Bromiley (Grand Rapids: Eerdmans; Devon, UK: Paternoster, 1985), 29.

24. Note also that in Ruth 2:10, 19, and 3:14 *nākar* denotes not only "to take notice" or "to pay attention to," terms of visual recognition, but also showing favor (cf. 2 Sam. 3:36).

is just as common (Judg. 18:3; Ezra 3:13; 1 Sam. 26:17). Less frequently, it involves the tactile senses (Gen. 27:23). In Job, the protagonist is unable to discern (4:16) what was heard, felt, and perceived (4:12–15). Arguably, the basic meaning of *nākar* includes physical apprehension, whether it be through sight, sound, hearing, or other means.[25]

The idea that discernment in the Old Testament emerges from human engagement with the world receives further amplification in the ways *bînâ* and its cognates are used. Also another common term, the broad meaning of *bînâ* includes discernment, insight, perception, and understanding. I want, however, to comment further on three distinct aspects of its usage. First, like the Pauline language for discernment in Philippians 1:9–10 and elsewhere, *bînâ* is often specifically connected to the senses and the processes of growth and development. *Bînâ* involves visual observation (Prov. 7:7) as well as auditory attention (cf. Dan. 12:8, where Daniel hears but does not discern or understand). It may consist further of the ability to assess the language, thoughts, and intentions of others, or the features of personal character (cf. Job 6:30—"Can my mouth not discern malice?" NIV). The Deuteronomist uses the word in Moses' speech that exhorts ancient Israel to "consider [*bînâ*] the generations long past" (Deut. 32:7 NIV)—to understand and learn from history itself. The discerning are the wise, the sages, the "men of learning" (Ezra 8:16 NIV). Whereas the "righteous care about justice for the poor, . . . the wicked have no such concern [*bînâ*, discernment or understanding]" (Prov. 29:7 NIV). This cluster of references gives the strong impression that discernment is a skill that is developed over time, one that is attuned to both the past and present features of the historical and social world and that enables understanding and appropriate action.

This leads, second, to a consideration of the relationship between discernment or understanding (*bînâ*) and wisdom (*ḥokmâ*). Yahweh promised Solomon "a wise [*ḥākām*, the adjectival form of *ḥokmâ*] and discerning [*bînâ*] heart" (1 Kings 3:12 NIV). In the same pericope, discernment appears also as the ability to listen closely (*shāmaʿ*, whose root word means "hearing" or "to hear")—a competency acquired only over a lifetime, as derivative from the

25. This is consistent with the Hebraic epistemology, where "to know" (*yādaʿ*) "expresses a multitude of shades of knowledge gained by the senses"; see R. Laird Harris et al., eds., *Theological Wordbook of the Old Testament*, 2 vols. (Chicago: Moody, 1980), 1:366.

journey toward sagehood—or as attentiveness to a people's condition (1 Kings 3:9). As a trait central to the proper governance of a nation and to the administration of justice, this connection between discernment and wisdom is thereafter prominently featured in the Solomonic tradition. The parallelism in Prov. 2:2–3, as a case in point, demonstrates what is reiterated throughout the biblical wisdom literature: that wisdom is synonymous with understanding (*bînâ*) and insight (*tĕbûnâ*) (cf. Job 28:12, 20, 28; Prov. 4:5, 7; 7:4; 8:14).[26] (By contrast, of course, the ways of the foolish and the simple are devoid of understanding or discernment [Prov. 9:6]; their lot is the disfavor of Yahweh [Isa. 27:11]). Given the setting of biblical wisdom in the ancient near Eastern context and the cross-fertilization of Israelite wisdom with her neighboring sage traditions, ancient Israel insisted that discernment is not a capacity peculiar to the people of God. Rather, discernment is (or should be) exercised by all those aspiring to sagacity, regardless of their relationship to the elect of God. Here, it is interesting to observe that in one of the wisdom psalms discernment precedes obedience to the law, rather than proceeds from reading the law (Ps. 119:34, 73). This is not what one would have expected to find in a Torah psalm, which would seem to want to subordinate wisdom, insight, understanding, and discernment to knowledge of the Torah. Discernment, however, is needed in order to walk according to the Torah and to obey its God! In biblical wisdom, then, a discerning person is the recognized sage, one skilled in making judgment, and full of spiritual, political, and moral insight.

The last aspect of *bînâ* I would like to emphasize is the tension between discernment as a gift from God on the one hand and as a native human capacity on the other. The gratuitous nature of discernment emphasizes the divine priority in conferring understanding and insight on human beings. The psalmist, for instance, tells of a prolonged period of agonizing over his faith that is finally alleviated only when the gift of understanding is conferred upon him after entering the sanctuary of God (Ps. 73:17). Daniel acknowledges angelic inspiration for his own discernment and understanding (Dan. 10:12–14). Other wisdom texts also anticipate the Pauline

26. Note also that understanding and wisdom are repeatedly personified in the biblical wisdom literature. In fact, they both are personified explicitly as the divine Spirit in Ecclesiasticus 24:9 and 23, "where the function of God's spirit mediated between God as wholly other, and the world" (ibid., 1:104).

distinction between spiritual and human wisdom, such as the familiar proverb "Trust in the Lord with all your heart and lean not on your own understanding [*bînâ*]" (Prov. 3:5 NIV). The source of true understanding and discernment is thereby specifically preceded by the fear and the knowledge of God (cf. Prov. 9:10).

That said, however, the reverse process may also be suggested. When Daniel acknowledges that God "gives wisdom to the wise and knowledge to the discerning [*bînâ*]" (2:21 NIV), he not only affirms the divine initiative but also asserts that the recipients of wisdom and knowledge are those who have previously and continuously either exercised their gifts or cultivated their natural abilities. The nuances of *bînâ* in this sense emerge when it is set in contrast to another Hebrew word for knowledge, *yādaᶜ*. As Louis Goldberg notes, the former "refers to knowledge which is superior to the mere gathering of data. It is necessary to know how to use knowledge one possesses. . . . [Whereas] *yādaᶜ* generally describes the process whereby one gains knowledge through experience with objects and circumstances[,] *bînâ* is a power of judgment and perceptive insight and is demonstrated in the use of knowledge."[27] Discernment in this framework is necessarily the outgrowth of experience aimed at successfully living and engaging the world. Within the broad scope of the Hebrew Bible, then, we find the emphasis both on discernment as a gift of God—what might be understood as the charism of discerning of spirits in the New Testament—and on discernment as an innate human faculty that needs to be developed. The tension is well articulated by Louis Goldberg:

> While understanding is a gift of God, it does not come automatically. The possession of it requires a persistent diligence. It is more than IQ; it connotes character. One is at fault if he doesn't have it and in fact, not to pursue it will incur God's punishment (Prov 2:1f.; Ruth 1:21f.). When one acts on the objective presentations of God's revelation, he will attain the ideal of the significance of understanding.[28]

An important distinction and a strategy for discernment proceed from these exegetical remarks. First, a biblical theology of

27. Goldberg, entry on *bîn* in Harris, 1:103.
28. Ibid., 1:104.

spiritual discernment needs to be articulated in both a narrow and a broad sense. More strictly defined, spiritual discernment is a gift of God by the Holy Spirit, perhaps of a somewhat permanent nature insofar as particular individuals are concerned, but at the very least related to concrete situations and for the specific purposes of providing insight and guidance and edifying the people of God. This is, perhaps, the most common Christian conception of discernment. The biblical data, however, suggests a much broader conception of spiritual discernment that emphasizes the processes of cultivating physical, cognitive, and affective sensibilities in order to more accurately perceive the assorted features of the natural world and of socio-institutional and interpersonal relationships and to guide one's actions in a responsible manner. Both senses of spiritual discernment are found in the Hebrew Bible and in the Christian Testament.

This distinction demands that specific attention be paid to how we should go about spiritual discernment. If discernment is solely a gift from God, there is not much we can do except pray that we are blessed with the gift if and when we need it. If, however, discernment requires cultivation as well as the continued and purposeful exercise of our human faculties, then we need to think more about how we should most effectively proceed. I suggest that the broader conception of discernment requires nothing less than that we aspire to be fully trained and equipped to engage the world in its fullness. Within this larger framework, the charismatic gift of discernment of spirits can certainly be an occasional experience functioning within a fully discerning spiritual life that gives attention even to the most trivial features of the world in which we live. Such perspicuity, I suggest, can also be understood as a hermeneutics of life.

Spiritual Discernment: Toward a Hermeneutics of Life

In this last section of the chapter, I make the transition from the biblical material to a more systematic theology of discernment.[29] I

29. I claim no credit for having originated the idea of spiritual discernment as a wide-ranging activity essential to the whole Christian life; my contribution is only to approach the topic from the standpoint of foundational pneumatology. Cecil M. Robeck Jr., "Discerning the Spirit in the Life of the Church," in *The Church in the Movement of the Spirit*, ed. William R. Barr and Rena M. Yocum (Grand Rapids: Eerdmans, 1994), 29–49, approaches the subject from the

propose to understand spiritual discernment in its broad sense as a holistic activity focused on the various dimensions of human life, which includes the charismatic experiences of discerning the spirits as enabled by the Holy Spirit. My focus in what follows, however, is on spiritual discernment in its expansive sense, with the proviso that for Christians, all discernment is sustained by our life led by and in the Spirit (Gal. 5:25). If hermeneutics is the discipline concerned with interpretive methods and reading strategies regarding texts, discernment is the discipline concerned with the perceiving and assessing of human life in the world. I will elaborate on this systematic claim from the viewpoint of phenomenology, charismology, and spiritual life.

A Phenomenology of Discernment

My argument to this point has highlighted the attention that needs to be paid to the appearances of things in order to accurately discern them. Concern with the appearances of things leads us to phenomenology. I need to insist, however, that I am not using the notion either of "appearance" or of phenomenology in their technical senses. Rather, in what follows, these terms should be understood in their obvious meanings. Phenomenology is simply the attempt to understand things as they manifest themselves to be—as they appear. I must make one caveat, however, regarding the notion of "appearance." Whereas this word implicitly refers to what is seen or what is visually engaged, I take it in the more

---

perspective of ecumenical ecclesiology. Chapter 11 of Simon Chan's *Spiritual Theology: A Systematic Study of the Christian Life* (Downers Grove, Ill.: InterVarsity, 1998), titled "The Discernment of Spirits," should not be read in isolation from the book. Donald Gelpi, *Discerning the Spirit: Foundations and Futures of Religious Life* (New York: Sheed & Ward, 1970), focuses on the features of authentic spirituality within a liturgical tradition and, in that sense, is a detailed examination of the broad thesis I am arguing here, albeit in a different context. Of course, the Ignatian tradition of spiritual discernment also contains a rich deposit of theological reflection; for an introductory overview, see Piet Penning de Vries, *Discernment of Spirits according to the Life and Teachings of St. Ignatius of Loyola*, trans. W. Dudok van Heel (New York: Exposition, 1973). In "Data for Theology," chapter 5 of her book *Theology in the Age of Scientific Reasoning* (Ithaca, N.Y.: Cornell University Press, 1990), Nancey Murphy argues for discerning within ecclesial frameworks by bringing the Edwardsian, Ignatian, and Anabaptist traditions of discernment into dialogue with the research methodology of philosopher of science Imre Lakatos. Finally, mention should be made of the connections between the theology of discernment I sketch here and that suggested from a process theological perspective: John B. Cobb Jr., "Spiritual Discernment in a Whiteheadian Perspective," in *Religious Experience and Process Theology: The Pastoral Implications of a Major Modern Movement*, ed. Harry James Cargas and Bernard Lee (New York: Paulist Press, 1976), 349–67.

holistic sense of a thing's being perceived or perceptible through the broad spectrum of human physiological sensation. This would, of course, include our ability not only to see but also to hear, smell, feel, touch, taste, and so on.

The hypothesis that reality is what it is by virtue of having both concrete form and dynamic or relational vector leads to the conclusion that discerning the inner—spiritual—aspect of any thing requires focused attention on its concrete particularities. The inner is revealed in the outer. Discernment of spirits therefore requires careful and intensive engagement with the phenomenon in question as it is revealed in its concreteness. One proceeds to the task of spiritual discernment only by concentrating on what is phenomenologically revealed to the broad range of the human senses. In short, only sensitive observation of the behaviors and manifestations of the thing in question enables one to pierce through its outer forms into its inner habits, dispositions, tendencies, and powers. (Remember that while "observation" is surely a visual metaphor, its use here is also inclusive of the various ways humans perceive and experience.)

Let us take, for instance, a "movement" (as we prefer to call ourselves) like the Assemblies of God (AG). What, if anything, is the "spirit of the AG"? Ultimately, one would hope, the spirit of the AG is none other than the Holy Spirit, the Spirit of Christ. However, can this be determined conclusively and if so, how? Does not a definitive answer to this question require a comprehensive assessment—discernment—of the AG as it manifests itself at various levels and in various forms? At the very least, discerning the spirit or spirits of the AG requires attention to its leadership (headquartered in Springfield, Missouri, along with its various offices and personalities, as well as the various national offices around the world), its churches (from Yoido Full Gospel in Seoul to First Assembly in the Bronx and everywhere in between), its programs (from Royal Rangers to Missionettes to Speed-the-Light), its educational arms (from its liberal arts colleges to its local-church-based Masters Commissions), its philosophies (of worship, liturgy, missions, etc.), and so on. In each case, however, there is clearly a complex nexus of forces that reveal themselves in a variety of forms. For our purposes we will focus for a moment on discerning the spirit of an AG Bible college.

Whatever we finally determine the "spirit" of this school to be, would not such an inquiry begin phenomenologically? We interview its board of trustees, president, faculty, staff, administration, students, and alumni. (We immediately encounter the complexity of the spiritual reality. Any one AG Bible school will have administration and faculty with terminal degrees from other academic institutions as well as various relationships and allegiances to other organizations, movements, institutions, etc. The "spirits" of these "others" are thereby influential through each individual, from the full-time and adjunct faculty, to the trustees, to the director of food services!) We critically assess the institution's stated mission, its philosophy, its academic program, its budget, its essential values, its advertisement and recruitment policies, and so on. We pore over administrative policy, catalogs, course syllabi, and other (institutional and faculty) publications. We visit chapels, classrooms, faculty meetings, the dining cafeteria, the library, the bookstore, the dorm rooms, and its homecoming basketball game. We participate in campus life, from academics to spirituality to mission. We inquire into its connections with the denomination's constituency and with local area churches, its influence and role in the local community, perhaps its relationship to the district office with which it is immediately affiliated, and certainly into the kind of successes its alumni have experienced. Do not graduates of an academic institution continue to shape the spirit of their alma mater by their accomplishments? (Also influential are the assessments of the outcomes of students who never graduate for one reason or other since shifts in policy and program often are made in response to these "failures.") What about the institution's donors and supporters? Such a process of investigation, and nothing less, reveals the "spirits"—the moving forces and powers—that give shape to what we see in the school's day-to-day activities and its ongoing vision and mission. And so far nothing has been said about how the broader Christian tradition, the liberal arts tradition, and the accreditation agencies have left their marks on the school. The complex togetherness of all these spiritual realities, it can be readily seen, is the "spirit" of this institution.

The objection may be raised that the inner spiritual realities of any thing cannot be exhaustively determined by focusing on that thing's outward forms. In response, however, I ask what kind of realities these may be that evade phenomenal manifestation? Are we any further along in discerning the spirit of any thing if we say that it is a reality that has no perceptible actualities? To proceed along these lines would seem to be symptomatic of our not having learned anything at all from the failure of Kant's noumenal *Ding an sich*. I am aware that if concrete forms are spatiotemporal in nature, then to assert that spiritual realities must have a correlative phenomenal appearance is to suggest not only that they (the spirits) are spatially and temporally discernible but also that they are, in a real sense, spatially and temporally bounded. At the same time, to concede that spiritual realities are spatially and temporally bounded is also to recognize that their concrete forms are dynamic modalities, perhaps exhibiting certain features at any particular point in time and other features—both continuous with and discontinuous with the previous sets—at later points in time. Our response to this should not be to deny that spiritual discernment focuses necessarily on phenomenal appearances but to insist that discernment is and should be an ongoing activity precisely because no phenomenon unveils the totality of its inner aspects all at once. We must recognize discernment as a dynamic process attuned to the basic phenomenal features of the world in which we live and to the diverse manifestations of any phenomenon over extended periods of time. Spiritual discernment cannot be anything less or simpler than this.

This way of putting it also suffices to meet the weaker objection that spiritual discernment is not necessarily derived from sensory perceptions of phenomena but is a direct intuitive perception of the inner aspects of things. I would argue that intuitive prehensions are simply the vague intimations obtained via sense impressions of things whose spatiotemporal formation and spiritual germination are still in process. What is intuited are the anticipated appearances of things based on their past and present phenomenal and spiritual trajectories. It is therefore incorrect, in my estimation, to say that intuitions of spiritual realities involve no sense perceptivity toward their concrete forms whatsoever. A more traditional manner of conveying a similar point is Thomas Dubay's saying that "the Spirit operates incarnationally"[30]—thus requiring that discernment proceeds not only from the "inner

30. See Thomas Dubay, *Authenticity: A Biblical Theology of Discernment* (Denville, N.J.: Dimension, 1977), 82–85, 167–72, quote from p. 157.

witness" an individual might receive but more importantly from the "outer verification" available through the thing's phenomenological manifestation.

A Charismology of Discernment

This leads naturally to the question of charismology (theology of the charisms) and of the charismatic gift of discernment. Even in its broad, but certainly in its more narrow sense, the experience of discernment raises the question of what is discerned. In my phenomenological summation, I discussed as an example the spirit of an academic institution. Not all spirits might be as benign as this one. Specifically, the gift of discernment of spirits brings to our attention the fact that besides the Holy Spirit and human spirits in the personal and corporate senses, there are also demonic spirits at work in the world.

Everything said from a phenomenological perspective also applies in our exercising the gift of the discernment of spirits—demonic or otherwise. Certainly, my exposition of the biblical concept of discernment supports this overall approach. As previously noted, the spirits of the antichrists were identifiable in or by the Johannine community precisely because they were manifest in concrete events, circumstances, claims, and so on. Other parts of the New Testament confirm my hypothesis. Legion's personality was evidenced in the life and activities of the Gerasene demoniac (Mark 5:2–5); the deaf and mute spirit displayed correlative behaviors in the little boy (Mark 9:17–25); Paul recognized the demonic reality behind the actions and vocation—loosely defined—of Elymas the sorcerer (Acts 13:6–11); the spirit of Artemis revealed herself as riotous, destructive, and opposed to the gospel of Christ (Acts 19:23–41). In each case, of course, recognizing and engaging with the demonic is part of the work of the Spirit in and through human agents. The paradigm here is that which took place on the Day of Pentecost: "All of them were filled with the Holy Spirit and began to speak [the human, manifest element] in other languages, as the Spirit gave them ability [the divine spiritual enabling]" (Acts 2:4). Why would the working of the demonic be any different? Non-manifesting spirits could not be said to exist in any meaningful sense, certainly in no palpable sense. These spirits, whatever else they might be, are at least irrelevant to the human condition and at worst a figment of our imagination.

The demonic, however, is real and confronts us at every turn and threatens us in every dimension of our lives. One could, of course, point to individual encounters with demons and label such as demonic possession, oppressions, or depressions. Or we could surely identify demonic forces—what Paul called "rulers," "authorities," "cosmic powers," and "spiritual forces of evil in the heavenly realms" (Eph. 6:12 NIV)[31]—behind atrocities such as terrorist activity, wars, socioeconomic and political forms of apartheid, racial discrimination and hate crimes, political corruption and injustice, the drug cartel, the glorification and perversion of sex and sexuality by Hollywood, the genocide of the Holocaust, and so on. These concrete actualities should be sufficient to convince us that the demonic does not refer to Casper-like spirits floating about in mid-heaven. If that were the case, we would certainly not be concerned with them since they would be no more than unverifiable noumenal entities wholly removed from, unconnected with, and uninfluential on the concrete world in which we live. On the contrary, our distress regarding the demonic stems from the fact that it intrudes in overt and conspicuous ways in our lives. It evidences itself in ways that shock us visually, stun our senses, horrify our imaginations, arouse our moral indignation, and motivate us to action.

It is this conviction that the demonic consists of both an inner dynamic field of force and an outer concrete form that enables discernment and also engagement and resistance, not by human might but by the power of the Spirit of God (cf. Zech. 4:6b). Spiritual warfare thus consists of such things as prayer, fasting, and exorcisms, which engage realities that are both spiritual and concrete. The very tangibility of the demonic is what enables a holistic understanding of spiritual warfare to emerge, one that includes, but is not limited to, the proclamation of freedom for those imprisoned, the healing of the sick, the opening of the eyes of the blind, and the liberation of the oppressed—whether considered in spiritual,

31. Cf. e.g., G. B. Caird, *Principalities and Powers: A Study in Pauline Theology* (Oxford: Clarendon, 1956); Hendrikus Berkhof, *Christ and the Powers*, trans. John H. Yoder (Scottdale, Pa.: Herald, 1962; Waterloo, Ont.: Mennonite Publishing House, 1977); Wesley Carr, *Angels and Principalities: The Background, Meaning, and Development of the Pauline Phrase* hai Archai kai hai Exousiai (Cambridge: Cambridge University Press, 1981); Clinton Arnold, *Powers of Darkness: Principalities and Powers in Paul's Letters* (Downers Grove, Ill.: InterVarsity, 1992); and Marva Dawn, *Powers, Weakness, and the Tabernacling of God* (Grand Rapids: Eerdmans, 2001).

social, or economic terms (cf. Luke 4:18–19). Besides the obvious spiritual practices and disciplines, spiritual warfare therefore involves concrete actions against the powers of injustice, destruction, and dehumanization.

In this framework, spiritual discernment involves both the identification of a thing's inner aspects and a well-conceived strategy of engagement. This strategy should take into account at least the dipolar structure of the demonic. We proceed, therefore, not only to exorcise the demon in the name of Jesus by the power of the Spirit but also to nurture the individual—and, it should go without saying, individuals-in-communities—to personal faith and spiritual health. Apart from seeing such fruits in the long run subsequent to exorcisms, we should be cautious that true liberation has been achieved. Jesus' saying about the return of the evil spirit to a person with seven others more wicked than itself (cf. Matt. 12:43–45) stresses the importance of growth in grace and the concrete living out of the lordship of Christ to the warding off of the demonic.

What, however, about criteria for distinguishing between spirits? The concern motivating this question, perhaps, is that redefining the demonic as having both inner and outer aspects might lead to the confusion of criteria for discernment. We might confuse, so the allegation continues, harmless phenomena with the truly demonic. Worse, we may not see the truly demonic in concrete events, circumstances, and actualities because they appear so innocent. Is it not more appropriate to clearly demarcate the material from the spiritual and to assess spiritual reality by means of spiritual methods and concrete phenomena by empirical methods appropriate to them?[32] I suspect, however, that such a clearly established dualism no longer appeals to most of us. If someone can explain what these supposed "spiritual methods of discernment" are and how they function completely apart from the kind of empirical processes the

32. Those who lodge this complaint might appeal to 1 Cor. 2:10–16. My initial response would be to contextualize this passage. Paul is contrasting, among the Corinthians, the carnal from the spiritual. His argument is that the former are in no position to judge the latter, but that the latter are equipped to make judgments "about all things" (NIV). Second, this passage says nothing about how such judgments are made from an anthropological perspective. My argument throughout this chapter, and especially in the second section, however, focuses on the processes and means through which such judgments emerge. I see no basis for using this passage against the overall thesis argued here. On the contrary, I submit that the spiritual person is precisely one who is keenly perceptive with regard to the phenomenal features of the many things in the world.

biblical authors suggest operate in our discerning, I would gladly admit that my foundational pneumatology is a defective hypothesis and in need of (perhaps severe) reformulation. As it is, however, I can make no sense of the claim that the discernment of spirits is a purely spiritual exercise. Spirits are manifest in concrete forms, and the discernment of spirits requires attention to the variegated forms that they take.

Spiritual Reality and Discernment

Against this background, let me sketch how discernment should transpire in the context of the spiritual life. So far I have suggested that discernment includes, in its broadest sense, perceptive attention to the wide range of natural, personal, and social phenomena we encounter and, in its narrower sense, similar attention focused specifically on distinguishing between the divine, the human, and the demonic. The former requires a sense of alertness that persists throughout the totality of the Christian life. Discernment in this sense is certainly spiritual—piercing through the outer forms that we encounter into their inner realities. Crucial to mature discernment for spiritual life in this broad sense is our faithful attention to and discrimination of all things on their own terms. By this I mean that we need to recognize things for what they are. Natural objects have their own forms, properties, and functions. Persons have their distinct forms, aspirations, capacities, and so forth. Corporate human entities need to be accurately assessed for what they are as institutions, networks, organizations, and the like, in terms of forms, and for what they do socially, politically, economically, religiously, and so on, in terms of functions.

What is important at this level is that the criteria for discernment needs to pertain to the things being discerned. It would be appropriate, for example, to apply moral and religious criteria to adult persons and religious organizations, less appropriate to apply the same criteria to teenagers or environmental groups, and completely inappropriate to apply them to infants or the work of mathematicians. Norms for discernment, in other words, need to be applicable to the things being discerned—to the specific forms and functions of such things' spatiotemporal modality. In short, discernment is particularistic in nature, focused on specific actualities and assessing such according to the norms and criteria appropriate to them.

By the same token, the specific charismatic gift of discernment builds on the more general processes of discernment as a whole. The whole point about the biblical charism of discernment of spirits is that we are enabled by the Holy Spirit to sort out whether or not and how the inner spirit of any thing is either influenced by or subjected to the Spirit or to the demonic. This involves recognition of the basic form and function of the thing in question. Is or is not the thing fulfilling its divinely appointed reasons for being? To the extent that it is, it might be appropriate to say that such a thing is fulfilling its created mandate. To the extent that it is not, however, this should occasion our paying closer attention to the features of the thing in order to determine the extent to which it has departed from its proper function. I would argue that evidence of demonic influence or infiltration consists in a thing's radical departure from its purposes and functions, thus affecting its relationships in a destructive manner. At the same time, it is important to emphasize the need for specificity in discernment.

To return to my example of an AG educational institution, one instructor may have come, over a period of time, to a theological position at some odds with the denomination, resulting in confusion among students and extensive discussion among the administration and the faculty. Such discussion, let us say, has reverberations through the denominational constituency, perhaps extending beyond local district and regional boundaries. The divisiveness that ensues may surely be a sign of demonic efforts to undermine the mission and integrity of the school as a Christian institution and of the denomination's witness to Christ and the gospel as a whole. It would be wrong, however, to demonize the denomination, the school, or even the department that oversees the instructor's position and course, at least in their entirety. It may even be erroneous to demonize the instructor since he or she may be fulfilling the school's mission of teaching with the most sincere of intentions. On the other hand, true spiritual discernment would surely not deny that insofar as the denomination's and the institution's witness of Christ to the world is hindered, there is a demonic element at work in and through this situation. In this instance, it may be much more apposite to delineate the divine and the demonic aspects of the situation and events at hand in their proper respects. In short, to discern a thing is to be sensitive to its complexity. Proper discernment allows us to engage the demonic influences on a thing at the right level, in the right places, and with the right methods, so that we are able to restore what is malfunctioning to its divinely ordered purposes.

Having said this, it should be clear that the development of criteria for discerning the outer and inner aspects of things is a complicated affair. It is difficult to develop definitive criteria for discernment. Biblical norms need always to be brought to bear. However, such norms have to be sensitively applied to the concrete world of things. I understand this process of application as a hermeneutics of life that is sustained by our living in and being led by the Spirit of God. This "life in the Spirit" therefore requires reading both Scripture *and* the world accurately in order to ensure the appropriate applicability of scriptural norms to the world. Biblical norms and criteria have to be correlated—to use Tillich's famous metaphor—to the thing in its spatiotemporal and relational context. To say, for instance, that we have a definitive or universalizable norm in the confession of the lordship of Jesus (cf. 1 Cor. 12:3) is to overlook not only the context in which this norm is forged (that of the congregational practice of charismatic gifts) but also the fact that it is nearly impossible for us to distinguish genuine from nominal or verbal confession of Christ (cf. Matt. 7:21–23). As a criteriological principle, the confession of the lordship of Jesus is a vague norm, requiring interpretive applications to determine if and how it can be brought to bear in discerning specific situations, events, and experiences.

I will return to this question of discernment in the context of the world religions in the next chapter. For now, however, I note that our criteriologies should be recognized for what they are: human constructions—our best efforts to discern the Spirit of God from the demonic in our world of flux—even as we attempt to faithfully rely upon, listen to, and follow the Spirit. To that extent, a humble and faithful reliance on God to shatter our preconceptions and assumptions is in order.[33] Because the material world permits only partial glimpses of the spiritual world, discerning the

33. The Russian theologian, Nicholas Berdyaev, admonishes us more straightforwardly that the question of *ultimate* criteria "can only be asked by the 'natural' man. For the criterion of our faith and the knowledge of God cannot be found apart from God and His manifestation in us and our relations with Him. He cannot exist in this lower natural world. In demanding an authoritative criterion which will convince us of the existence of God and enable us to discern what is divine in the world, we are looking for support not to God Himself and to divine reality, but to the lower natural reality of the exterior world" (*Freedom and the Spirit*, 26).

spirits will always be inherently ambiguous. Our norms and criteria can never be exhaustive because foundational pneumatology—concerned as it is with the wide range of human experience and the broad scope of the historical process—resists conclusive articulation.[34]

I have attempted in this chapter to sketch a theology of discernment within the larger framework of a foundational pneumatology that is consistent with the biblical concept of discernment in general and spiritual discernment in particular. The latter seems to me to support two distinctions: that there are, on the one hand, two kinds of discernments in Scripture—the charism of discernment of spirits more specifically and the exercise of spiritual discernment more generally, although both are enabled by the Spirit of God—and, on the other, that the means of discerning the spiritual or inner aspect of any thing is through careful perceptivity to its concrete or outer phenomenal features. These distinctions, I suggest, both corroborate and are confirmed by the metaphysical/theological assertion of Word and Spirit—*logos* and *pneuma*—being intrinsic to all things.

What, then, are the practical implications of the theses argued here? First, we should all be cautioned about assuming a dualism between the spiritual and the material realms. A fully trinitarian vision of reality, I think, enables us to overcome either the tendency toward bifurcation of Word and Spirit or the subordination of either to the other.[35] Second, we should all be encouraged to "strive for the greater gifts" (1 Cor. 12:31) and in that sense actively cultivate the ways of the Spirit in our lives so that we develop the capacity for specific charisms. If in fact the aptitude for spiritual

34. In the words of Harold Johnson Green, "'Pneumatology' must not claim to be a science. Though there are no doubt certain pneumatological findings (the object of which is the word and its essence), there is no pneumatology as a science" ("The Word and the Spiritual Realities: A Translation of and Critical Introduction to Ferdinand Ebner's *Das Wort und die Geistigen Realitäten* and a Comparison with Martin Buber's *Ich und Du*" [Ph.D. diss., Northwestern University, 1980], 58). Green's study is one of the few accounts in the English language of Ebner's "pneumatological fragments" (the subtitle of Ebner's book). For Ebner, to speak of Word and Spirit was to speak of the Logos-in-relation-to-the-world. Ultimately, however, Ebner's christology overwhelms his pneumatology, but that may actually be a characteristic of the unfinished nature of his "fragments."

35. See, e.g., Killian McDonnell's "Pneumatology Overview: Trinitarian Guidelines for Speaking about the Holy Spirit," *Catholic Theological Society of America Proceedings* 51 (1996): 188–98, for a lucid discussion of this point.

discernment in general is part and parcel of the specific charismatic gift of the discernment of spirits, then it would be foolish for us to think of ourselves as competent regarding the latter if we pay no attention to perceiving the most basic features of our phenomenological world. Finally, however, to "strive for the greater gifts" requires our continuous submission to the Spirit of God and our rejection of the demonic forces of this world. The foundational pneumatology of discernment developed here supports the notion that humans are material and spiritual beings who are open to the transcendent. Whether we align ourselves with the Spirit of God or with the spirits of this world or of the devil and his minions is, in one sense, in our hands. To choose the former, however, is to commit ourselves to combating the latter, and we cannot hope to be successful in this task apart from being sufficiently adept at discerning the inner spirits of things.

7

Transitions

The Pneumatological Imagination and Discernment in the World of the Religions

The detour to discuss a theology of discernment in the preceding chapter is one of the initial but important steps in any attempt at becoming adept at apprehending the ways and deeds of the Spirit of God in the world. In this final chapter, I want to apply the insights gained so far to developing a criteriology for discerning the Spirit(s)—the Holy Spirit and whatever other spiritual realities there may be—in the religions. This will lead to the discussion of comparative religion and comparative theology. I will conclude by charting the way forward for a pneumatological theology of religions. In many ways, as we shall see, the proposals laid out in this book constitute no more than sketching a mandate for an extensive research program for the future.

The Quest for a Criteriology of Religious Discernment

The major question for any pneumatological theology of religions that has emerged so far is the question of discernment. How is the Holy Spirit to be distinguished from other spirits in the religions?

What criteria should be employed in the discernment process, and who decides this? What is the role of christology, and what is the normative character (at least for Christians) of christological criteria in discerning the Spirit's presence and activity in the world of the religions? In light of the discussion in the preceding chapter, I contend that discerning the religions is an ongoing process requiring both the charismatic (gracious) activity of the Spirit of God on the one hand and the hard work of phenomenological and theological comparison on the other. I take up the former aspect in this section.

The Hermeneutics of Life and the Religions

The discussion so far has opened up the necessary space for conceiving and executing a pneumatological approach to the religions. The overarching categories for reflection derive from the pneumatological symbol itself. The Holy Spirit is the primary theological symbol for the presence and activity of God in the world. As noted, however, pneumatology in its broadest sense includes the diversity of human, social, and even demonic "spirits." This requires a third category flexible enough to accommodate this pluralistic realm of the spiritual. I propose that in addition to the categories of divine presence and divine activity, a pneumatological theology of religions has to engage this reality of greater or lesser divine presence and activity or, alternatively, the fact of divine absence or the demonic.

What renders the task of discerning the divine from the demonic complex is that lived reality is seldom clear-cut. Our own personal experience testifies to the fact that we frequently find ourselves conflicted (cf. Rom. 7:14–24). We struggle intensely to "take every thought captive to obey Christ" (2 Cor. 10:5b). There is, as St. Paul noted, a perennial battle both within and without ourselves—understood individually and corporately or ecclesially—against the wiles of the devil, the principalities and powers of this world (cf. Eph. 6:11–12). In other words, the demonic is fully at work, not only in the lives of those of other faiths, but also in our own. And if we cease to be vigilant, whatever victories we experience today in discerning and exorcising the demonic will be lost tomorrow when it reenters our lives in more deadly form than before (Matt. 12:43–45). Spiritual discernment, in short, is a never-ending process.

A robust sense of discernment is therefore needed in order to engage the various dimensions of human experience in all of their interconnectedness and complexity. Herein lies the injunction toward developing a hermeneutics of life. This is the case because while we may attempt to isolate our religious practices—for example, by separating sacred spaces and times out from our profane existences and reserving the former for ritual, liturgical, and other religious expressions—the habits, convictions, and values nurtured in and through these practices are pervasive across the rest of our lives. We deceive ourselves if we think that only rituals or devotional practices are religious activities since in reality they are complex human constructions that are intimately tied to the cultural, social, and political dimensions of our lives.[1] That is precisely what "religious practices" are: practices that connect our ultimate concerns with the rest of our experience. Further, it is also the case that whatever else the devil might be up to, demonic operations are certainly not limited to the private spaces and times devoted to religious activity. So yes, discernment of the religions needs to pay attention to specifically religious experience in all of its complexity, and we can do so only through a broadly conceived and engaging hermeneutics of life.

The importance of the pneumatological categories can now be clearly stated. Whereas the category of *divine presence* marks the truth, goodness, beauty, and holiness that characterizes the reality of God, that of *divine absence* registers the destructive, false, evil, ugly, and profane existence of the fallen and demonic world. The symbol of *divine activity* is thus dynamic and mediational, calling attention to the fact that things move continuously either to or away from their divinely instituted reason for being. Clearly, given the nature of the world's religions, it is imperative that all three pneumatological categories should be kept in play. Needless to say, the object of theological discernment is to identify the presence or absence of divinity at various levels of any religious phenomenon at any particular point of space-time. As important, however, is the capacity to follow the trajectory of that phenomenon's movement and historical evolution—whether that be identified in moral, religious, spiritual, or theological terms—precisely what

1. On this, see the work of Catherine Bell, *Ritual Theory, Ritual Practice* (New York: Oxford University Press, 1992); and idem, *Ritual: Perspectives and Dimensions* (Oxford: Oxford University Press, 1997).

the category of divine activity points to. Any judgment, especially a negative one, rendered today regarding a religious phenomenon may not be applicable tomorrow because that phenomenon may not be the same.[2] I am convinced that the Achilles' heel of any pneumatological approach to theology of religions will be its failure to develop a criteriology of discernment adequate for the dynamic complexity of lived human religious experience.

In order to demarcate with greater precision just what these categories—divine presence, divine activity, and divine absence—do and do not accomplish, let me insert a caveat at this point. The goal of a pneumatological theology of religions can never be to state dogmatically or precisely: "This is where the Spirit of God is!" This is the case for at least two reasons. First and foremost is the fallibility and finitude that accompanies all human knowledge. Second, while Christians who believe in the charismatic gift of discernment of spirits can and should earnestly desire this gift, it is surely the case that even if God does all things through Word and Spirit, the full manifestation of Word and Spirit in the world has been distorted, muted, and even effaced by sin.

This effacement also explains the ambiguity of the spiritual world—the fact that all experiences and things are, at least potentially if not actually, a site of spiritual conflict. In other words, things in the world—including the rituals, doctrines, myths, texts, communities, practices, and morals of all religious traditions—do not reflect Word and Spirit in a pure manner. Rather, every thing, and more specifically every religious reality and event, reflects not only Word and Spirit to a greater or lesser degree but also human and perhaps even demonic activity to various degrees as well. At least epistemologically and phenomenologically (if not ontologically), divinity, humanity, and the demonic cannot be understood

2. See, e.g., the fascinating story of the movement of a New Age group toward Eastern Orthodoxy from the 1960s–1980s described by Phillip Charles Lucas, *The Odyssey of a New Religion: The Holy Order of MANS from New Age to Orthodoxy* (Bloomington and Indianapolis: Indiana University Press, 1995). Better known in evangelical circles is the movement of the Herbert W. Armstrong–founded Worldwide Church of God from heterodoxy to orthodox Christianity; see Joseph Tkach, *Transformed by Truth* (Sisters, Ore.: Multnomah, 1997), and J. Michael Feazell, *The Liberation of the Worldwide Church of God* (Grand Rapids: Zondervan, 2001). On an empirical level, both movements can only be described as a dynamic convergence of various cultural and religious influences with different manifest trajectories at different times. And, of course, the history of religion is filled with the cross-fertilization of religious traditions, the emergence of new orthodoxies from older movements, the apostatizing of groups, and the dying out of traditions.

separate from each other; each derives part of its significance and reality from the other two. Spiritual discernment, therefore, cannot stop at labeling any religious reality only as divine, human, or demonic since none of these features inhere purely in the events of human history. Rather, incisive discernment should be able to point out where God the Spirit is or is not at work, as well as where and how other spirits are at work in the same thing.

Still, it is certainly the case that Christians are called to be discerning. So we cannot take leave of this task simply because of its complexity and (in some senses) indeterminacy. Discernment, however, requires criteria, norms, and means to make discriminations. Do not Christians have the Scriptures, and the normative life, death, and resurrection of Jesus through which to discern the presence and activity of God in the world?

The Pneumatological Paradigm and the Christological Criterion

We observed earlier (chapter 4) that the affirmation of the distinctiveness of the Spirit's economy sought to liberate theology from the categorial constraints of christology. This attempt may be what motivated the tempering of christological criteria between Khodr's two WCC addresses. While ultimately the metropolitan's vision understood the two economies as much more connected than disconnected, he sought to affirm the permanence of the religions within the *oikonomia* of the Spirit. And while the Spirit's relatively distinct mission certainly does not vitiate the ethical criteria proposed by Samartha, it seemingly supports his suggestion that the marks of interiority and inwardness are self-evident and self-defining within the various traditions. The concept of interiority is sufficiently vague that it can be made more specific by the various traditions on their own terms. Finally, Dupuis's recognition that the turn to pneumatology is not merely a christological detour may even invigorate his project of developing a theology of non-Christian scripture in that his explicit christological categories could in fact be supplemented by categories that arise out of the various traditions themselves. Such a move, justified by an understanding of the relative but distinct economy of the Spirit, would do far less violence to the integrity of the other traditions. It is on this basis that Knitter recognizes the value of construing the relationship between the two economies as one of openness:

> Our faith affirms the hope that the relationship between the genuinely different economies will be one of ultimate complementarity. How this complementarity will express itself—whether in particular instances the work of the Spirit in the religions will be "fulfilled" or "included" in the Incarnate Word of the Gospel, or whether the "Yes" given to us in Christ will be clarified and completed by the Spirit given to others—such questions can be answered only *in the relationship*, only in the dialogue.[3]

We also noted, however, that in each case—Khodr's, Samartha's, Dupuis's, and Knitter's—the turn to pneumatology appeared to have been temporary, perhaps resulting ultimately in the U-turn to christology. Certainly, it may be too early to expect a comprehensive pneumatology of religions since the efforts of Dupuis (and others exploring questions about whether or not the scriptures of other traditions are indeed conduits of divine revelation)[4] are best understood as initial attempts in that direction. And it is undeniably the case that to traffic in a pneumatological theology of religions does not lessen the brunt of the issues connected to the economy of the Son. What it demands is clarification of the relationship between the two economies even while it may act as a neutralizing factor against the traditional Latin domination of the Second Person over the Third. The hypothesis of foundational pneumatology advanced in this book suggests that there is a universal and coextensive relevance of the Word and Spirit, understood in one sense, perhaps, in the two dimensions of church and world. Yet even this proposition needs to be qualified, given the intrinsic relationship between pneumatology and ecclesiology in the Christian Scriptures.

So, at this point the Christian norm of Jesus Christ reasserts itself: "No one can say, 'Jesus is Lord,' except by the Holy Spirit" (1 Cor. 12:3 NIV); and, "By this you know the Spirit of God: every spirit that confesses that Jesus Christ has come in the flesh is from God, and every spirit that does not confess Jesus is not from God. And this is the spirit of the antichrist, of which you have heard that

3. Paul F. Knitter, "A New Pentecost? A Pneumatological Theology of Religions," *Current Dialogue* 19 (1991): 39 (emphasis Knitter's).

4. See, e.g., Kevin McNamara, "Is There a Non-Christian Revelation?" in *Evangelization, Dialogue and Development: Selected Papers from the International Theological Conference, Nagpur (India) 1971*, ed. Mariasusai Dhavamony, Documenta Missionalia 5 (Rome: Universita Gregoriana Editrice, 1972), 147–55.

it is coming; and now it is already in the world" (1 John 4:2–3). Here, it may seem that those of us exploring a pneumatological approach to the religions are confronted decisively with the finality and normativity of Jesus Christ. On the one hand, one might admit that pneumatology is subservient to christology after all, at least insofar as discerning the Spirit is concerned. On the other hand, does it serve to finally resolve the relationship between pneumatology and christology by subordinating the former to the latter? Is it not the case, for instance, that both these scriptural formulas need to be understood in their contexts—of Corinthian enthusiastic excess and abuse on the one hand, and Ephesian encounters with Gnosticism on the other? In a very real sense, are not both formulas designed to engage with intra-Christian disputes, to identify imposters "within the fold" rather than outside, and to deal with ecclesial problems? If so, should these be applied to the question of discerning the Spirit "outside" the church, and if so, why and how?

While I believe it wise to be cautious even in this respect, I do not believe that the significance of these texts applies only to intra-Christian contentions. Two guidelines, however, should be observed in deploying these formulas to discerning the religions. First, no formula can be sacrosanct, especially if it is understood in a simplistic manner. After all, Jesus himself warned that there will be those who will call him "Lord" but do not know him since their lives do not bear the appropriate fruit (of the Spirit of God, it should be added, according to Gal. 5:22–23; cf. Matt. 7:15–23). The formal norm of Jesus Christ is therefore applicable only by and through the power of the Spirit. So while discerning the Spirit is intimately connected with the Christ, this should not be understood in a way that subordinates the Spirit to Christ—as in, "Ah, here is a confession of Jesus as Lord, and therefore we can be certain of the presence and activity of the Spirit!" in a simplistic sense—or that renders the Spirit subservient to the Word. Rather, Word and Spirit are mutually defining as the "two hands of the Father."[5] This should alert us to the processive, ambiguous, and dialectical nature of discernment.

5. Here I confess my sensitivity to the Eastern Orthodox critique that the *Filioque* clause has translated in the Western church to a subordination of the third article of the creed to the second. Of course, the danger of reverse subordination presents itself as well, and we need to be continuously mindful of it. The comments in this note also apply to what I say in the next paragraph in the text.

Second, all formulas are propositional abstractions derived from narratively structured experiences. And, since all criteriologies are constituted by formulas, they also are abstractions. As vague generalities, criteriological abstractions are always in need of specified testing against particular cases in order to determine the appropriateness and manner of their applicability in those concrete circumstances. Further, such testing is always a triadic activity of interpretation, with regard to the generality of the criterion, with regard to the thing being discerned, and with regard to the respects, intentions, and so on, of the activity of discernment. Since the things to be discerned are historical phenomena, they are dynamic realities that require ongoing engagement and repeated discernment. In the process, the criteria of discernment are themselves given new significance as they are brought into contact with different phenomena and situations than that through which they had previously emerged. This is the unavoidable result of the hermeneutical circle or process. In some instances, however, the newness of the significance for understanding the criterion is itself of such radical discontinuity that it is fair to say that a new criterion appears. In short, there is a complex history to any criterion in particular, as well as to entire criteriological frameworks (worldviews, one might call them), which requires our understanding and acknowledging the discernment of Spirit(s) to always be *in via*.

Criteriological Questions

There are really two interrelated sets of questions regarding discernment that have percolated implicitly and persisted explicitly throughout this investigation. The former is an intra-Christian matter concerned with the theology of *salvation*: Is it possible for the unevangelized to be saved, and if so, how? While important, this question is not the immediate focus of this book, and I will not address it directly now. The latter set of questions concerns the theology of *religions*: Is it possible that the religions are infused with general revelation? Is it possible that the religions mediate salvation? What is good, noble, true, or even salvific about the religions? Discernment here involves a number of issues, intersecting at various levels. In terms of comparative method, the question arises whether it would be justifiable to interpret the diverse religious traditions according to foreign (in this case, Christian) categories.

Perhaps, but that such comparisons would be viable should not be taken for granted. The concept of "general revelation," for instance, is a distinctively Christian one, and it may prove difficult to demonstrate that the religions bear within themselves the fruit of general revelation as understood by Christians, if general revelation be defined within a Christian theological framework. In this case, would it be surprising if one did not find the religions attesting to general revelation? Goodness, nobility, and truth are all defined variously by the religions. Gautama's insistence on the tragic character of existence can be said to parallel Qohelet's dictum that "all is vanity." Yet to equate them both without acknowledging the profoundly different visions between the Buddhist cosmology and the Hebrew theistic worldview is methodologically unpardonable.

The notion of "salvation" is also not as easily transferable across religious boundaries as one might think. In fact, the reason the question of whether or not the religions mediate salvation has persisted throughout the inclusivist-exclusivist debate is probably because it is a misunderstood one. "Salvation" has not proven to be an innocent comparative category simply because there are a diversity of ailments diagnosed by the religions and a correspondingly diverse number of cures.[6] To affirm that the religions mediate Christian salvation (something about which the Catholic Rahner is ambiguous and the evangelical inclusivist Pinnock has repeatedly denied) would not only distort the religions as they understand themselves but also wrongly change the parameters of the discussion and the nature of the stakes involved. For then the question that proponents of this concept would need to answer is no longer whether or not religion is salvific but whether or not this or that religious tradition, practice, ritual, or doctrine mediates specifically Christian salvation.

The dialogue may eventually proceed to the point where this question cannot be avoided, but at the present stage, I want to suggest that it is prematurely posed. The discernment presently required is not so much that which identifies what is good, true, noble, and salvific in the religions but that which comprehends how goodness, truth, nobility, and salvation as Christians understand

6. On this point, see Joseph A. DiNoia, *The Diversity of Religions: A Christian Perspective* (Washington: Catholic University of America Press, 1992), 34–64; S. Mark Heim, *Salvations: Truth and Difference in Religion* (Maryknoll, N.Y.: Orbis, 1995), part 2; idem, *The Depths of the Riches: A Trinitarian Theology of Religious Ends* (Grand Rapids: Eerdmans, 2001).

them are or are not applicable to the various religions. In short, the religions need to be discerned in such a manner that adequate descriptive categories are formulated that will both avoid diluted reductionisms of the religions and generate legitimate comparisons across the diverse traditions.

The mutual concerns of Knitter and his predecessors about discerning the Spirit may therefore point the way forward. For Knitter, the attractiveness of the pneumatological turn lies in its capacity to both justify and encourage interreligious dialogue with the partial objective of discerning the extent of complementarity between other traditions and Christianity. Because the economy of the Spirit is related to but not identical with that of the Word, Christians can relate to those in other faiths "as others without having to reduce them, either at the beginning or end of our conversations, to our Christian categories. Any relationship between Christianity and the religions that does occur will be between two really different economies."[7]

Now, Alister McGrath is correct in what he affirms when he admonishes against importing "a set of criteria from outside the Christian revelation and allow[ing] that to become of normative importance in evaluating the religions. We must develop a Christian response on the basis of a Christian set of criteria."[8] Christian criteria are certainly needed to enable Christians to discern the important (i.e., redemptive) features of religious experience. And, for purposes of Christian self-understanding, Christian criteria certainly are deployed to understand other faiths. In one sense, we can do no other. Yet in another sense, just as McGrath resists the imposition of other religious norms in the Christian evaluation of other faiths, in the context of the interreligious dialogue, should he not also be cautious about the Christian imposition of Christian norms in the mutual evaluation of human religious experience in general? Does not the interreligious dialogue require a kind of confident spiritual maturity that is nevertheless self-critical about the finite, fallen, and perspectival character of human understanding, including one's own? And would the utilization of solely Christian criteria and norms be able to generate this kind of self-critical perspective

7. Knitter, "A New Pentecost?" 37 (emphasis in original).

8. Alister McGrath, "Response to Clark H. Pinnock," in *More Than One Way? Four Views on Salvation in a Pluralistic World*, ed. Dennis L. Okholm and Timothy R. Phillips (Grand Rapids: Zondervan, 1995), 131.

since, as the saying goes, the fact that we see through our spectacles makes it difficult for us to criticize them? If so, how would such self-critical perspectives arise? Would not other perspectives be needed to locate the blind spots of one's normative worldview?

My point is that while Christians, like everyone else, can only begin with what they have, meaningful participation in the interreligious dialogue requires that one be open at least to assessing other traditions, including their criteria and norms, on their terms. This is what it means to understand the religious other. In the process, their perspectives can be brought to bear on our own thinking, a sort of checks and balances system. Does not the proverb of iron sharpening iron apply to engaging those beyond the boundaries of one's (faith) community, as well as those within it (cf. Prov. 27:17)? This is what I believe Knitter and others are exhorting us to do: engage the other as other (sin excepted, although perhaps the Christian understanding of sin will itself be transformed through the crucible of interreligious exchange). In that sense, more complex and sophisticated descriptive categories need to be developed in order to respect the importances and the particularities of the different traditions, even while these same categories, which emerge during the course of interreligious engagement, could act as catalysts for the self-critical reflection that always needs to occur with regard to one's home tradition.[9]

Of course, some conservative Christians may not believe in the value of the interreligious dialogue to begin with. Given the fallenness of human rationality, they would protest, the possibility of learning something substantively new about the gospel is minimal at best. Certainly, this would not justify the prolonged exposure to other faiths that interreligious encounter demands. In response, however, I would suggest that while the depravity of human beings in general and of human rationality in particular are valid components of Christian doctrine, this would not be the appropriate point of departure for authentic interreligious engagement for at least two reasons. First, this a priori approach begs the question

9. Minimally, what is needed are both normative criteria that arise out of the home tradition and what may be called "generic criteria," which may have application across cultural and religious tradition. I would argue that to the extent that Christian norms are applicable to non-Christian faiths, and Buddhist norms to non-Buddhist faiths, and Islamic norms to non-Islamic faiths, etc., we will continue to develop such "non-generic" criteriologies. On this point of specific versus generic criteria, see Dale Cannon, *Six Ways of Being Religious: A Framework for Comparative Studies of Religion* (Belmont, Calif.: Wadsworth, 1996), esp. 119–27.

regarding the battle of the religions and therefore evades the very thing that needs to be argued in the interreligious dialogue: the superiority of one explanatory system over any other. Second, such a fideist position undermines claims to truth since truly depraved rationalities would not be able to receive even the truth of divine revelation itself but would have to remain finally agnostic about all the interpretations of alleged divine revelation.

Since I am not writing directly to this particular audience, I will assume that those who have followed the argument so far see interreligious dialogue as a valuable intentional activity for Christian academicians and other intellectuals on the one hand and as a by-product of living in increasingly diverse neighborhoods and being employed in religiously plural workplaces on the other. Further, I have already suggested that dialogue is not exclusive but rather constitutive, at least in part, of mission (chapters 1 and 2), and I will reaffirm this below. For the moment, however, it is necessary to reemphasize the call of Pinnock and others for a more sustained dialogical engagement with the empirical religions in order to develop the criteria and comparative methodology required for discerning what is good, true, and noble (and perhaps even salvific?) in other traditions.

The discussion so far has led us into the thickets of the interreligious dialogue. At the same time, Christian participation in the interreligious dialogue cannot be simply an affirmation of religious otherness. Christians are called, as agents of the gospel, to be catalysts of transformation and harbingers of the kingdom of God. Further, as led by the Spirit, ours is a calling to discern the Spirit's presence and activity in the world in general and in the world of the religions more specifically.

Comparative Religion and Comparative Theology

The question of how to discern the religions so far has focused on the criteria for discernment. In what follows, I will argue that discerning the religions involves developing skills not only for recognizing heterodoxies but also for identifying heteropraxis. As such, interreligious discernment requires the full repertoire of tools developed by *Religionswissenschaft*, or the academic study of religion. And, insofar as Max Müller (the recognized founder of the modern study of religion) is correct in that the person who knows only one religious tradition knows none, discerning the religions and the interreligious dialogue also requires competence in comparative religion and comparative theology.[10] So a pneumatological theology of religions needs to reengage not only the academic study of religion in all of its complexity but also the disciplines of comparative religion and theology.

Reengaging the Study of Religion

I have argued throughout this book that the overarching goal of a pneumatological theology of religions is the ongoing activity of discerning the Holy Spirit and the diversity of spirits in the world of the religions. This goal has three aspects: to understand the religions as a human phenomenon in all of its diversity; to understand the relationship between the divine and this human phenomenon; and, to distinguish, where possible, the divine and the human from the demonic. The religions are no exception to the rule argued in the previous chapter that discernment of spiritual realities proceeds necessarily through their concrete, outer manifestations. To get at the inner spirits of the religions therefore demands (at least) a phenomenology of religion. This is an empirical task requiring an interdisciplinary approach, and interpreting the data theologically is an ongoing comparative project. Let me briefly expand on each of these points.

Discerning the Spirit(s) in the world's religions has to begin with the empirical actuality of these traditions and therefore requires an interdisciplinary methodology designed to engage that multidimensional phenomenon. This is in part because "religion" is itself a constructed category through which human beings order their lives with regard to the things that matter most. In that sense, there is a certain sort of numinousness to religion, which is why there is often the sense that we cannot investigate it directly. Instead, as Ninian Smart has labored to describe it, we explore religion best by paying attention to its phenomenologically manifest dimensions (to the extent we can separate those out for identification) such as its doctrines, rituals, myths, ethics, politics, sociality and materiality.[11]

Theologians who attempt to understand the phenomenon of religion therefore rely on historians, anthropologists, sociologists,

10. On Müller, see Eric J. Sharpe, *Comparative Religion: A History*, 2d ed. (La Salle, Ill.: Open Court, 1986), chap. 2.

11. Cf. Ninian Smart, *Dimensions of the Sacred: An Anatomy of the World's Beliefs* (Berkeley: University of California Press, 1996); and *Worldviews: Crosscultural Explorations of Human Beliefs*, 3d ed. (Upper Saddle River, N.J.: Prentice-Hall, 2000).

psychologists, practitioners of other faiths, and so on to familiarize them with the object of their reflections. In other words, one can no longer discern the religions in the earlier, superficial sense from a priori commitments. As such, alongside the histories of Christianity, of Christian theology, and of dogmatic theology, those who would render judgments on the non-Christian faiths would need to be armed with a variety of tools derived from the academic study of religion: history of religion, philosophy of religion, phenomenology of religion, sociology of religion, psychology of religion, anthropology of religion, religion and the arts, religion and culture, and so on.

At the same time, theologians should also listen to those pastoral agents and missionaries who work within environments that sustain such traditions. Certainly they cannot exclude personal observation and participation, even as theologians themselves cannot ignore their own personal experiences with a religious tradition. For this reason, they should also heed the testimonies of those—both insiders and outsiders—who have firsthand experience of a tradition. Otherwise, one theologizes alone in an ivory tower, far removed from the empirical reality of the world's religious traditions. Getting at that empirical reality is a complex and arduous task beyond the capacities of any one human being.

In short, our awareness of the religiously plural world that characterizes our time requires that theologians look to and learn from the work of other specialists of religion, including those agents of the gospel who have devoted a lifetime to understanding the people, culture, and religions amidst which they fulfill their calling. It should not be a case of either/or with regard to *Religionswissenschaft* or missiology but rather a case of both/and. A relevant and true theology of religions builds on an empirical engagement with the world of the religions, and such has to be developed from diverse perspectives and approaches.[12]

Toward a Theory of Comparison

But what then does one do while gathering data? Inevitably, one categorizes the data as one proceeds. Fair categorization, however, requires that one pay attention to the categories emergent

12. This is not a new argument but a well-established methodological dictum since the work of Lonergan; see also Gerhard Ebeling, *The Study of Theology,* trans. Duane Priebe (Philadelphia: Fortress, 1978), and J. Wentzel van Huyssteen, *The Shaping of Rationality: Toward Interdisciplinarity in Theology and Science* (Grand Rapids: Eerdmans, 1999).

from within the religious tradition one is engaging. In other words, a faithful and true interpretation of Buddhism, for example, must pay close attention to the ways in which Buddhists understand and engage each other, the world, and that which is, in their perspective, ultimately real. Its depiction of Buddhism should be recognized and accepted by Buddhist practitioners as authentic to their experience and tradition. As Christians would not want their experiences interpreted in other—for example, Buddhist—terms (at least not without the opportunity for response and rebuttal), so also should Christians always be cautious of imposing foreign categories on religious others.

But the pneumatological categories themselves derive from specifically Christian reflection on the world's religions. And if from a pneumatological perspective the data is supposed to illuminate, finally, divine presence, activity, and absence, how then does one bridge the gap from the categories of the religious other to the pneumatological categories? One does so by doing comparative theology. My conviction is that theology of religions can proceed only as a rigorously constructed comparative enterprise.

This activity of comparison has been recently analyzed by Robert Cummings Neville.[13] Neville describes the process of comparison as necessarily involving the registration of what is important in things compared as defined on their own terms. Importance, in Neville's theory, is a complicated notion about the value of things. A thing's value or importance arises out of its own *haecceity*—the fact that it is—and has objective and subjective aspects. The former relate to its functions, achievements, and structured relations to other things, while the latter derive from the perspective of any experiencer of the thing. Registering importance in all of these respects is crucial for avoiding a reductive analysis of the thing.

There are, however, two related complicating factors: the value-ladenness of all thinking and theorizing and the lack of adequate comparative categories.[14] With regard to the first, it is inescapable

13. In this section, I draw from Robert Cummings Neville; see his *Normative Cultures* (Albany: SUNY Press, 1995), chaps. 2–3; and *The Truth of Broken Symbols* (Albany: SUNY Press, 1996).

14. Here, I supplement Neville's ideas with those of Jonathan Z. Smith, especially his "In Comparison a Magic Dwells," in Smith, *Imagining Religion: From Jonestown to Babylon* (Chicago: University of Chicago Press, 1982), chap. 2; and *Drudgery Divine: On the Comparison of Early Christianities and the Religions of Late Antiquity* (Chicago: University of Chicago Press, 1990).

that all thinking about anything begins within the hermeneutical circle. Because all comparisons emerge from finite perspectives, they are therefore conducted with (oftentimes unconscious) biases that inevitably leave out what is of import in the things compared, thus distorting the conclusion. This distortion can be alleviated only by allowing what is important to be represented by the thing itself prior to the imposition of theoretical constructs or, that being practically impossible, approaching the thing compared from as many vantage points as possible, thus allowing a more synoptic vision of its importances to emerge. When applied to the task of religious and theological comparisons, discerning the Spirit(s) requires that dialogue partners be allowed to define the parameters and categories of their traditions or, lacking that, that attention be paid to as many voices regarding the other tradition as possible.

The second and related complicating factor is the lack of adequate comparative categories. There are actually two issues here. The first is that our categories are inevitably biased, usually toward that part of the things compared that we are either more favorably disposed toward or more knowledgeable of. Again, what we need to do is approach the other thing from a variety of angles prior to forming our comparative categories. The generality of these categories actually forms the framework within which the criterion for comparison and contrasts are defined. In terms of the interreligious dialogue, it means that we need to listen empathetically before we proceed toward discriminations. Discerning the Spirit(s) in the religions necessitates the application of christological criteria at some point in the process, but the integrity of the other tradition needs to be respected as well, and that can only occur if we begin with what it represents as being important about itself and conclude by ensuring that nothing considered valuable on its own terms has been lost in the process.

The second and more important issue related to our lack of adequate comparative categories is that the existing comparative categories we have tend to be either overly specific on the one hand or insufficiently specific on the other so that the results of the comparative exercise turn out to be of limited value. Neville's proposal is to emphasize the importance of vagueness in the formation of comparative categories. Following Peirce, Neville defines a vague category as "one to which the law of excluded middle does not apply."[15] At the vague level, things that are perhaps otherwise starkly contrasting can be unified without doing violence to their integrity, and they can then be fruitfully contrasted as specified by their importances.

Dupuis, for example, is to be applauded for focusing on a doctrine of sacred scripture. The notion of sacred scripture is sufficiently vague that it can potentially be applicable to the Confucian or even Taoist canons. Yet Dupuis moves too far too fast. First, he proceeds to limit the suitability of the category by defining it in (Christian or theistic) terms of divine revelation. This immediately removes from consideration scriptural canons from non-theistic traditions (like Theravada Buddhism). Then, while he does allow for the possibility of understanding the Qur'an, at least in its parts, as an authentic word of God and Muhammad as a genuine prophet,[16] he unfortunately relegates to a few meager notes discussion of the Hindu and Buddhist scriptures. This exercise in comparison therefore fails on two counts. On the one hand, what began as a sufficiently vague category was abruptly delimited by a less-than-neutral subcategory, and on the other hand, the adequacy of the new category remains questionable as long as it engages only one comparative instance and is not sufficiently tested against a greater variety of cases. This example demonstrates that the process of discernment is always in danger of being abruptly terminated and that often either the results are hastily assembled without a thorough consideration of all the available evidence or the evidence has been assessed only within a limited framework of interpretation.

The New Comparative Theology

Building on Neville's work, it is clear that effective religious and theological comparisons should do two things: they should lift up what is important in the things compared as determined by criteria identified in their own terms, and they should elicit, via

15. Neville, *Normative Cultures*, 96.

16. Jacques Dupuis, *Jesus Christ at the Encounter of World Religions*, trans. Robert R. Barr (Maryknoll, N.Y.: Orbis, 1991), 170. On the possibility of understanding Muhammad as a genuine prophet, see also Hans Küng's dialogue with Josef van Ess, in Küng et al., *Christianity and the World Religions: Paths of Dialogue with Islam, Hinduism, and Buddhism*, trans. Peter Heinegg (New York: Doubleday, 1986), 24–28; and Kenneth Cragg, *Muhammad and the Christian: A Question of Response* (Maryknoll, N.Y.: Orbis; London: Darton, Longman & Todd, 1984).

categories that are neutral to the things compared, an analysis of similarities and contrasts. Certainly one of the goals of comparative religion and theology is to identify points of convergence or divergence between religious traditions. And in this regard, it is important to note that this generation of comparativists is finally getting beyond the facile comparative phenomenological work of previous thinkers like Otto, van der Leew, and Eliade and engaging in deeper and much more substantive hermeneutical, philosophical, and, ultimately, theological comparisons and contrasts.[17] Briefly stated, the new comparativism moves from comparison of phenomena and texts (here considered as written documents) to the comparisons of subtexts and contexts, including the practices and purposes that give meaning to texts (here considered in their complexity as events inscribing a way of understanding the world). In short, the new comparison turns out to be a comparison of worldviews and (to use Wilhelm Dilthey's phrase) world-and-life views.[18]

To see this difference, consider the kind of sophistication with which we have come to understand a central aspect of Christian faith, namely the notion of scriptural revelation.[19] Many Christians have traded in the dictation theory of inspired Scripture for the belief that inspiration extends to the entirety of the canonical process. Yet upon closer examination, this process is itself rather complex. Scripture emerged through the variegated sacramental, liturgical, and devotional life of the early Christians, the emergent and always developing episcopate, the patristic oral and written traditions, iconography, and so on. In other words, the notion of

17. For some of the differences between what I call the "old school comparativism" and the new comparativism, see Kimberly C. Patton and Benjamin C. Ray, ed., *A Magic Still Dwells: Comparative Religion in the Postmodern Age* (Berkeley: University of California Press, 2000); and Robert Cummings Neville, ed., *The Comparative Religious Ideas Project*, 3 vols.: *Ultimate Realities*; *Religious Truth*; *The Human Condition* (Albany: SUNY Press, 2001).

18. See Wilhelm Dilthey, "The Types of World-View and Their Development in the Metaphysical Systems," in David E. Klemm, *Hermeneutical Inquiry*, vol. 2: *The Interpretation of Existence*, American Academy of Religion Studies in Religion 44 (Atlanta: Scholars Press, 1986), 33–54. Note also the emerging awareness of this requirement in ethnographical, anthropological, sociological, and cultural studies; see, e.g., Robin Horton and Ruth Finnegan, eds., *Modes of Thought: Essays on Thinking in Western and Non-Western Societies* (London: Faber & Faber, 1973).

19. In what follows, I draw from William J. Abraham, *The Divine Inspiration of Holy Scripture* (Oxford: Oxford University Press, 1981), and *Canon and Criterion in Christian Theology: From the Fathers to Feminism* (Oxford: Clarendon, 1998); also, Telford Work, *Living and Active: Scripture in the Economy of Salvation* (Grand Rapids: Eerdmans, 2001).

"scripture" itself leads to the rich fabric of the lived-experience of early (patristic) Christianity. Strive as one may, Scripture makes no sense apart from the ecclesial life and history that names it and through which it endures.[20] In the present context, the Christian doctrine of Scripture makes no sense apart from Christian practices, liturgies, and thickly described ways of being in the world.[21]

This sophisticated hermeneutic of Scripture itself, of course, needs to be applied in any attempt to understand the sacred textual traditions of other faiths.[22] It simply will not do to say that other scriptures are not inspired by God and are therefore not revelatory at all. That may indeed be the case. However, the scriptural convictions of other faith communities now have to be understood within the richness of their lived historical experiences and contexts. The performatory aspects of other scriptural canons will need to be understood along with their pedagogical value. Textual criticism, as well as rigorous analysis of the relationship between the canonical and commentarial traditions of other faiths, will need to be undertaken. The various logics that undergird the authority and inform the reading of different sacred texts demand clarification. The results will be a greater understanding not only of what other scriptures say but also why and how it is said. In sum, the function and role of scripture in the various religious traditions of the world will be better understood.[23]

20. I draw here also from Edward Farley's concept of ecclesial duration as referring to the complex way of life that sustains Christian beliefs and practices; see Farley, *Ecclesial Reflection: An Anatomy of Theological Method* (Philadelphia: Fortress, 1982), esp. chaps. 10–12; and Farley and Peter C. Hodgson, "Scripture and Tradition," in *Christian Theology: An Introduction to Its Traditions and Tasks*, ed. Peter C. Hodgson and Robert H. King (Philadelphia: Fortress, 1982), 35–61.

21. This is the truth of George Lindbeck's cultural-linguistic theory of religion; see Lindbeck's *The Nature of Doctrine: Religion and Theology in a Postliberal Age* (Philadelphia: Westminster, 1984).

22. Cf., e.g., Harold G. Coward, *Sacred Word and Sacred Text: Scripture in World Religions* (Maryknoll, N.Y.: Orbis, 1988); Miriam Levering, ed., *Rethinking Scripture: Essays from a Comparative Perspective* (Albany: SUNY Press, 1989); Wilfred Cantwell Smith, *What Is Scripture? A Comparative Approach* (Minneapolis: Fortress, 1993); and Harold G. Coward, ed., *Experiencing Scripture in World Religions* (Maryknoll, N.Y.: Orbis, 2000).

23. For a superb example of how Christian theology can engage another canonical tradition, in this case Hinduism, as textually, ritually, and practically lived out, see Francis X. Clooney, *Thinking Ritually: Rediscovering the Purva Mimamsa of Jaimini* (Vienna: Sammlung De Nobili Institut für Indologie der Universität Wien, 1990); *Theology after Vedanta: An Experiment in Comparative Theology* (Albany: SUNY Press, 1993); *Seeing through Texts: Doing Theology among the Srivaisnavas of South India* (Albany: SUNY Press, 1996); and *Hindu Wisdom for All God's Children* (Maryknoll, N.Y.: Orbis, 1998).

The forces of globalization we currently experience not only require but also facilitate such in-depth engagement with religious otherness.[24] And in fact, such engagements are two-way streets—genuine dialogues that produce authentic transformation in both parties. Buddhists, for example, are engaging with Christians at the deepest theological levels. The recent *Buddhist Theology: Critical Reflections by Contemporary Buddhist Scholars* (1999) shows that whereas previous generations have been quick to assume that Buddhist reflection on ultimate issues is "theological" since that is what Western reflection on ultimate issues has been called, the contributors to this volume, who are Buddhists who not only recognize that many branches of Buddhism are non-theistic, but who also have been trained in theistic traditions.[25] What they call "Buddhist theology," then, is not the acknowledgment that Buddhists are "anonymous theists" after all but the recognition of the need to explore how the various Buddhist traditions should or should not engage the questions, concerns, and issues that are raised by theistic traditions. This requires, of course, not only a deep understanding of the home tradition (in this case, Buddhism), but also sophisticated views of theistic traditions in order to determine how appropriate it is to compare and contrast the ultimate reality views, values, and commitments of Buddhists with those of theists.

In the process of studying in depth the historical and contextual frameworks that shape the scriptural functions of other faiths, the perspectives of religious insiders will need to be consulted. As a result, what is of importance to religious others will emerge. This is the kind of interreligious and intercultural comparative work that allows, indeed requires, that the religions be

24. And, of course, this kind of in-depth compativism is taking place with greater and greater frequency. The Faith Meets Faith series published by Orbis Books has produced, to date, over twenty-five titles featuring a variety of comparative interreligious projects.

25. Roger Jackson and John Makransky, eds., *Buddhist Theology: Critical Reflections by Contemporary Buddhist Scholars*, Curzon Critical Studies in Buddhism 7 (Richmond, Surrey, England: Curzon, 1999). Other representative volumes of this Buddhist-Christian dialogue include John B. Cobb Jr. and Christopher Ives, eds., *The Emptying God: A Buddhist-Jewish-Christian Conversation* (Maryknoll, N.Y.: Orbis, 1990); and Paul F. Knitter and Roger Corless, eds., *Buddhist Emptiness and Christian Trinity: Essays and Explorations* (New York: Paulist Press, 1990). This two-way dialogue is also beginning to feature evangelical voices—Russell Bowers, *Something or Nothing? Nishitani's "Religion and Nothingness" as a Foundation for Christian-Buddhist Dialogue* (New York: Peter Lang, 1995).

taken seriously on their own terms.[26] Only through this laborious process will comparative categories adequate to the thickly described experiences of people of faith be generated, will hypotheses sufficiently sophisticated to the realities of religious experiences and to verification or falsification be developed, and will truths general enough to be meaningfully grasped across cultures and religious traditions and yet specific enough to deal with experiences on the ground be won.

For Christians, however, this kind of cross-cultural and cross-religious dialogue, hermeneutics, and comparison is all the more significant since it is part and parcel of our asking and attempting to answer questions regarding whether or not and how the Holy Spirit is present and active in the religions. And, engaging this question itself has to be understood as a Spirit-led process of encounter with religious others who are not entirely devoid of the Spirit of God, according to the central axioms of a pneumatological theology of religions (chapter 2). Theology of religions therefore needs to be comparative theology that proceeds from multiple conversational starting points: that of the practitioners, that of a diversity of scholars from various disciplines, and that of a diversity of perspectives of theologians or intellectuals representing the various traditions, all of whom are reflecting from both within and without the traditions in dialogue. This multifaceted conversation is necessary to protect oneself against ideological or personal bias in interpreting and categorizing the religious other. It is also the process through which one translates the symbolic content of Christian faith into different religious (and cultural) contexts. In short, it is the means through which Christian theologians tentatively determine the presence and activity of the Spirit in the lives, practices, and beliefs of the world's religious traditions.

26. For more on the complexity, sophistication, and direction of the current discussion of intercultural and interreligious hermeneutics, see, e.g., David Tracy and Frank E. Reynolds, eds. *Myth and Philosophy*, SUNY Series: Toward a Comparative Philosophy of Religions (Albany: SUNY Press, 1990); and Thomas Dean, ed., *Religious Pluralism and Truth: Essays on Cross-Cultural Philosophy of Religion* (Albany: SUNY Press, 1995). My own comparativist vision is modeled in part after Robert Cummings Neville, *Behind the Masks of God: An Essay toward a Comparative Theology* (Albany: SUNY Press, 1991); and Francis X. Clooney, *Hindu God, Christian God: How Reason Helps Break Down the Boundaries between Religions* (Oxford: Oxford University Press, 2001), esp. chaps. 1 and 6.

Whither Pneumatological *Theologia Religionum?* Toward the Systematic Reconstruction of Christian Theology in Global Context

We are almost at the end of this leg of our theological voyage. In what follows, I will attempt to trace the trajectory of the Spirit's leading as I have been able to discern it so far, recapitulate a pneumatological theology of religions's most problematic features, and chart its potential future course.

Looking Backward

The introductory chapter laid out the basic terms of the debate, commented on the state of the *theologia religionum* discussion, specified the guiding questions, even while setting to one side other important issues not addressed in depth in the book, identified the prospective audiences, and outlined the argument.

In chapter 2, I began the argument in earnest by laying out the basic biblical data regarding pneumatology that informs this project. There, the Spirit's work in creation, re-creation, and final creation was delineated in order to establish the spatial and temporal ubiquity of the Spirit's presence and activity in the world directed toward the eschaton. From there, the basic axioms of a pneumatological theology of religions were explicated within a trinitarian framework: that the Spirit of God is universally present and active; that the Spirit of God is the life breath of all human interpersonal and communitarian activity; and that the world's religions have their place in the divine providence for divine purposes. In one sense, this entire book is focused on developing the proper questions concerning these purposes and attempting to discern just what such purposes may be.

Chapter 3 pursued in greater detail the first two axioms of this pneumatological *theologia religionum*. There, the concept of foundational pneumatology was introduced as a way to get at both the ontological question regarding the Spirit's presence and activity and the epistemological question regarding our engaging this reality within the various publics and discourses of theological encounter. The idea of a pneumatological imagination was also introduced to model a way between the universal fact of human knowing and the particular and traditioned ways of such knowing. I attempted to demonstrate the plausibility of both the foundational pneumatology hypothesis and the pneumatological imagination construct as specifically emergent from the Pentecostal and charismatic experience.

Chapters 4 and 5 traced four previous proposals toward a pneumatological approach to the religions: that of the Orthodox Khodr, the Protestant Samartha, the Catholic Dupuis, and the evangelical Pinnock. Each traveled a different route in engaging the religions theologically. This inevitably included reflection on both the christological and soteriological questions. Yet with regard to a pneumatological *theologia religionum*, the primary question that emerged from these chapters was that concerning discernment. How is the Spirit to be discerned in the religions, and how are other spirits to be discerned in the same? In short, how are the religions themselves to be discerned?

This question was then taken up in detail. Chapter 6 argued that discernment in general includes the charismatic gift of discernment of spirits but that all discernment proceeds empirically through an investigation of the basic phenomenological features of the world and of human experience. Only by doing such investigation is one able to pierce through the outer manifestations of any thing into its inner spiritual reality. As such, Christian discernment in general should be characterized as a hermeneutics of life that is dynamic in paying attention to the temporal and modal qualities of things, concretely focused on the particularities of what is to be discerned, and sophisticated in terms of the criteria and categories brought to bear in the process of discernment.

This theory of discernment has been elaborated on in this chapter with regard to theology of religions. Here, I have argued that discerning the religions needs to proceed empirically—and as such, within an interdisciplinary methodological framework—and comparatively—in ways that enable the religions to be taken seriously on their own terms in order to facilitate the emergence of adequate comparative (and therefore discerning) categories.

Assessing the Situation

Before moving ahead with the overarching question of discerning the religions, I think it is important to redress an important set of questions with its corollary concerns that may be lingering as a potential problem for pneumatological *theologia religionum*. This set of questions may be simply framed with regard to the *Filioque*, since it basically concerns the relationship of pneumatology to christology in this project. This question, of course, is not new. It has been a perennial source of tension, going as far back as Irenaeus's view of the Word and the Spirit as the "two hands of God" and evidenced throughout the history of Christian dogmatics. Irenaeus's dictum has been generally assumed as summarizing the biblical distinction underlying the differentiation between the christological and pneumatological missions. Yet, at the same time, because this early Christian apologist understood the economies of the Son and the Spirit to be integrally related, he also insisted that "where the Church is, there is the Spirit of God; and where the Spirit of God is, there is the Church" (*Against Heresies* 3.24). This question of the relationship of the Spirit to Christ and to his church has been replayed down through the ages in the *Filioque* debate. In terms of the historical formulas, is the Spirit solely "from the Father," "from the Father and the Son," "from the Father of the Son," or even "from the Father through the Son"? The result of this debate may be pertinent to the question of whether or not a pneumatology of religions is possible. If indeed the *Filioque* is reasserted, pneumatology may remain subordinated to christology, thereby minimally securing the fulfillment theory—the notion that other faiths, including Judaism, are valid only as anticipations of the Christian revelation and therefore are fulfilled by Christ—and perhaps reinforcing the Catholic doctrine of *extra ecclesiam nulla salus*.

As previously discussed, however, there is growing agreement in the West regarding the dogmatic illegitimacy of the *Filioque* particularly in light of its intrusion into the creed outside the recognized conciliar processes. Rejection of the *Filioque* may free up some room for a development of a pneumatology of religions as a distinct or at least related stream in the history of salvation. Yet in a very real sense, removing the *Filioque* is just the beginning of the adjustment of a religious vision, leading to a complete reassessment of traditional formulations of christology, pneumatology, ecclesiology, and missiology.

There are many other aspects of this particular issue that have not been considered. I am certainly not arguing for a view of the economy of the Spirit as completely sovereign or unrelated to that of the Son. I am, however, affirming that the turn to pneumatology may allow for more neutral categories to emerge when attempting to discern the presence and activity of the Spirit in other traditions.

Christological criteria will always remain and have their place, but they may perhaps be enhanced by other criteria, thus retaining the integrity of the other tradition. How else should discernment proceed if not by first paying serious attention to the "object"—I use this conceptually, realizing that often, discerning the religions includes discerning persons and personal activities—of discernment as radically other? Of course, discerning the demonic is itself not unambiguous. More often than not, as the Orthodox like to say, "we can only know with some assurance where the Spirit is, rather than where the Spirit is not" (the latter being divine absence).[27] In that case, certainly we can proceed only with confidence as we are enabled to discern the Spirit precisely as the Spirit of Jesus. The question is whether or not we can learn anything substantively new from engaging seriously with religious otherness and, if so, whether or not this will, ultimately, transform our own capacity to recognize the face of Jesus. Another way to pose this question is to ask whether we as Christians ever encounter other faces that are only and generically human rather than religiously formed and expressive.

My own sense, as should be clear from this volume, is that the latter is always the case. Religiousness is not incidental to personal self-identity and not something that may be discarded at will. Even conversions, as radical as they may be, carry over former values, perspectives, and commitments, even if they proceed, at times, unnoticeably.[28] So, the interreligious dialogue turns out to include what Raymond Panikkar calls the "intra-religious" dialogue, the dialogue that occurs in the heart of every person who wrestles with two or more religious ways of being in the world and

27. For this saying, I am indebted to my friend Father Andrew Jaye formerly of St. Mary's Orthodox Church in Minneapolis, Minnesota. This finds confirmation in Sergius Bulgakov, *The Bride of the Lamb*, trans. Boris Jakim (Grand Rapids: Eerdmans, 2002), 313, which deserves to be quoted at length: "An even greater abstention from judgment is appropriate with regard to non-Christians. On the one hand, we know that Christ's Incarnation and Pentecost are universal. Their efficacy extends to all people without exception: all humankind is the body of Christ. On the other hand, it pleases the Lord to shroud in obscurity the ways of salvation and the eternal destinies of those to whom, in our age, the holy gospel has not been revealed and baptism has not been given, which perhaps is not even their fault but ours. The Church does not judge those on the outside but keeps silent about them, leaving them to God's mercy. Her practical attitude toward them consists of the duty of preaching. . . ."

28. See, on conversion, Lewis Rambo, *Understanding Religious Conversion* (New Haven: Yale University Press, 1993); and Donald Gelpi, *The Conversion Experience: A Reflective Process for RCIA Participants and Others* (New York and Mahwah, N.J.: Paulist Press, 1998).

with the fact of religious plurality in general.[29] At this level, getting at the criteria for what is true, holy, beautiful, and good is a complex intersubjective process. Yet discern we must. It may turn out to be the case that discernment in this model will reveal the other tradition to be destitute of the Spirit of God. However, even in that instance, is it not within the province of the Spirit to avail himself to that tradition through the very process of dialogue itself as such occurs at many levels?

My argument is that this kind of discerning comparativism is absolutely central to the contemporary Christian engagement with other faiths. Yet we cannot judge the other without first understanding the other; and all our judgments—which we inevitably must and do make from day to day—should be held tentatively, subject to the ongoing processes of engagement and discernment. I am optimistic, however, that the power of the pneumatological symbol lies in its calling attention to and accentuating every and all particularities, and that precisely because of its universality. The doctrine of the Spirit thus requires that Christians take the empirical particularities of historical religious traditions seriously as data for theologizing. A pneumatological approach to the religions demands reflection not only on Christian sources but also on the sources provided by the religions themselves. Pneumatology therefore leads to global theology, which methodologically includes the important tasks of comparative religion and comparative theology.[30]

Looking Ahead

What, then, should a Christian theology that sustains an intensive dialogue with the religions of the world look like? Here, let me lay out in brief what I see as the task for Christian systematic theology in the twenty-first century global context. First, Christian theology is concerned with the truth. Truth, however, arises out of

29. Raimundo Panikkar, *The Intrareligious Dialogue* (New York: Paulist Press, 1978); cf. also David J. Krieger, "Methodological Foundations for Interreligious Dialogue," in *The Intercultural Challenge of Raimon Panikkar*, ed. Joseph Prabhu (Maryknoll, N.Y.: Orbis, 1996), 201–23; and Leonard Swidler, *After the Absolute: The Dialogical Future of Religious Reflection* (Minneapolis: Fortress, 1990), esp. 52–53.

30. Here, I am in basic agreement with James L. Fredericks, *Faith among Faiths: Christian Theology and Non-Christian Religions* (New York: Paulist Press, 1999), that the way forward for Christian theology of religions is through the hard work of intercultural and interreligious comparisons and contrasts.

the dialectical relationship between divine revelation and human reception and interpretation. All Christians have responsibility for grappling with the truth. But wrestling with the difficult question of truth is compounded when confronted by the question of the non-Christian faiths.[31] Since Christians in Asia, Africa, and Latin America now far outnumber Christians in Europe and North America, Christian theology should work hard to include these non-Western readings of the gospel itself in order to understand the truth of divine revelation.[32]

This means, second, that to the extent the non-Western world is religiously infused with Hindu, Taoist, Confucian, Buddhist, and other traditions of belief and practice, the gospel will itself be read and reread through those lenses.[33] If we naïvely push ahead with our efforts to contextualize the gospel in the non-Western world as if these non-Western religious ways are not deeply embedded in the languages and sociocultural practices of these peoples, should we be surprised if Christianity is rejected in the long run? This has certainly been the case in Japan, for instance, where after centuries of missionary activity, the church remains practically nonexistent. Of course, our ignoring other faiths could also result in an unconscious assimilation of tenets contradictory to the gospel. This is irresponsible religious syncretism, which we

31. See, e.g., Mortimer Adler, *Truth in Religion: The Plurality of Religions and the Unity of Truth* (New York: Macmillan, 1990); Wolfhart Pannenberg, "Religious Pluralism and Conflicting Truth Claims: The Problem of a Theology of the World Religions," in *Christian Uniqueness Reconsidered: The Myth of a Pluralistic Theology of Religions*, ed. Gavin D'Costa (Maryknoll, N.Y.: Orbis, 1990), 96–106; Keith Ward, "Truth and the Diversity of Religions," in *The Philosophical Challenge of Religious Diversity*, ed. Philip L. Quinn and Kevin Meeker (New York and Oxford: Oxford University Press, 2000), 109–25.

32. On this point, see also John B. Cobb Jr., "Global Theology in a Pluralistic Age," *Dharma World* 14 (1987): 31–37; Don A. Pittman, Ruben L. F. Habito, and Terry C. Muck, eds., *Ministry and Theology in Global Perspective* (Grand Rapids: Eerdmans, 1996); and William R. Barr, ed., *Constructive Christian Theology in the Worldwide Church* (Grand Rapids: Eerdmans, 1997).

33. Cf. Gerald McDermott, "What If Paul Had Been from China? Reflections on the Possibility of Revelation in Non-Christian Religions," in *No Other Gods before Me? Evangelicals and the Challenge of World Religions*, ed. John G. Stackhouse Jr. (Grand Rapids: Baker, 2001), 17–36; "The Spirit at Work in Asia Today: A Document of the Office of Theological Concerns of the Federation of Asian Bishops' Conferences," FABC Paper no. 81 [http://www.ucanews.com/html/fabc-papers/fabc-81.htm] (1998); Chwen Jiuan A. Lee and Thomas G. Hand, *A Taste of Water: Christianity through Taoist-Buddhist Eyes* (New York: Paulist Press, 1990); Paul J. Griffiths, ed., *Christianity through Non-Christian Eyes* (Maryknoll, N.Y.: Orbis, 1990); John C. England and Alan J. Torrance, eds., *Doing Theology with the Spirit's Movement in Asia* (Singapore: ATESEA, 1991); and Kyoung Jae Kim, *Christianity and the Encounter of Asian Religions* (Zoetermeer, Netherlands: Uitgeverij Boekencentrum, 1994).

should rightly be cautious of and reject.[34] The problem, however, is that of distinguishing between valid forms of contextualization and invalid ones. This process involves, as I have argued in this book, extensive interreligious and intercultural engagement and comparative religion and theology at its depths rather than on its surfaces.

Alternatively, of course, we should take the Word-made-flesh (John 1:14) and the Spirit poured-out-on-all-flesh (Acts 2:17) seriously in developing what could be called either an incarnational or a "pentecostal" pneumatological model of contextualization (chapter 1). To do so would be to ask what the gospel might look like if its primary dialogue partners are not Plato, Aristotle, Kant, Hegel, or Whitehead, but rather the Buddha, Confucius, Lao-tzu, Chuang-tzu, Nagarjuna, Shankara, Ramanuja, Chu Hsi, Dogen, Wang Yang Ming, and so on. These thinkers are not religiously neutral, of course; but then neither are any in the so-called philosophical tradition in the West. More important, where are we able to receive divine revelation in its purity apart from all cultural-linguistic "contamination"? The truth of the matter is that theological reflection has to continuously negotiate the dialectic between revelation and enculturation since divine revelation comes always-already inculturated, even as the Word-made-flesh was a first-century carpenter who was also male, Jewish, and a Nazarene and the Spirit is poured out, not on all people in the abstract, but on real people in particular places and times.

I have argued in this book that it is a pneumatological approach to the non-Christian faiths that provides the most rigorous theological, methodological, and epistemological rationale for engaging religious otherness in a serious, in-depth, and discerning manner. Of course, the proof is in the pudding, and the value and promise of a pneumatological *theologia religionum* will need to be determined in the long run by the results this research project delivers. The long-term result of the dialogical quest for truth driven by a pneumatological theology of religions will, I believe, be a thoroughly reconstructed Christian theology that will have passed over into the other faiths and returned home transformed

34. But note the call for a "theologically responsible syncretism" by Walter J. Hollenweger, *Pentecostalism: Its Origin and Development Worldwide* (Peabody, Mass.: Hendrickson, 1997), chap. 11; cf. Jerald Gort et al., eds., *Dialogue and Syncretism: An Interdisciplinary Approach* (Amsterdam: Editions Rodopi; Grand Rapids: Eerdmans, 1989).

in such a way as to be able to speak the gospel effectively and meaningfully in a world context generally and in the context of the diversity of religions in particular.[35]

The goal of reconstructed Christian systematic theology that takes the world religions and other non-Christian faiths seriously, however, cannot be the product of one person's reflections.[36] I envision my own contribution to this project as one of testing the specifics of the pneumatological paradigm against the empirical reality of the world religions. In other words, I want to ask what the pneumatological categories of divine presence, divine activity, and divine absence, for example, would look like when brought into dialogue with the religious symbols of the non-Christian faiths. With regard to Buddhism, for example, these categories lead to the comparison of metaphysical and ontological visions, of soteriological analyses, and of the role and function of the demonic.[37] Application of the pneumatological categories need to be tested against the

35. The model for this kind of theological work remains John B. Cobb Jr., *Beyond Dialogue: Toward a Mutual Transformation of Christianity and Buddhism* (Philadelphia: Fortress, 1982); cf. also John S. Dunne, *The Way of All the Earth: Experiments in Truth and Religion* (London: Collier Macmillan, 1972).

36. Tillich was moving in this direction at the end of his career (see Paul Tillich, *The Future of Religions* [New York: Harper & Row, 1966]), even while Pannenberg has long called for Christian theology to be done in light of the history of religions even if he himself has not succeeded in heeding his own advice (see Wolfhart Pannenberg, "Toward a Theology of the History of Religions," in his *Basic Questions in Theology: Collected Essays*, vol. 2, trans. George H. Kehm [Philadelphia: Fortress, 1971], chap. 4; and idem, *Systematic Theology*, trans. Geoffrey W. Bromiley, vol. 1 [Grand Rapids: Eerdmans, 1991]). Yet still, progress has been made. See, e.g., Wilfred Cantwell Smith, *Towards a World Theology: Faith and the Comparative History of Religion* (Philadelphia: Westminster, 1981); Paul Varo Martinson, *A Theology of World Religions: Interpreting God, Self and World in Semitic, Indian and Chinese Thought* (Minneapolis: Augsburg, 1987); Leonard Swidler, ed., *Toward a Universal Theology of Religion* (Maryknoll, N.Y.: Orbis, 1987); Ross N. Reat and Edmund Perry, *A World Theology: The Central Spiritual Reality of Humankind* (Cambridge: Cambridge University Press, 1991); David J. Krieger, *The New Universalism: Foundations for a Global Theology* (Maryknoll, N.Y.: Orbis, 1991); Catherine Cornille and Valeer Neckebrouck, eds., *A Universal Faith? Peoples, Cultures, Religions, and the Christ*, Louvain Theological and Pastoral Monographs 9 (Louvain: Peeters; Grand Rapids: Eerdmans, 1992); Ninian Smart and Steven Constantine, *Christian Systematic Theology in a World Context* (Minneapolis: Fortress, 1996); and Wayne Teasdale, *The Mystic Heart: Discovering a Universal Spirituality in the World's Religions* (Novato, Calif.: New World Library, 1999); cf. also Hugo Meynell, "The Idea of a World Theology," *Modern Theology* 1.2 (1985): 149–61.

37. For preliminary comparative studies on the latter two categories, see my "Technologies of Liberation: A Comparative Soteriology of Eastern Orthodoxy and Theravada Buddhism," *Dharma Deepika* (forthcoming); and "The Demonic in Pentecostal-Charismatic Christianity and in the Religious Consciousness of Asia," in *Asian and Pentecostal: The Changing Face of Christianity in Asia*, ed. Allan Anderson and Edmond Tang, Journal of Pentecostal Theology Supplemental

world religious traditions—Hinduism, Taoism-Confucianism, Islam, Judaism—as well as against the phenomenon of new religious movements.

In this book I have assessed the promise as well as the potential problems and pitfalls of a pneumatological theology of religions. While the turn to pneumatology certainly does not eliminate the need to grapple with christological issues, it is far too early to conclude what a renewed form of christology would look like if the pneumatological paradigm charted here is taken seriously. My purpose here, however, is motivated by my conviction that the Spirit blows wherever the Spirit wills (John 3:8). I have therefore attempted to keep the vision for a pneumatological theology of religions afloat and perhaps to blow a gentle breeze upon its sails. The entire project is still in its infancy. I maintain, however, that discerning the presence and activity of the Spirit in the religions is central to this endeavor, and we are in desperate need of more adequate categories in order to conduct more viable theological comparisons across religious lines. Is it too far-fetched to hope that a pneumatological approach to the religions will prove to be more of a conduit that advances the formation of *theologia religionum* and the interreligious dialogue and our understandings of the human condition than we have so far realized?

Series (New York: Continuum, forthcoming). I hope to incorporate, revise, and extend these inquiries in a book-length manuscript currently in progress and tentatively titled, "Does the Wind Blow through the Middle Way? Pneumatology and the Christian-Buddhist Dialogue."

Scripture Index

Author Index

Subject Index